Listening to Ourselves

SUNY series in Living Indigenous Philosophies

Agnes B. Curry and Anne Waters, editors

LISTENING TO OURSELVES

A MULTILINGUAL ANTHOLOGY OF AFRICAN PHILOSOPHY

EDITED BY

Chike Jeffers

FOREWORD BY

Ngũgĩ wa Thiong'o

SUNY PRESS

Published by
STATE UNIVERSITY OF NEW YORK PRESS
Albany

© 2013 State University of New York

All rights reserved

Printed in the United States of America

No part of this book may be used or reproduced in any manner whatsoever without written permission. No part of this book may be stored in a retrieval system or transmitted in any form or by any means including electronic, electrostatic, magnetic tape, mechanical, photocopying, recording, or otherwise without the prior permission in writing of the publisher.

For information, contact
State University of New York Press
www.sunypress.edu

Production and book design, Laurie Searl
Marketing, Anne M. Valentine

Library of Congress Cataloging-in-Publication Data

Listening to ourselves : a multilingual anthology of African philosophy / edited by Chike Jeffers.
pages ; cm — (SUNY series in living indigenous philosophies)
Includes bibliographical references and index.
ISBN 978-1-4384-4743-8 (hardcover : alk. paper)
ISBN 978-1-4384-4744-5 (paperback : alk. paper) 1. Philosophy, African. I. Jeffers, Chike, 1982-
B5305.J44 2013
199'.6--dc23

2012037138

10 9 8 7 6 5 4 3 2 1

IN MEMORY OF EMMANUEL CHUKWUDI EZE

1963–2007

Contents

Foreword: A Historic First

Ngũgĩ wa Thiong'o

This book, *Listening to Ourselves*, edited by the Caribbean-Canadian intellectual, Chike Jeffers, is a historic intervention in the debates about African philosophy. Its publication signals that the tradition of Africans writing philosophy in European languages might change. By putting together essays on philosophy in six different African languages (Dholuo, Gĩgĩkũyũ, Akan, Igbo, Wolof, and Amharic), and on different themes, ranging from morality to ontology to questions of time, Chike Jeffers has laid to rest the questions as to whether written modern philosophy is possible in African languages.

The collection also demonstrates what should be obvious: that translation is one way by which the accessibility of resources in African languages can be ensured. Philosophizing in African languages directly, conversation among African languages, and then across other languages through translations is the only way by which Africa can add originality to the wealth of human knowledge, enriching the world the way it once did in Old Egypt. It also puts a serious dent into the absurdity of the concept and practice of philosophizing in European languages and then calling it African philosophy. African philosophy has been restored to its linguistic identity.

I hope that the work of Chike Jeffers is just the beginning of more to come. Now is the time. Africa has waited long enough. Whatever the ultimate effect of his historic intervention, Jeffers has joined a long line of diasporic intellectuals from Marcus Garvey to W.E.B. Du Bois to Frantz Fanon to Walter Rodney, among others, whose actions and thought have had a transforming impact on Africa and Africa-related worlds. And, of course, all lovers of philosophy will enjoy these essays.

Acknowledgments

When I had the idea for this anthology, I was in my first year of graduate school. In April 2005, I ran into Emmanuel Eze at the meeting of the Central APA (American Philosophical Association). This presented me, I felt, with an excellent opportunity: Eze had had a track record of editing important anthologies in African philosophy and so I figured he might be interested in bringing my unique idea to fruition. As it turns out, he found the idea very interesting but also looked at me and said: "Why don't you do it?" I had never considered that possibility.

I therefore must begin by thanking the late Professor Eze for inspiring me to put this anthology together myself. It saddens me greatly that he passed away not only before seeing its appearance, but also before he could edit the English translation of his essay.

I next want to thank all the other contributors and translators who decided to join this presumptuous young grad student in carrying out such an unorthodox project. I must single out Souleymane Bachir Diagne, who was also co-chair of my dissertation committee. In many ways, my accomplishments in academic life have been a product of the warm support and useful guidance I have received from this man who, I think it is generally agreed, is one of the nicest people on Earth. Bachir, merci beaucoup!

Charles Mills, the other co-chair, has also been a great support from the very beginning—as a matter of fact, he was there in April 2005 when I first spoke with Eze about the idea. Thanks also to my committee members Robert Gooding-Williams (to whom, if I am not mistaken, I described the idea even before talking to Eze) and Penelope Deutscher. Thanks to the Department of Philosophy at Northwestern University, where I completed my PhD, and to the Department of Philosophy at Dalhousie University, where I am now fortunate enough to hold a tenure-track position. And a great big thanks to the general community of scholars who are interested in or who are practitioners of Africana philosophy, especially those such as Lucius Outlaw, Albert Mosley, and Lewis Gordon who precede me in being diasporic scholars deeply invested in philosophy from the Continent (note to those who may be confused: my name is Igbo but I myself am not . . . I am a Canadian of Caribbean heritage who happens to be a dedicated Pan-Africanist!).

Very special thanks, of course, to Anne Waters and Agnes Curry for believing in this project and taking it on as part of their book series. Their great patience with me and encouragement along the way has been vital.

I am grateful to Kalajine Anigbogu and Love Ghunney, who made extremely valuable contributions to the editing of Emmanuel Eze's and Kwasi Wiredu's essays, respectively. I thank Katherine Faull, executor of Eze's estate, for her permission to publish Eze's essay. Messay Kebede's essay, although commissioned and written for this anthology, has also appeared in the *International Journal of Ethiopian Studies*, Vol. III, No. 1 (Winter/Spring 2007): 29–39. I thank Elias Wondimu and Tsehai Publishers for the permission to reprint it.

My heartfelt thanks to one of Africa's greatest writers and thinkers, Ngũgĩ wa Thiong'o, for his gracious foreword. I am humbled by and grateful for his extremely kind words.

Finally, I wish to thank my parents (Denise and Francis Jeffers), my siblings (Adom and Asha Jeffers), my family and friends generally, and lastly, the three people with whom I am so blessed to share my daily life: my wife, Tina Roberts-Jeffers, whose love and support have sustained this project for as long as we have been together; Aminata Lilla Jeffers, my gorgeous little girl; and Ayo Jelani Jeffers, my brand new baby boy.

Introduction

What lies within the pages of this book is a revolutionary moment in African philosophy: the first multilingual collection of African philosophy in indigenous African languages. The seven essays collected here are in six different languages from five different countries. Each has been translated into English by a scholar or scholars who are native speakers of the essay's tongue; the translations are included here on facing pages. In this introduction, I will first contextualize this achievement and then introduce and discuss the anthology's contents.

In *Moving the Centre,* Kenyan writer Ngũgĩ wa Thiong'o argues that there have been three types of literary traditions in Africa. The first is oral literature (or "orature").[1] The songs, poems, drama, proverbs, riddles, and sayings that constitute this tradition represent a rich and ancient heritage. The tradition is also a living one: through it, Ngũgĩ claims, African languages have been kept alive "in their most magical form."[2] The second tradition is that of Africans writing in European languages (generally the languages of their now former colonizers). Though he does not announce this in the present context, Ngũgĩ is extremely important to the development of this tradition: his first novel, *Weep Not Child* (1964), published under the name James Ngugi, was the first novel in English by an East African. Since then, however, Ngũgĩ has undergone one of the most remarkable transformations in modern literature: by the 1980s, he renounced English as a language for creative writing and vowed to publish all such work in an African language, particularly Gĩkũyũ (the language of his people).

Thus, in *Moving the Centre,* Ngũgĩ articulates a sharp critique of the Europhone tradition, arguing that while it has performed the anti-Eurocentric function of "re-drawing the images of the world as previously drawn by the literature of Europe," it has at the same time "continued and even aided in that Eurocentrism by its very choice of languages."[3] The third tradition, then, Afrophone writing, is the stream of African literature of which Ngũgĩ has become the greatest champion. Despite problems associated with literacy levels, opportunities to publish, the existence of literary criticism, orthographical confusion, the multilingual nature of most African countries, hostile governments, and the concentration of genius in the Europhone stream, Ngũgĩ believes that "writing in African languages still holds the key for the positive development of new and vital traditions in African literature as we face the twenty-first century."[4]

The debate surrounding the use of African languages has not remained an issue for novelists, playwrights, and poets alone. Ghanaian philosopher Kwasi Wiredu, one of the most celebrated African philosophers, writes in his book *Cultural Universals and Particulars* that his profession must eventually begin contributing to the third tradition: "Sooner or later . . . African philosophy will have to be done in an African language or African languages."[5] Wiredu associates the fact that the philosophical education of professional African philosophers has generally been in the languages of the colonizers with the danger of what is known as "colonial mentality."[6] An undisturbed colonial mentality is the fate of any African philosopher who never critically interrogates the conceptual frameworks inherited through this education and who never makes any effort to explore the resources inherent in indigenous African conceptual schemes. To do both of these things, on the other hand, is to participate in the fight for what Wiredu calls "conceptual decolonization."[7]

Wiredu demonstrates this by looking at the concept of truth, arguing that trying to translate controversies surrounding the relation between *truth* and *fact* into his native Akan runs into the difficulty that the same phrase expresses both concepts ("*nea te saa*" = "that which is so").[8] He concludes that debates in English about truth versus fact constitute an example of a philosophical problem that is "tongue-dependent."[9] He does not claim that such problems are therefore not real problems, but they are therefore less fundamental than more universal problems—such as the question of what it means for something to be so.

Until now, Wiredu's championing of philosophizing by means of African languages has remained in the above form: utilizing Akan translations of terminology to explore philosophical problems. He has not, however, made "the Ngũgĩ switch," as we might call it: he has not switched to publishing all of his work in Akan. Asked about this in an interview, Wiredu responds: "I fear that I am not as important as Ngũgĩ, so that if I wrote texts in Akan I do not think anybody would be going to translate them."[10] Going beyond this humility, he mentions the issue of the number of languages in Ghana alone, making the decision to write only in Akan something that would cut him off from many readers in his own country, to say nothing of the rest of Africa and the world. He concludes that "it is just not practicable now for us to work exclusively in our own languages."[11]

This is a claim with which I agree, and the following collection of essays is *not* an attempt to set up intellectual walls of division, forcing African philosophers to write only for the tiny audiences that would result from working *exclusively* in their own languages. Not making the move to exclusivity, however, does not preclude inaugurating a new and vibrant tradition of publication in indigenous African languages by professional African philosophers. This is exactly what this anthology aims to do: its collection and translation of African language work in philosophy serves to (1) advocate and exemplify the value of mining the linguistic and conceptual resources which Africa's languages have to offer Africa's philosophers, and (2) normalize what ought to at least be an option for African philosophers of the future.[12] This anthology seeks, in other words, to take the next step in the development of African philosophy as an institution: going beyond talking about the use of African languages to actually producing compelling work in those languages, along with translations so that the wider world will benefit as well.

The first piece in the volume is by Souleymane Bachir Diagne of Senegal, proclaimed one of the world's twenty-five most notable thinkers by the French magazine *Le Nouvel Observateur*. He addresses in Wolof the very issue I mentioned in relation to Wiredu: truth. When thinking about the topic, Diagne found himself drawn to the same format as Plato: the philosophical dialogue. He therefore presents us with an exchange between a woman named Soxna and her male friend Ngóór in which they interrogate the concept of truth and its relation to tradition. Is truth to be identified with tradition, that is, with what the ancestors taught? What is the opposite of truth? What is the relationship between the truth of Islam and the traditional beliefs of non-Islamic ancestors? Soxna and Ngóór seek and find reasonable answers to these three questions.

The second essay is by Ethiopian philosopher Messay Kebede, acclaimed author of *Africa's Quest for a Philosophy of Decolonization*. Writing in Amharic, Kebede explores the relationship between conceptions of time and the process of modernization. After connecting the question of time to the question of the meaning of life, he describes the unique combination in the Ethiopian tradition of cyclical and teleological conceptions of time: while the observance of the natural world produced a cyclical view of life, Ethiopia's Orthodox Christian tradition provided the country with a goal-oriented eschatological outlook. Kebede turns to the sacred text of the *Kebra Negast* to explain how these seemingly opposing conceptions of time were reconciled in such a way as to place Ethiopia at the center of history. He argues that, in the modern period, Ethiopia's failure to prosper has been intimately related to its rejection of the traditional combination of conceptions in favor of a Eurocentric teleological understanding of history and time.

Three of this anthology's essays are by philosophers from Kenya, and two of those are in the Luo language (also known as Dholuo)—which is, incidentally, the ancestral language of the forty-fourth president of the United States, Barack Obama. The first essay in Luo is by D. A. Masolo, whose *African Philosophy in Search of Identity* is among the most thorough and insightful overviews of the field. Here, Masolo examines the nature of proverbs as linguistic phenomena. He argues that they are not propositions, as they do not make claims about the world that are true or false. Offering a wide variety of examples of Luo proverbs and differentiating between simple and complex types of proverbs, Masolo aims to show how they are general impressions and reflections that transmit wisdom that is useful to the community, rather than case-specific statements that could be disproven by pointing out discrepancies between their literal meaning and events in the world.

The second essay in Luo is by F. Ochieng'-Odhiambo, who has previously written on topics such as sage philosophy (a unique form of African philosophy involving interviews with wise people, which originates in Kenya). He turns his eye here to traditional naming practices among the Luo, in an effort to delineate the philosophical stance on language and personhood that underlies these practices. The Luo tradition rejects a conception of naming according to which names serve only to pick out individuals; a name is meant, rather, to express significant information about the name-holder. Ochieng'-Odhiambo describes four levels of naming: naming at birth, which is determined by the circumstances of birth; naming children after dead relatives, often on the basis of dreams; naming that displays kinship relations among the living; and praise names, acquired over the course of life, which Ochieng'-Odhiambo compares to proverbs and riddles. It is interesting to note the many points of connection between this essay and Masolo's, perhaps signaling a common sense of direction for Luo philosophy.

The third essay by a Kenyan philosopher is significant for at least two reasons: it is in Gĩkũyũ (also known as Gĩgĩkũyũ), the same language in which Ngũgĩ has been writing his Afrophone work, and it is by a woman, which is important because women are severely underrepresented in African philosophy. Betty Wambui's essay is a contribution to the philosophy of gender. The impetus for her reflections was an assertion by a friend that, among the Gĩkũyũ people, women, children, goats, and land are regarded as one and the same thing. Wambui attempts to investigate the validity of this claim by tracking the life experiences from birth to adulthood of women and men in traditional Gĩkũyũ society, carefully noting similarities and differences in the treatment of the two sexes and seriously considering arguments both for and against the perception of inequality. She gives special consideration to traditional society's categories of exceptional women, such as barren women who were allowed to marry other women and women who did not get married at all. Her conclusion is nuanced and resists simplification.

The anthology's penultimate essay is by the late Nigerian philosopher Emmanuel Chukwudi Eze, best known for having edited a number of classic anthologies in African philosophy and philosophy of race as well as the journal *Philosophia Africana*. We are proud to be able to honor Eze's memory by including this essay in Igbo, which is one of the last things he wrote before joining the ancestors. Eze's metaphilosophical piece concerns itself with the relationship between language and thought. He frames the discussion by raising the question of why it might be useful to do philosophy in Igbo, which leads him to make use of the anthology's titular reference to the idea of *listening to ourselves*. Exploring the ways in which philosophy can listen to itself in the Igbo language, Eze makes use of idiomatic Igbo expressions to produce insights concerning topics such as the dialogical form of thought, the concept of intellectual property, the importance of cultivating an open culture, and the presence of unity and diversity within and across persons and cultures.

Finally, it is very fitting that we close with a contribution from Kwasi Wiredu, whose calls for conceptual decolonization played a large part in inspiring this anthology. Wiredu's essay in Akan (also known as Twi) is an exercise in ethical theory. He aims to build an account of good and evil that properly incorporates the importance of both consequences and intentions and that captures both the universal and culturally variable aspects of morality. He specifies what we call the Golden Rule as the "First Law" of human conduct and examines how it provides the foundation for morality by serving to harmonize individual and community interests. Then, looking at what determines the goodness or badness of acts that do not contravene the First Law, he offers a standard of promoting well-being which he compares and contrasts with John Stuart Mill's utilitarianism. Turning to the importance of cultural context, Wiredu discusses the variability of custom and gives special attention to the Akan notion of *musuo,* which has sometimes been translated as "taboo." Wiredu argues that the word should not be translated in this way, which leads him to discuss the role of religion in morality.

It may help prepare the reader for what follows to embark upon a brief discussion of some notable tendencies within the anthology's essays that we can, I think, see as directly linked to the fact that they are written in indigenous languages. These tendencies, I would argue, emerge as a result of the perspectival shift engendered by leaving behind English or French and attempting to philosophize in the language of one's ancestors and kin. One is likely to find these tendencies present and prominent in the anthology in ways that make it differ from other anthologies in African philosophy and, more importantly, from other works by the same philosophers whose work is collected here.

I will begin with the tendency, arguably present to some degree in every essay, toward an attitude of *deference to tradition.* Deference need not be understood here as total and uncritical submission, although uncharitable readings of some essays would perhaps charge them with displaying that extreme. Deference, when not taken so far, can be understood as a form of deep respect that commits one to giving at least the first word to the object of deference, if not always the last word. This is precisely what we find in the essays within this volume. There is a palpable sense of the need for humility before tradition, of the need for some recognition of tradition's authority, in the work collected here. This is entirely appropriate for an anthology motivated by the goal of demonstrating how philosophy looks and sounds when articulated in indigenous African languages, the tongues within which African traditions appear and gain shape most naturally not as caricatured barbarisms or exotic curiosities but as the necessary background and grounding for habitual forms of thought, expression, and action.

And yet, as I have said, tradition's authority need not be seen as total and unquestionable. Tradition is the starting point for discussion, and in many of the essays, we find that the discussion develops in ways that include raising suspicions about and offering criticisms of certain aspects of tradition or common ways of understanding those aspects. I firmly believe that this represents one of the most important and fruitful methodologies for African philosophy as a discipline: the investigation and articulation of ideas drawn from what is seen as traditional, followed by the application of a critical eye that aims to praise and keep what is best while criticizing and rejecting that which is unacceptable.

Related to the theme of deference to tradition is the *religiosity* that features prominently in a number of essays. The first two essays, for example, can each be read as in some sense taking for granted a background commitment to Islam and Christianity, respectively. The foregrounding of these two religions may strike some readers as ironic and as contrary to the volume's commitment to upholding the value of African traditions, but it is important to remember the presence of Islam in West Africa is many centuries old and Christianity has been a dominant religion in Ethiopia for nearly two millennia. We should therefore be careful and flexible with how we define what is and what is not traditional in Africa. The important point to note here, however, is that the treatment of these religions as part of the necessary background for philosophizing in Wolof and Amharic is best understood as part of what is involved in depicting the arising of philosophical discourse in these linguistic contexts as authentically as possible. It is not simply a language that is at stake in any of the essays in this volume, but rather an entire culture and the way that culture structures the world. Religious commitments are central to many worlds in Africa, and they are therefore the most natural starting points for asking the fundamental questions to which philosophy seeks answers. Once again, though, we need not worry that the authority of religion is such that these starting points are shielded from the questions they inspire being subsequently turned back upon them. Diagne's piece, for example, is masterful in its subtle encouragement of questioning and its discouragement of an uncritical, fundamentalist approach to Islamic faith.

The last notable feature upon which I would like to comment in anticipation of any consternation on the part of the reader is the discourse of *race,* or, more precisely, of *African-European difference*. It should surprise no one that explicit or implicit comparisons between Africans and those who colonized them are common in these essays, as they are in discussions of African philosophy generally. And yet, such comparisons can sometimes be jarring to those who are extra-sensitive to the need to avoid generalizations, especially when the comparisons present themselves as comments on the differences between "races"—take, for example, the talk of black people and white people, their initial encounter and their different approaches to naming, in Ochieng'-Odhiambo's essay. But one would be quite clearly mistaken if one took Ochieng'-Odhiambo to be simply essentializing and homogenizing people according to racial classifications, as his essay is tightly focused on communicating the specificities of naming practices among his particular people, the Luo. His talk of black-white difference is resonant, then, of the larger context within which his investigation of the customs of a single ethnicity takes place: a world shaped and indelibly marked by the colonial encounter. The figure of the European looms here, as elsewhere, as a sort of challenge to self-knowledge: what matters is not what can be said about the entire history of the European subcontinent and those descended from its inhabitants but rather what to make of the lasting effects in Africa itself of the presence of the *mzungu,* the *toubab,* the *oyinbo,* the *obruni* (to use just a few of the names in African languages for *white people*).[13] The struggle for self-knowledge necessarily includes attempts to distinguish African and European characteristics, although carefulness in doing so is of course warranted.

In closing, I want to note the significance of this anthology's being published as part of a series on "Living Indigenous Philosophies." The essays within it bear a special relationship to the genre of African philosophy known as "ethnophilosophy," a term closely associated with Paulin Hountondji of Benin, whose negative use of it to describe works claiming to express the philosophy behind traditional African cultures deeply impacted the direction of the field. One of Hountondji's objections to ethnophilosophy is that he sees it as an "extraverted discourse": a case of attempting to intervene in a Western conversation by setting oneself up as a spokesperson for a people already presumed to not be part of the conversation.[14] The essays in this volume, no matter how ethnophilosophical they might be by virtue of excavating the philosophical content of traditional cultures, automatically evade this particular criticism by addressing themselves first and foremost, by virtue of the languages in which they are written, to an African public. They are thus prime examples of *living indigenous African philosophy*: they participate in and aim to enrich a tradition of thinking deeply in African languages that has hitherto been primarily oral. In this manner, they communicate on a number of levels, to all Africans who are interested in philosophy, a vital anti-Eurocentric message: let us listen to ourselves!

NOTES

1. Ngũgĩ wa Thiong'o, *Moving the Centre: The Struggle for Cultural Freedoms* (London: James Currey Ltd, 1993), 18.

2. Ibid., 19.

3. Ibid.

4. Ibid., 21.

5. Kwasi Wiredu, *Cultural Universals and Particulars* (Bloomington: Indiana University Press, 1996), 3.

6. Ibid., 4.

7. Ibid., 136.

8. Ibid., 107.

9. Ibid., 101.

10. "Decolonization, Multilingualism, and African Languages in the Making of African Philosophy: Kwasi Wiredu in Dialogue with Kai Kresse," <http://them.polylog.org/2/dwk-en.htm>.

11. Ibid.

12. It is worth noting at this point the sad irony that while all of this anthology's contributors are African philosophers in the sense that they are philosophers from Africa, none of them currently hold positions at African universities. All except one work (or, in the cases of the deceased and the retired, worked) at universities in the United States, and the exception works at a university in the Caribbean. A majority of them have, however, held positions at African universities at some point in the past, and their moves to the United States and elsewhere thus form part of the unfortunate brain drain Africa has experienced as its institutions of higher education have been affected by structural adjustment and other detrimental factors.

13. "*Mzungu*" is Kiswahili, "*toubab*" is used in Wolof and a number of other West African languages, "*oyinbo*" is Yoruba, and "*obruni*" is Akan.

14. Hountondji, *The Struggle for Meaning: Reflections on Philosophy, Culture, and Democracy in Africa*, trans. John Conteh-Morgan (Athens, OH: Ohio University Press, 2002), 95.

Listening to Ourselves

Dëgg ak ludul dëgg

Waxtaan diggante Soxna ak càmmiñam Ngóór

Suleymaan Basiir Jaañ

Soxna. Nga baal ma ma laaj la, Ngóór, lu waral, ñaare, béppub kàddu gu waay di dëggal di dëgëral, da naan Wolof Njaay a ko wax ?

Ngóór. Wax nga dëgg, Soxna. Soo gisee ñu fent benn boroom xamxam bu la kenn munul ni jamono jii la juddu, berëb sàngam, diw ak diw jur ko, mu yaroo faa, dëkk fee . . . ci gàttal daal amul dara lu ko màndargaal ludul tudd na 'Wolof' sant 'Njaay,' booba dafa am lu tax ak lu muy tekki.

S. Waaw lu tax?

Ng. Ni ma ko gisee moo di dañu la bëgg won rekk ni kàddu gi ñu ni Wolof Njaay a ko wax, kàddu la bu dëggu ba ñépp war cee ànd nangu ko. Kenn waru koo weddi. Dinaa la wax nak man ni ma firee 'Wolof Njaay.'

S. Nan?

Ng. Moo di rekk bépp boroom xel.

S. Yaakaaroon naa ni danga naan mooy rekk mag ñu jëkk ña, maanaam suñu maam yi ñu jiitu.

Ng. Waaw, li nga wax itam noonu la, waaye batay benn la, soo ko seetloo. Su ma nee 'Wolof Njaay' mooy rekk maam yi, booba dama bëgg wone ni kàddu yi maam yooya bàyyi dëgg la bu sax ndax cosaan lañu sukkandiku. Su ma nee itam Wolof Njaay du kenn kudul yow, di man, di keneen, di ñun ñépp feek ñoo ngiy jëfee xel, li ma wax mooy ni kàddu gu ñu ni Wolof Njaay la sosoo dafa di kàddu gu dëppook xel, loolu war tax ñu nangu ko. Ñàkk koo nangu li muy wone mooy ñàkk xel.

Truth and Untruth

A Conversation Between Soxna and Her Friend Ngóór

Souleymane Bachir Diagne, *Columbia University*
Translated by Omar Ka, *University of Maryland, Baltimore County*

Soxna: May I ask you, Ngóór, why everyone who wants to emphasize the truth of what he is saying affirms that Wolof Njaay said it?

Ngóór: You're right, Soxna. There is a reason and a meaning why people would come up with some wise person of whom they are unable to provide a birth date, a birth place, who were his parents, where he was raised, where he lived. . . . In short, there is nothing that identifies him except that his first name is "Wolof" and his last name "Njaay."

S: So what is the reason?

Ng: In my opinion, they just want to show you that a saying attributed to Wolof Njaay must be well founded in order to be universally accepted. Nobody should be able to deny it. I will now tell you how personally I interpret "Wolof Njaay."

S: How?

Ng: It just means someone who thinks.

S: I thought you were going to simply say the ancestors, that is, our great-grandparents who came before us.

Ng: Yes, what you say is correct, but it is still the same as what I said if you think about it. If I say "Wolof Njaay," it means the great-grandparents. I want to show here that the sayings that those ancestors left are founded in truth and are rooted in tradition. If I also say that Wolof Njaay is none other than you, me, someone else, or all of us, as long as we use our ability to think, I mean that a saying attributed to Wolof Njaay is a saying that results from thinking, which is why we should accept it. Denying it shows a lack of thinking.

S. Dégg naa la. Waaye dafa mel na war nañoo mëna gisee neneen, tàggale ñaari maana yii nga ni benn lañu. Ndax dama yaakaar ni soo ne lëf dëgg la ngir cosaan, yaa ngi naan li tax ñu jàppee ko noonu dafa fekk ñu wara roy maam yi ci xalaat ak ca la ñu gëmoon daan ko jëfee. Mel na ma ni la mag ñi daan nañu muslu ci dëmm, koon war nañu leen déggal te jàpp ni dëmm lu am la. Ndaxam tey soo nee dëmm am na ndax maam yi daan nañu ci muslu, jàpp naa ni amoo xel. Li ma jublu ci bile misaal mooy lii: Su ma nee dëmm amul, xel munul nangu lu ni mel bokk ci mbindeef yi, booba maa ngi naan cosaan mën na dëggal loo xam ni jamono dina dox ba xel dootu ko nangu.

Ng. Waaw, koon loo yaakaar ni moo fi indi tur wi?

S. Wax ji yëpp a ngi noonu nak. Waaye léeb wone na ni lëf mën na am tur te di rekk lu ñu fent. Nangu naa nak ni mbirum dëmm bokkul ak lu ñu rekk léebu. Donte bañ nga ni dëmm am na munoo weddi ni yenn feebar yi fajkat yi dañu koy féetale dëmm mbaa seytaane. Su ko defee mën nga ni rekk li ñu tuddee dëmm du dara lu moy li mbiral yenn jàngoro yu ñu gisaluloon beneen ngirte. Yaakaar naa ni tey doktoor yi mën nañu wax ci yooyu jàngoro leneen ludul di tam nit ñi.

Ng. Ey waay ñi ñu tam ci lu teguwul fenn ludul jàngoro yu ñu ni dëmm a ko waral!

S. Kenn rawu ci sama mbokku Ndar-Ndar yi nak. Waay waay Yàlla na Yàlla baal doomu Ndar yi ci gaaw tamaate. Li ñuy mën gan yépp de, ku ñu xamul foo bokk rekk tam nañu la!

Ng. Waaw ñiy jaafur nak di waxal seen bopp ni dëmm lañu?

S. Maa ngiy ñëw. Jaafur ba it du dara ludul feebar moomit. Tàngat di jiiñ sa bopp lu nekk ci jàngoro doomu Aadama yépp la am. Soo bokkee nak xeet bu gëm ni dëmm am na, ci biir feebar bi, su sa xel mu muuru di seet lu rëy looy jiiñ sa bopp, yaakaar na ni mën na jàpp dëmm.

Ng. Li nga wax daal mooy koon du dëmm moo waral nit ñi gëm ne am na; waaye gëm ga ko nit ñi gëm moo ko amloo?

S. Foofu sax nak laa jëmoon! Góor gi Aamadu Ampaate Ba mos na léeb bii léeb: dafa ni bukki, ci mën fen bi ñu ko xamee dafa yóoxu joxoñ ne xeewal a nga fale di xaar; ba wax ja tasee ba fu mu jublu rekk gis ñu samp seen xél jëm fa mu joxoñoon, mu ni "waaw, man tee maa dem seet ba xam ndax xeewal newul foofa? Ñii ñépp àndandoo daw jëm fa kat, war naa am dara." Mën nga jàppee wax maye waaye la mu tekki gën na xóot te mooy li nga wax léegi: gëm mooy waral dëgg ñaare, donte li ñu gëna jàpp mooy ni dëgg ay waral gëm.

S: I hear you. But it seems as if we should be able to see it another way, by separating the two meanings you say are the same. I think that if you say something is true because of tradition, you are also saying that the reason why we should see it that way is because we should emulate the ancestors in their thinking and their beliefs. For instance, the ancestors used to seek protection from sorcery, so we should listen to them and conclude that sorcery does exist. In fact, today if you say that sorcery exists because our ancestors used to seek protection against it, I would conclude that you do not think. This is where I am going with this example: if I say that sorcery does not exist, that reason cannot allow for such a thing to exist among creatures, I am saying then that tradition might consider as truth something that might no longer be acceptable to the mind in present times.

Ng: Then what do you think is at the origin of that word *sorcery*?

S: That's precisely the whole issue. Folktales show that something might have a name and still be imaginary. I concede that sorcery is not the same as a folktale. Although one might refuse the existence of sorcery, one cannot deny that some illnesses are said by healers to be caused by sorcerers or evil. In that case, you can just say that what is called sorcery is nothing other than what marks certain illnesses for which we have not yet found a cause. I am sure that these days doctors can say something about those diseases other than to accuse people of sorcery.

Ng: Alas, how many people have been accused of sorcery for no reason other than a lack of explanation for certain illnesses!

S: On this point, nobody can rival my friends from Saint-Louis. May God forgive them for their quick accusations. As much as they are hospitable, if they do not know where you are from, they will accuse you of sorcery!

Ng: How about people who get in a trance and accuse themselves of sorcery?

S: I am getting to that. The trance also is nothing but an illness. Accusing yourself of all kinds of things is one of the human diseases. If you then belong to a community that believes that sorcery exists and you get sick, if your unconscious mind is looking for something important of which to accuse itself, I think it can find sorcery.

Ng: You are then saying that it is not because of sorcery that people believe it exists, but that it exists because people believe it does?

S: That is exactly where I was going! Mr. Amadou Hampate Ba once told this story: he said that Hyena, like any good liar, announced that there was some treasure waiting at some location to be picked up; when the rumor spread, and he saw that everywhere he turned people single-mindedly were heading in the direction he had indicated, he said: "Maybe I too should go and check whether or not there is a treasure there? If all these people are running together in that direction, there must be something." You can always say it is a tale, but it has a deeper meaning that you just articulated: belief leads to truth, although what we usually think is that truth leads to belief.

Ng. Waaw nañu bàyyi waxu dëmm te . . .

S. Xanaa danga ragal?

Ng. Ragal lan?

S. Damay kaf. Waaye xam nga dañu naan dëmm soo koy tudd rekk dafa fekk sorewul . . .

Ng. Fii de maak yow rekk a fi nekk di waxtaan. Xanaa ak gune gile tëdd ci sa wet, sa sët bi Suleymaan, di ñu déglu mel na dafa bëgg mëna nettali li ñuy wax. Déglul bu baax, Suleymaan, dégg nga?

Suleymaan. Waaw, maam.

Ng. Soxna, dama xalaat léegi, bi ñuy wax ci dëgg ak gëm, benn baat ci Alxuraan. Ndax Yàlla ci téereem bu tedd wi dafa ci wax yonnent bi, *sallalaahu alayhi wa salam*, ni ko: "Te su ñu leen tarilee suñuy aaya ak ni ñu leeree, ñu naan, lii du dara lumoy nit kese bu leen bëgga tàggaleek li seeni maam daan jaamu." Dinga ko fekk ci saar bi ñu naan Saba, di fanweer ak ñent ci saar yi; aaya bi nak mooy ñent fukk ak ñetteel. Bii aaya laa indi, waaye am na yeneen yu ni mel di wone ni cosaanu maam ya mooy liy tax doomu Aadama xàmmee, dëgg të ko.

S. Maa ngi daldi gis li la taxa xalaat baatu Alxuraan bii nga indi . . .

Ng. Dafa dëggal li nga waxoon léegi bi nga nee liy taxawal dëgg xel la, du cosaan. Ndax ñii Alxuraan ni ba dëgg dikkee ci ñoom nanguwuñu ko xàmmee, dara taxu leena gëlëm ludul ŋoy ca la seen maam yi nekkeewoon. Koon mu mel ni fii ñu tollu ci suñu waxtaan wii, ñépp dañu wara ànd jubóo ci ni Wolof Njaay mbaa Cosaan mbaa maam yi nee nañu taxul wax ja di dëgg.

S. Waaw ma ni, su dul dëgg koon lan la?

Ng. Aa! Loo bëgga wax foofu?

S. Deet, xam nga soo firee baatu Alxuraan bi nga indi léegi, mu tekki ni dëgg ba mu dikkee dafa randal la mu fa fekk di cosaan. Ma di laaj: la mu fekk lu mu, su dul dëgg? Walla book negal ma jaare li may wax neneen: nooy waxee li safaan dëgg?

Ng. Maanaam?

S. Xam nga guddi moo safaan bëccëg? Lëndëm ak leer safaanoo? Danga naan itam biir ni biti, ni lëf ni tus, mën nañu topp yeneen ak yeneeni kàddu yu ni mel. Ma di la laaj, soo jàppee dëgg mu mel na leer, ban baat ngay jàpp mu mel ni guddi?

Ng: Now let us stop talking about sorcery and . . .

S: Are you scared?

Ng: Scared of what?

S: I am just kidding. But as you know, they say that if you talk about sorcery, that means it is not too far . . .

Ng: Right here, it is only you and I talking. And maybe this child lying down next to you, your grandson Suleymaan, who is listening to us as if he wants to be able to report our conversation. Listen carefully, Suleymaan, you hear?

Suleymaan: Yes, grandpa.

Ng: Soxna, as we were talking about truth and belief, I just thought about a passage in the Koran. In His blessed Book, God tells the prophet, Peace Be Upon Him: "And when we recite to them our verses in all their clarity, they say: 'this is nothing but a human being trying to detach you from what your ancestors used to worship.'" You will find this passage in the chapter called Saba, the thirty-fourth chapter; it is the forty-third verse. I brought up this verse, but there are similar ones which show that ancestral traditions are the reason why human beings know the truth but do not recognize it.

S: I am starting to see how you thought about the passage of the Koran that you brought up . . .

Ng: It supports what you said earlier about truth being sustained by thought, not by tradition. Those who according to the Koran did not want to recognize the truth when it came to them, nothing blinded them except holding tightly to what their ancestors believed. Thus, it seems that, at this point in our conversation, there should be a consensus that what Wolof Njaay, or Tradition, or the ancestors say, does not make something true.

S: But then, if it is not truth, what is it?

Ng: What do you mean?

S: You know, if you interpret the passage of the Koran that you just brought up, it means that when truth arrived, it displaced what it found there, that is, tradition. Here is my question: Did it find there anything other than truth? Or let me put it another way: What do you call the opposite of truth?

Ng: Say it again?

S: You know that night is the opposite of day? Dark the opposite of light? One also says inside versus outside, something versus nothing; we can keep on adding many other pairs of this kind. I am asking you, if you associate truth with light, which word would you associate with night?

Ng. Yaakaar naa ni sama tontu mooy doon ni baat yi safaan dëgg bare nañu. Biy jëkk ñëw ci xel xëyna mooy 'fen'; yaakaar naa ni mën nga itam ni ludul dëgg mooy 'leeb'; 'juum' itam safaan na dëgg . . .

S. Waaw xanaa amuloo benn kàddu kese bu ñu mën ni ma ngoog, bii moo safaan dëgg , ni guddi mel ak bëccëg?

Ng. Déedéet. Gis nga li waral lim gi, mooy bu nekk ci ñetti baat yii ma wax benn maanaa ci maanaawu dëgg la safaan. Mu mel na su ma nee "wax jii du dëgg, fen la" dama jàpp ni am na ku tey, xam dëgg ba noppi di waxee neneen: ku wax lu amul te xam ni amul, kookaa ngay fen, di kàcc, di nar, yii baat yëpp bokk li ñuy tekki.

S. Waaw, boobu di 'fen.' Jàpp naa ni ku juum fenul?

Ng. Déedéet. Ndax ki juum dafa wax lu amul, fekk yaakaaroon na ni noonu la. Mel na ku juum ci woññi xaalis ni la nàngam a ngii, fekk li mu woññi ëpp na mbaa mu yees. Su ko defee ngir tappale mbaa caay-caay, fen dafay daadi dugg; waaye su dee ku munul woññi bu baax mbaa ku mel na man di magal, juum lay doon ndax jubluwu ci naxaate ak njublaŋ. Mu des 'léeb.' Bii moom leer na, ndax soo ne 'léeb' yaa ngi naan lu ñu fent, indi ay bàyyima yuy wax, mbaa ay rab ak yu ni mel; doonte léeb day faral di ëmb dëgg bu ñu bëgg xamal gune yi, ngir yee leen ci àddina, kenn jàppul ni xeet buy soppaliku beneen xeet lu am la. Noonu nga mën ni léeb, maanaam lu ñu fent, moo safaan dëgg.

S. Xanaa book ñetti baat yii safaan dëgg am nañu lu leen boolee?

Ng. Ni ma ko gisee mooy lii: dafa mel na ab fittkat buy diir lëf. Ñaar ay am, mu dal mbaa mu moy. Li ma namm ci misaal mi mooy wax bu dëggu dafa mel na fitt wu dal: mooy wax ja dëppook li am. Lu dul dëgg nak mooy li moy li am: su ko moyee ci kaw tey, moy ma dafay firi fen; su ko moyee ci kaw doyadi, njuumte la moy moomu tudd; su fekkee nak ni dafa won gannaw li am, fent beneen tëralinu àddina, booba léeb lañuy wax, booba du rekk moy: li am dafa jaar nii, léeb jaar nale. Koon daal mel na ni baatu 'moy' mooy reen bi boole baatu 'fen,' 'juum' walla 'léeb.'

Ng: I guess my answer would be that there are not many words that are the opposites of truth. The first one to come to mind is maybe "lie"; I guess you might also say that what is not truth is a "tale"; "mistake" also is an opposite of "true."

S: So you do not have any single word that we could say is the opposite of truth, just as night is the opposite of day?

Ng: No. You see, the reason why I gave a list is that each of these three words represents one of the meanings of the opposite of truth. It is similar to saying "this sentence is not true, it is a lie"—I imply that there is someone who knows the truth but purposely speaks otherwise: someone who says something he obviously knows is not true, he is lying [*fen*], he is hiding the truth [*kàcc*], he is deceiving [*nar*], all these words share the same meaning.

S: All right, that is "lie." Then someone who is mistaken is not lying?

Ng: No. Because someone who is mistaken is not telling the truth, but he thinks he is doing so. Like someone who makes a mistake counting money and gives you a certain amount, which may be more or less than the real amount. If the reason for that is mischief or cheating, then the right word is lying; however, if it is because he does not count well or he is forgetful, as I am, he would be mistaken because he had no intention to deceive or trick. The remaining item is "tale." This one is easy to deal with because when you talk about a tale, you are talking about something that is invented, animals that can talk, or spirits, or things of that sort; although tales often involve some truth that we want our young to know, in order to make them understand the world, no one would agree that a given species can transform into another. In that sense, you can say that a tale, that is, something that is invented, is the opposite of truth.

S: Can we say then that these three words that are the opposite of truth have something in common?

Ng: This is how I see it: It is like an archer who is aiming at something. There are two possibilities, either he hits the target or he misses. What I like in this analogy is that a statement that is based on truth is like an arrow that hits its target: it is a statement that agrees with what is real. Then, what is not truth is something that misses what is real: if it misses it intentionally, that miss translates as a lie; if it misses it because of ignorance, that miss is called a mistake; finally, if it turns away from what is real, inventing another view of the world, we will talk about a tale, and it is not just a miss: what is real goes one way, and a tale goes the other way. Therefore, it looks like the notion of "miss" is the root that is common to the words *lie, mistake,* or *tale.*

S. Nii nga faramfàncee mbirum baat yi safaanoo dëgg leer na. Yaakaar naa ni mën nañu ko waxee nii: dëgg mooy yoon wi am, ludul dëgg mooy li teggi yoon wa am te ñu rëdd ko. Te sax soo ko seetee, 'dëgg' ak 'yoon' am nañu fu ñu bokkee maanaa mi ñu ëmb. Soo nee nàngam du dëgg du yoon, dafa mel na danga wax ni dëgg mooy yoon, yoon di dëgg; rax ci dolli itam nàngam du dëgg du yoon li muy tekki, mooy jëf ju ñaaw, ju moy li ñu doon séenu. Koon dëgg du rekk li am, li wara am la itam. Ba ku def lu warul, ñu ni la li nga def du dëgg, dafa teggi yoon wa.

Ng. Waaw, yaakaar naa ni maanaab 'dëgg' ak 'ludul dëgg' xaw na gëna leer.

S. Koon ma dellusi ci li tax ma laajoon la ludul dëgg lu mu doon. Xam nga baatu Alxuraan bi nga indi dafa ni ba dëgg dikkee dafa dàq li fi newoon di cosaan. May laaj nu ñu wara jàppee maam ya jiitu? Ndax soo ko seetee, ludul Alpulaar yi ak Saraxulle yi nga xam ni bi ñu duggee ci diine Lislaam yàgg na, waaso yu bare bi ñu tuubee yàggul; soo jëlee Wolof yi, ci jamono Seriñ Tuubaa mbaa Maam Maalik lañu sumboxloo ci Lislaam; soo jëlee Joolaa mbaa Seereer waxi noppi: bi ñu duggee ci Lislaam mbaa ci diine Kercen démb la. Balaa Lislam walla diine Katolig di agsi ci suñu gox yii, li doon suñu cosaan, diine ak xam-xam ak jëfin yi fi amoon, ndax dañu leen di rekk féetalee ci 'ludul dëgg,' lu wàcc yoon, gannaaw yoon benn la?

Ng. Gis naa fi nga jëmsiwoon. "Ndax dëggu diine dafa neenal cosaan?" mooy li ngay seet.

S. Ma ngook! Waaye negal ma yaatal porobalem bi, won la ni nii nga ko tëralee benn la rekk ci anam yi am ci li ma bëgg sax sax ñu sottante ci xel. Muy dëgg ak jamono. Ndax lëf dina doon dëgg, jamono di dox ba mu soppaliku, ñu gisee ko lu dëppootul ak li wara ne: te juboo nañu ci ni dëppook li wara ne moo firi dëgg.

Ng. Bi nga nee "dëgg ak jamono" danga ma indil sama emisioŋu xarit bi ci rajo *Wal Fajri*, Siidi Lamin Ñas. Mooy emisioŋ "diine ak jamono." Du dinga ko déglu?

S. Bu baax sax! Ñàkkul sax moo ñëw ci sama xel ba ma wax li ma wax. Gis nga li Siidi Lamin jublu ci emisioŋ bi nga wax, mooy batey li may laaj. Ndax Siidi dafa bëgg xool ni dëggu diine doonee lu dul soppiku, ba noppi di itam luy ànd ak jamono. Wax ji yépp a ngook.

S: The way you explain the words opposite of truth is clear. I think we can describe it in the following terms: the truth is the path that exists, the untruth is what deviates from the path which is delineated. Indeed if you look at it, "truth" and "path" share in some way the meanings which they convey. If you say that something is "not the truth nor is it the path," it is like saying that the truth is the path and the path is the truth; in addition, the expression "Something is not the truth nor is it the path" also refers to a bad act that deviates from what was expected. So the truth is not only what is, it is also what should be. Consequently, when someone does something wrong, he is told that what he did is not the truth, it deviates from the path.

Ng: Yes indeed, I think the issue of "truth" and "untruth" is a little clearer.

S: In that case, let me come back to the reason why I asked you what untruth was. As you know, the passage of the Koran that you brought up says that when truth came, it replaced what was there before, which was tradition. I am asking how should we consider the people that came before us? If you look at it, except for the Fulani and the Soninke who came to the religion of Islam a long time ago, many communities converted recently; the Wolof converted en masse in the times of Serigne Touba and Mame El Hadj Malick; the same is true of the Diola and the Serer: they came to Islam and Christianity recently. How should we consider what were our existing traditions, religion, knowledge, and ways of doing things before Islam or Christianity came to our shores? Should we just classify them as "untruths," deviations, since the path is one?

Ng: I see where you are going. "Does religious truth nullify tradition?" is what you are looking for.

S: That's it! However, let me broaden the problem and show you that, the way you formulated it, this is just one of the issues concerning which I happened to want to exchange ideas with you. It is about truth and time. Something might be true, but with the passage of time it might change and be seen as not corresponding any more to what should be; however, we have agreed that what corresponds to what should be is what defines truth.

Ng: When you said "truth and time," you reminded me of my friend Sidy Lamine Niasse's talk show on *Wal Fajri* radio. It is the show "Religion and the Times." You do listen to it, don't you?

S: Yes indeed! It is even possible that this was what came to my mind when I spoke. You see that Sidy Lamine's goal in the show you mention is related to what I am asking. Sidy wants to examine how religious truth is something immutable, and at the same time is something that agrees with the times. This is the whole issue.

Ng. Gis nga, su ñu dellusee ci ni nga waxeewoon léegi bi nga nee "ndax dëggu diine dafa neenal cosaan?" dama ci bëgg joxe tontu boo xam ni ñaari anam la. Benn mooy ni diine ci boppam moo tontu ne déedéet. Soo jëlee diine Lislaam, dafa wax ni li ko indi mooy dëggal aada yu rafet yu mu fekk, dindi rekk lu ñaaw, te boo seetee, mooy batey lu xel nanguwul, lu dëppoowul ak li wara ne. Koon ci benn wàll dafa dàq cosaan, waaye ci beneen dafa ko beesalaat, gën koo taxawal.

S. Waaw kay! Lii la xel gëna mëna nangu: ni rekk ni nit ñi fi nekkoon di suñuy maam, nañu daan xalaatee, nañu daan gisee, nañu daan jëflantee ci seen biir, ci seen digganteek saxayaay yi, bàyyima yi, doomu Aadama yi, seen digganteek seen boroom, loolu yépp réer lawoon, lu jiitu yoon feeñ, neexula nangu.

Ng. Dëgg la. Ma bëgg yokk ni mbir mi du rekk diine Lislaam. Diine Kerecen itam wax na lu ni mel. Góor gi Seŋoor daan na wax di waxaat ni cosaanu doomu askan wi du lu Kiriscanism wara randal: dafa ciy seey, and ak moom, dugg ca baatin ba. Ma dikk léegi ci li doon ñaareelu anam bi ma doon wax. Gis nga baatu Alxuraan bi ma indiwoon séddalewul rekk diine ak cosaan. Ndax soo ci bàyyee xel te seetaat ko, ña daan taafantoo cosaan ak aada ngir bañ diine, mooy ñi nga xam ni tey ni ñu gisee diine ak ni ñu ko déggee ca déggin ba gëna xat, dara wuutalewu leen ak ñooñu daan wax ni dañu bëgg ŋoy ci li maam yi daan jaamu, walla book ci ni maam yi daan jaamoo.

S. Koon war nañu mëna juboo ni cosaan taxul di dëgg, dëppook xel ak dëppook jamono moo tax ñu naan dëgg.

Ng. Mel na na noonu lañu mujjee kay.

S. Waaw koon maa ngiy yàqq waxtaan wi. Ñàkkul sax am na yeneeni xalaat yu ma dikkal ci biir waxtaan, lu mel na maanaawu 'jamono' . . . Waaye xanaa dañu koy aj fii, dem ba beneen ndax mi ngiy guddi. Aywa, Suleymaan, aywan dem nak.

Ng. Baax na Soxna. Ba beneen.

Ng: You see, going back to what you said earlier, that is, "Does religious truth nullify tradition?" I would like to give it a two-pronged answer. First, religion itself will say no. If you take the religion of Islam, it says that its purpose was to reaffirm the good traditions already present and to take away only the bad ones; if you think about it, those are again the unreasonable ones, the ones that do not agree with what should be. Therefore, on one hand it replaces tradition, but on the other hand it renews it, it reinforces it.

S: Yes indeed! This is what makes more sense and is easier to accept than to say that all that preceded the true path was wrong: the way our ancestors were thinking, the way they were seeing things, the way they were relating to one another, to plants, to animals, to their Creator.

Ng: That's true. I want to add this is not only the case with Islam. Christianity also says something similar. Former President Senghor often used to say that the people's tradition is not something that Christianity should displace: it should melt into it, go with it, penetrate its essence. I come now to the second aspect that I was talking about. You see, the Koranic verse I mentioned does not distinguish only between religion and tradition. If you play close attention, those who used to take tradition and custom as a pretext to refuse religion are no different than those who today have a very narrow view and understanding of the religion; nothing distinguishes them from those who used to say they wanted to partake in what their ancestors were worshipping, or worship the way their ancestors were worshipping.

S: Then we can come to an agreement that tradition is not enough for us to talk about truth, we should say making sense and agreeing with the times.

Ng: It seems indeed like a logical conclusion.

S: I will stop our conversation here then. There may be some other thoughts that occurred to me during the conversation, such as the meaning of "time". . . . We will just have to leave it at that for the time being, as it is getting late. Suleymaan, let us get on our way.

Ng: Good, Soxna. Till next time.

የኢትዮጵያ ጊዜ ግንዛቤና ዘመናዊነት

መሳይ ከበደ

ፈላስፎችን የሚያስማማ አንድ ነገር ቢኖር የጊዜ ምንነት የፍልስፍና እምብርት ጥያቄ መሆኑ ነው። ምዕራባዊውን ዓለም እንደ ምሳሌ ብንወስድ፤ ስለ ጊዜ ሳይመራመር የቀረ ታዋቂ ምዕራባዊ ፈልስፋ የለም። የጀርመኑ ፈላስፋ፤ ማርቲን ሃይደገር፤ የጊዜ ጥያቄን እንብርትነት ሲያመለክት፤ "ጊዜ ተብራርቶ የኑባሬ ማንኛውም ግንዛቤና ትርጓሜ አድማስ መሆኑ በትክክል መታወቅ አለበት" ብሏል።[1] እንዲሁም በፈረንሳዊው ፈላስፋ ሃንሪ በርግሶን አባባል፤ የፍልስፍና ጥያቄዎች አስቸጋሪ የሆኑበት ዋናው ምክንያት "ዕውኑን ጊዜ ስለማናስብ" ነው።[2] የጊዜ ጥያቄ በጣም ግራ አጋቢ በመሆኑም ነው አንዳንድ ፈላስፎች ጊዜ ዕውን ያልሆነ የውሸት ዕይታ ነው ያሉት። ለምሳሌ ፓርመኒዲዝ የተባለው የጥንታዊ ግሪክ ፈላስፋ ኑባሬን ከጊዜ ውጪ ማሰብ እንዳለብን ሲያስርዳ፤ "ቀድሞ ወይም ወደፊት አይኖርም፤ ሁሌም በአንድነት መቼም ሳይቋርጥ ያለ ነውና" ሲል ተናግሯል።[3]

የዚህ ፅሑፍ ዋና ዓላማ አስቸጋሪ የሆነውን የጊዜ ጽንሰሐሳብ ኢትዮጵያውያን[4] እንዴት ይመለከቱትል የሚል ነው። ጊዜ የፍልስፍና ወሳኝ ጥያቄ በመሆኑም አመለካከቱን መመርመር የኢትዮጵያ የዓለም አመለካከትን ሥር መሰረት ያስጨብጣል። በተለይም የጊዜ ግንዛቤ ከታሪካዊ አስተሳሰብ ጋር የተሳሰረ በመሆኑ ኢትዮጵያውያን ምንነታቸውንና ዓላማቸውን እንዴት እደተረጎሙ ያመለክታል። በያዙት ዓላማ አንጻርም እንዴት ዘመናዊነትን እንደተቀበሉት ይጠቁማል። የአቀባበሉ ሁኔታ ደግሞ ለምን ዘመናዊነትን በኢትዮጵያ ለማስፈን እንዳልተቻላቸው አብሮ ይናገር።

ጊዜና ኑባሬ

ጊዜን ዋናና አስቸጋሪ ጥያቄ የሚያደርጉትን ምክንያቶች በአጭሩ እንመልከት። ስለ መኖር በተመራመርን ቁጥር ምርምሩ ጊዜ ምን ማለት ነው? ወደሚል ጥያቄ በቀጥታ ይቀየራል። ኑሮ መጀመሪያና መጨረሻ ያለውና በተለያዩ ተለዋዋጭ ሁኔታዎች የሚያልፍ ክስተት ነው። ተፈጥሮ የሆነ ሁሉ መጀመሪያ እንዳለው ሁሉ መጨረሻውም አይቀሬ ነው። እንዲሁም የሚኖር ነገር

The Ethiopian Conception of Time and Modernity

Messay Kebede, *University of Dayton*
Translated by Bethlehem Hailu Dejene, *Northwestern University*

If there is one thing that philosophers agree upon, it is that the meaning of time is a central philosophical question. If we take the Western world as an example, there is no famous philosopher who has not investigated time. The German philosopher Martin Heidegger, to indicate the centrality of time, writes: "The central problematic of all ontology is rooted in the phenomenon of time correctly viewed and correctly explained."[1] Likewise, according to the French philosopher Henri Bergson, the main reason that philosophical questions are difficult is because "we do not think real time."[2] The fact that the question of time is very confusing has led some philosophers to claim that time is an unreal, illusory notion. For example, the ancient Greek philosopher known as Parmenides, in order to explain that we have to think of being as outside of time, says that "it is neither was nor will be, it simply is—now, altogether, one, continuous."[3]

The main intention of this essay is to ask how Ethiopians perceive this difficult notion of time.[4] Because time is a decisive question for philosophy, to examine how it is perceived allows us to understand how Ethiopians have seen the world. Particularly, as the conception of time is tied up with historical thinking, it can show us how Ethiopians have interpreted their identity and their goals. The goals they espouse indicate how they have received modernity. In return, how they received modernity should inform us about why it has been so impossible to modernize Ethiopia.

BEING AND TIME

Let us look briefly at the reasons for the importance and difficulty of the question of time. Whenever we seek to study life, our inquiry leads us directly to the question: "What is the meaning of life?" Life is a phenomenon that has a beginning and end but which also passes through various changing situations. As everything that is natural has a beginning, it is natural that it has an end. Furthermore, since everything that lives experiences growth, it goes through

ሁሉ በእድገት ሁኔታ ውስጥ ስለሚያልፍ የማያቋርጥ መለዋወጥን ያሳያል። የመኖር ባሕርያት የሆኑት የመጀመር፤ የማደግ፤ የማርጀት፤ የማለቅ ሁኔታዎች ሁሉ የጊዜ መግለጫዎች ናቸው።

እዚህ ላይ የሚነሳ አስቸጋሪ ነጥብ አለ። አንድ ነገር ሲለዋወጥ ምንነቱን ያጣል ካልን ሥለ ነገሩ የምንሰጠው ብያኔ ትክክለኛነት አይኖረውም። ምክነቱም ነገሩ ቋሚ ባህርይ ስለሌለው በተለዋወጠ ቁጥር ብያኔያችንን ይሽረዋል። መለዋወጥ የሚያስከትለው ዓለም በሰው ልጅ አእምሮ ሊታወቅ አይችልም የሚል ድምዳሜ ይሆናል ማለት ነው። በተጨማሪም፤ ሳያቋርጥ የሚለዋወጥ ነገር አለ ማለት ፍች የሚሰጥ አነጋገር አይመስልም። አሁን ያለው ሲለወጥ፤ መኖሩ የት ይገባል፤ ምን ሆነ ይባላል? ባዶ ሆነ የምንል ከሆነ፤ ባዶ የሌለ ነገር ስለሆነ እንዴት ያለው ወደ ምንም ይቀየራል? በመሆኑም አለ መባልና ጊዜ አብረው የሚሄዱ አይመስሉም።

የለም፤ ነገሩ ሲለወጥ ባህሪው አይቀየርም የምንል ከሆነ ደግሞ፤ ጊዜ እውነታ የሌለው ክስተት ይሆናል። ነገሩ ካልተለወጠ በጊዜ ውስጥ ማለፉ ያመጣው ድርጊት የለም ማለት ነውና። በመሆኑም የምናየው መንቀሳቀስና መለዋወጥ የቁም ቅዥት ይሆናል።

ከዚህም ችግር አልፈን በመሄድ መኖርን በትክክልና በተሟላ መልኩ ለማሰብ ስንሞክር ከዘለዓለማዊነትና ከለውጠቢስነት ጋር ይዛመድብናል። ኑሮ ፍጹም የሚሆነው መጀመሪያና መጨረሻ ሳይኖረው፤ ከማደግና ከመለዋወጥ የጸዳ ባሕርይ ሲያሳይ አይደለምን? ተፈጥሮ ተፈጣሪ እንደ መሆኑ፤ እሱን ሊፈጥር የሚችለው ኃይል እራሱ ከጊዜ የወጣ መሆን አይኖርበትምን? ስለዚህ ነው ፍጹም መኖርን እግዚአብሔር የምንለውና ዋና ባሕሪውንም ከጊዜ ሂደት ውጪ የምናድርገው።

የመኖር የማይጣጣሙ ባሕርያትን ለማስታረቅ ስንነሳ ጊዜን እንደ ሂደት ወይም ጉዞ እናስባለን። መጀመሪያ ያለውና ተለዋዋጭ የሆነ ኑሮ የሚያከናውነው ግብ ወይም ዓላማ ስላለው በጊዜ ውስጥ ይጓዛል። ይህ አባባል አንድ የሐሳብ አቅጣጪ ይከፍታል። የመለዋወጥ ምስጢር ዓላማን ማስፈጸም ከሆነ፤ አንዱ ዓላማ ወደ ላቀ የመኖር ደረጃ መሸጋገር ሊሆን ይችላል። የዓላማው መከናወንም ወደ መኖር ፍጹም ደረጃ ሊያሸጋግር ይችላል። በሌላ አባባል፤ የጊዜ ምስጢር ዘለዓለማዊነት ይሆናል ማለት ነው።

የጊዜ ጥያቄ ከመኖር ጋር የተሳሰረው የመኖርን ፍች ወይም ምስጢር ገላጭ በመሆኑ ነው። ሃይደገር እንዳለው፤ የጊዜን ጥያቄ ማብራራት የመኖርን ምስጢር መፍታት ነው። ለዚህም ነው ሰዎች ጊዜ ግብ አለው ለማለት የበቁት። ጊዜ ግብ ሲኖረው ሂደት ይሆናል፤ ሂደቱም የኑሮን ግብ ያስፈጽማል። ለምሳሌ የክርስትናና የእስልምና ሃይማኖት ተከታዮች ሁሉ የጊዜ ሂደት ዘለዓለማዊነት ያዘጋጃል ይላሉ።

የኢትዮጵያ ሁኔታ

የኢትዮጵያ የጊዜ ግንዛቤን የምንጨብጠው ጊዜ የኑሮን ትርጉም አብሳሪ መሆኑን ስንቀበል ነው። ግንዛቤውንም ማመንጨት ያለብን ከነበሩበት ሁኔታ በመነሳት እንዴት ኢትዮጵያውያን የመኖራቸውን ፍች ቀመሩ ብለን በመጠየቅ ነው። ከነበሩበት ሁኔታ ካልተነሳን የምናገኘው ውጤት ከመኖር ፍች ምርመራ ጋር የተገናኘ አይሆንም። እንዲሁ ብቅ ያለ ሐሳብ ነው ከማለት በስተቀር ኑሮንና ጊዜን በጥምር መመልከት አያስችለንም።

uninterrupted change. The processes of beginning, growing, aging, and ending, which are the characteristics of life, are thus expressions of time.

There is a difficult point that needs to be raised here. If we say that when something changes, it loses its essence, our judgments about this thing will be incorrect. Since it has no permanent characteristics, our judgments are falsified each time the thing changes. Continuous change leads, therefore, to the conclusion that the world cannot be known by the human mind. Furthermore, to say that continuous change is real does not seem to make sense. When what exists changes, where does its previous existence go—what can we say happened to it? If we say that it has become nothing, since nothing is nothing, how can something change into nothing? Accordingly, being and time do not seem to go together.

On the other hand, if we say that when a thing changes, its nature does not change, then time is a phenomenon without reality. For unless the thing itself changes, the fact that it has passed through time is without consequence. Therefore, the movement and the change that we see is nothing but an illusion.

Going further, when we attempt to think of life correctly and in its fullness, then it coincides with eternity and immutability. Does not life become absolute when it has neither beginning nor end and is free from the characteristics of growth and change? Since nature is created, does not the power that creates it have to be outside of time? This is why we say Absolute Life is God and why we place it outside temporality.

When we try to reconcile the incongruent characteristics of life, we think of time as a process and a journey. Living, which has a beginning and which involves change, has goals and aims and thus it passes through time. This approach opens a new direction of thought. If the secret of change is the accomplishment of goals, then one of the aims could be to accede to a higher level of life. The accomplishment of this aim could lead to life's absolute level. In other words, the secret of time is the state of eternity.

The question of time is tied to life because it reveals the meaning or secret of life. As Heidegger says, to dwell on the question of time is to unravel the secret of life. This is what makes people say time has a goal. When time has a goal, it becomes a process; this process accomplishes the goal of life. For example, adherents of Christianity and Islam say the process of time prepares us for the state of eternity.

THE ETHIOPIAN SITUATION

We can grasp Ethiopia's understanding of time when we accept that time reveals the meaning of life. We must gain this understanding by examining how Ethiopians, starting from their situation, arrived at the meaning of life. If we do not start from their situation, our elucidation will not be connected with an inquiry into the meaning of life. It would fail to tie time to the meaning of life, thereby making the latter into a thought that just popped up.

We know that Ethiopia's situation turned the question of existence into a major concern. For a country that has existed as a lone island of Christianity for centuries, life inevitably holds a precarious character. In particular,

የኢትዮጵያ ሁኔታ በከፍተኛ ደረጃ መኖርን ጥያቄ ያደርግ እንደነበር እናውቃለን። ለብዙ ዘመናት ብቸኛ የክርስቲያን ደሴት ሆና ለተቀመጠች አገር መኖር አጠራጣሪ መልክ መያዙ አይቀርም። በተለይ በኃያላን እስልምና ተከታይ አገሮች መከበብና አልፎም የወረራ ጥረት መጋለጥ ለመኖር የሳሳ ጠባይ ስጥቷል። ኑሮን የተረጋገጠ ለማድርግና አበረታታች ተስፋ ለመፍጠር ልዩ የታሪክ ግንዛቤ መቀመር አስፈላጊ ሆኗል። ይህም ታሪክ ለኢትዮጵያ ልዩ ተልዕኮ በመስጠት በድል አድራጊነት እስከመጨረሻ እንደምትቆይ ማረጋገጥ ይኖርበታል። የጊዜ ሂደት ተልዕኮውን መፈጸም ሲሆን የመኖር ፍችንም አብሮ ይሰጣል። የዚህ ድል አብሳሪ ታሪክ ግንዛቤ ዋና ምንጭ ክብረ ነገሥት የተባለው መጽሐፍ ነው።

እንደሚታወቀው ሁሉ የንግሥት አዜብና የንጉሥ ስለሞን መገናገኘት ሁለት ቁም ነገሮችን አስከትሏል። አንዱ የኢትዮጵያ ንጉሥ የሚሆነው የምንሊክ መወለድ ሲሆን ሁለተኛውና ዋነኛው ደግሞ የታቦት ጽዮን ወደ ኢትዮጵያ መወሰድ ነው። የታቦቷን መወሰድ እንደተረዳ ንጉሥ ስሎሞን በቀጥታ እንዲህ ብሏል፤ "የከበረችው የጽዮን ልጅ ክብር ተነስቷል። የጎስቋላዋ የኢትዮጵያ ልጅ ክብር ከፍ ብሏልና"።[5] ከፍተኛ ብስጭትና ሓዘን ውስጥም ንጉሥ ስሎሞን በመውደቁ የትንቢት መንፈስ እንዲህ ሲል ጠይቆታል፤ "ይህ በእግዚአብሄር ፈቃድ ሆኗልና በአባትህ በዳዊት ዙፋን ላይ ለሚቀመጠው ለበኩር ልጅህ ነው እንጂ ለባእድ የተሰጠች አይደለችምና ለምን እንደዚህ ታዝናለህ?"[6] ይህ የክብረ ነገሥት አባባል በትክክል የሚያስቀምጠው እግዜር ኢትዮጵያን ለልዩ ዓላማ ማጨቱን ነው።

የኢትዮጵያ የጊዜ ግንዛቤ ለአገር ልዩ ዕጣ በመለገስ ብቻ አልተወሰነም፤ የግልሰቦችን ኑሮና ማህበራዊ ሥፍራንም ያጠቃልላል። የግለሰቦች ኑሮ በጣም ተለዋዋጭ፤ በብዙ ውጣ ውረዶችና አጋጣሚዎች የሚያልፍ እንደመሆኑ፤ ይህ ተቀያያሪ ሁኔታ ፍች የሚኖርው ወደ አንድ ግብ ሲጓዝ ብቻ ነው፡፡ የዚህ ግብ አፈጻጸም የጊዜ ሂደት ይሆናል። በተለይም፤ ጊዜ የሚራመደው በአንድ አቅጣጫ ወደፊት በመሄድ ነውን ለሚለው ጥያቄ ኢትዮጵያውያን የሰጡት መልስ የአመለካከታቸውን ፍሬ ነገር ይጠቁማል።

የጊዜ ተፈራራቂነት

የኢትዮጵያ የጊዜ ግንዛቤ በትትክል እንዲገባን አንድ መሠረታዊ መነሻ መቀበል አለብን። እሱም እንደ ማንኛውም ቅድመ ዘመናዊ አመለካከት ኢትዮጵያውያን ጊዜን የተመለከቱት እንደ ተደጋጋሚ ክስተት ነው። ይህን ሐሳብ ሊሰጣቸው የቻለው በመጀመሪያ ደረጃ የተፈጥሮ ሁኔታ ነው። ተፈጥሯዊ ክስተቶች በሙሉ ይፈራረቃሉ። ቀን በማታ፤ ማታ በቀን ይተካል። ክረምት ሲያልፍ በጋ ይመጣል፤ በጋ ሲሄድ፤ ክረምት ይተካል። ሙቀት ወደ ቅዝቃዜ፤ ቅዝቃዜ ወደ ሙቀት ይሸጋገራል። ሕይወት ወደ ሞት፤ ሞት ወደ ሕይወት ይቀየራል።

ልክ እንደ ተፈጥሮ ግለሰባዊና ማህበራዊ ኑሮም የጊዜን ተፈራራቂነት ያረጋግጣል። ዛሬ የተደሰተ ነገ ያዝናል፤ ተመልሶም ይደሰታል። አባት ልጅ ሲወልድ፤ ልጅ ደግሞ አባት ይሆናል። ዛሬ የተነሳ ነገ በወደቀው ይተካል። ሀብታሙ ሲደኸይ ድሀ የነበረው ይከብራል። ንጉሥ ሲሞት ሌላ ንጉሥ ይመጣል።

the fact of being surrounded by powerful Islamic countries and exposed to attempts at invasion gave life a perilous meaning. To give life certainty and to conjure up encouraging hope, it became necessary to create a special understanding of history. By giving Ethiopia a special destiny, this history would confirm that Ethiopia will exist victoriously until the end. While the passage of time accomplishes this goal, it also provides the meaning of life. The main source of the understanding of this victory-proclaiming history is the book known as the *Kebra Negast.**

As is well known, the meeting of Queen Saba (Sheba) and King Solomon brought forth two important consequences. While one was the birth of Menelik who eventually became the king of Ethiopia, the second and more important outcome was the taking of the Ark of the Covenant to Ethiopia. When King Solomon discovered the disappearance of the Ark, he said directly: "The glory of the revered son of Zion has been removed, while the glory of the son of wretched Ethiopia has been raised."[5] Since King Solomon fell into deep disappointment and sadness, the spirit of prophecy asked him: "This hath happened by the will of God, and as the Ark has been given to your first son who sits on your father David's throne rather than a stranger, why are you so sad?"[6] This quote from the *Kebra Negast* shows precisely that God assigned Ethiopia a special role.

Ethiopia's understanding of time is not limited to assigning a special destiny to a country; it includes individuals' lives and social status. Since the life of the individual is constantly changing, since it passes through many highs and lows and incidents, this changing situation finds meaning only when it moves toward a goal. The accomplishment of this goal becomes the process of time. Above all, the answer that Ethiopians have given to the question of whether time moves forward and in one direction points to the essence of their outlook.

CYCLICALITY OF TIME

To comprehend the Ethiopian conception of time correctly, we need to accept a basic point of departure. That is, like any premodern view, Ethiopians saw time as a repetitive occurrence. What enabled them to attain this idea, on the first level, was the condition of nature. All natural phenomena are cyclical. Day is substituted for night and night for day. When winter passes, summer arrives; when summer leaves, winter replaces it. The warm becomes cold, the cold warm. Life changes into death and death into life.

Like nature, individual and social life confirms the cyclicality of time. One who is happy today is saddened tomorrow, and goes back to being happy. When a father gives birth to a son, the son becomes a father. The one who has been promoted will be replaced tomorrow by the one who has been demoted. When the rich turns poor, the poor becomes rich. When a king dies, another king comes.

የኢትዮጵያ የጊዜ ግንዛቤ በትክክል የሚያንጸባርቀውን የከበደ ሚካኤልን አንድ ግጥም እንመልከት። የግጥሙ አርእስት "ሁሉም የሆነ ነው" የሚል ሲሆን፤ ከግጥሙ ውስጥ አለፍ አለፍ እያልን ብንጠቅስ የሚከተሉትን ሓሳቦች እናገኛለን።

ሰሎሞን ብሎናል ደጉ ተመልካች
አዲስ ነገር የልም ከፀሓይ በታች

ልበ ተላላ ሰው ዘላለም ይሞኛል
እስኪ ረግቶ ያለ ምን ነገር ይገኛል?
የተማመኑበት እየሆነ ፈራሽ
ሲፈጸም ይገኛል ያልታሰበው ጭራሽ
ደካማ ይጠናል ኀይለኛ ሲዋረድ
ቡቃያ ይለማል ያፈራው ሲታጨድ
ሰፊው ይቀንሳል ጠባቡ ሲሰፋ
ጨረቃ ታምራለች ፀሓይ ስትጠፋ
ሀብታሙ ሲደኸይ ድኻ ሰው ይከብራል
አንዱ ሲደፈርስ ሌላውም ይጠራል
ከእንቅልፉ ሲነቃ ቀድሞ የፈዘዘ
የሞቀው ይሄዳል እየቀዘቀዘ
ትንሹም ትልቅ ነው ትልቁም ትንሽ
መጥፎውም መልካም ነው መልካሙም ብላሽ
እንደ ሕልም ታይቶ ያልፋል እንደ ጥላ

የዚህ ዓለም ነገር ምንም የለው መላ
ተፈራራቂ ነው አዲስ ነገር የለም።[7]

ከዚህ ግጥም የምንረዳው መሠረታዊ አመለካከት ሁሉ ነገር የሚፈራረቅ በመሆኑ ምንም አዲስ ነገር የለም የሚል ነው። የሚታዩት ለውጦች ሁሉ የነበረውን፤ የታየውን የሚመልሱ እንጂ አዲስ ነገር የሚያመጡ አይደሉም። የጊዜ ተፈራራቂነት የሚያስከትለው ሌላ ዋና ሐሳብ ሁሉ ነገር ከንቱ እንደሆ ነው። ምንም ነገር ስለማይቆይ፤ ብሎም ወደ ተቃራኒው ስለሚለወጥ፤ ሁሉ ነገር አንጻራዊ ነው። በዚህ ዓለም ውስጥ ምንም ፍጹማዊ ነገር ስለሌለ ሕይወታችን አላፊና ተቀልባሽ ሁኔታዎችን በማሳደድ መወሰን የለበትም። በመሆኑም የጊዜ ተፈራራቂነትን የሚያጋልጠው ነገሮች እራሱን የቻለ ንባሬ እንደሌላቸው ብቻ ሳይሆን ወደ ተቃራኒዎቻቸው በመለወጣቸው እራሳቸውን የመምራት ችሎታ እደሌላቸው ጭምር ነው።

ይህም በመሆኑ እነዚህን ነገሮች ሁሉ መናቅና መሸሽ አለብን ማለት አይደለም። እንደ አመጣጣቸው በጸጋ መቀበል እንጂ፤ ምክንያቱም የጊዜ መፈራረቅ የሚያመለክተው የእግዜርን ፍጹም ኃይል ነው። እግዜር ይሰጣል፤ መልሶም ይወስዳል። አንድን ሲሾም ሌላውን ይሽራል። አንድን ጌታ ሲያደርግ ሌላውን ያደኸያል። የነገሮች ቋሚነት ማጣትና ወደ ተቃራኒዎቻቸው መለወጥ የእግዜር መኖርንና የዓለም በእሱ ፈቃድ ብቻ መገዛትን ይጠቁማል። የነገሮች

Let us look at one of Kebede Mikael's poems, which correctly reflects Ethiopia's understanding of time. The title of the poem is "Everything Is Deja Vu." Here are some representative thoughts:

> Solomon, the fine observer, told us
> There is nothing new beneath the sun
>
> The naive person is constantly fooled
> Is there anything that stays the same?
> While that which you have put your trust in crumbles
> The unplanned is found happening
> The weak becomes strong while the powerful is humiliated
> Young plants grow while fruits are reaped
> The wide shrinks, while the narrow expands
> The moon becomes beautiful when the sun disappears
> When the rich becomes poor, the poor becomes wealthy
> When one thing becomes murky, another clears up
> The one who was sleepy wakes up
> The warm becomes colder
> The small is big, the big small
> The bad is good, the good bad
> It appears like a dream and passes like a shadow
> The nature of this world is unpredictable
>
> In the past, in the future, and today in this world
> There's nothing new; everything is cyclical[7]

The basic outlook we find in this poem is that, since everything is cyclical, there is nothing new. All the changes that are seen only replace what was previously seen; they do not bring anything new. The other important thought that is produced by the cyclicality of time is that everything is vain. Since nothing stays permanently and even changes into its opposite, everything is relative. Since there is nothing absolute in this world, our lives should not be limited to chasing transient and reversible conditions. Therefore, what the cyclicality of time exposes is not only that things do not have independent existence; the fact that things change into their own opposites also shows that they do not have the capacity to direct themselves.

Even so, we should not denigrate and avoid these things. Rather, we should accept them graciously as they come, because the cyclicality of time evinces the absolute power of God. God gives and takes back. While He appoints one, He demotes another. While He makes one a lord, He impoverishes another. The lack of permanence in things and their transformation into their opposites points to the existence of God and the fact that the world is ruled only by His will. The other lesson the cyclicality of things teaches us is not to be trapped by arrogance because we happen to be wealthy and

ተፈራራቂነት ሌላው የሚያስተምረን፣ በለጸግን፤ ሥልጣን ተቀዳጀን ብለን በትዕቢት ስሜት እንዳንጠመድ ነው። ትዕቢት ለራስና ለነገሮች አስመሳይ ነጻነት በመሥጠት የአምላክን ገዢነት የሚያድበሰብስ ዲበአካላዊ ውዥንብር ነው።

ጊዜና እድል

እዚህ ላይ የኢትዮጵያን ልዩነት መመልከት ያሻል። ቅድመ ዘመናዊ አመለካከቶች ሁሉ ጊዜ ተፈራራቂ ነው ቢሉም አመለካከታቸው በአመዛኙ ያተኮረው ተፈጥሮአዊ ክስተቶች ላይ ነበር። ኢትዮጵያውያን ግን ሐሳቡን ወደ ማህበራዊ ኑሮ በማዛር የጊዜ ተፈራራቂነት በሕብረተሰብ ውስጥም ይታያል ብለዋል። የግለሰቦች ማህበራዊ ሥፍራ ቋሚ አለመሆኑ ብቻ ሳይሆን ይቀለባበሳልም እስከማለት ደርሰዋል። የከበደ ሚካኤል ግጥም እንደሚናገርው፤ ሀብታሙ በድህው ይተካል፤ ደካማው ኃይለኛ ይሆናል። በቋሚ መደቦች በተከፋፈለ ማህበረሰብ ውስጥ ቋሚ ሥልጣንና ማህበራዊ ሥፍራ የለም ማለት የሚገርም አነጋገር ነው። የሰዎች ማህበራዊ ማዕረግ ይፈራረቃል ማለት በቋሚነት የሚያዝ ከፍትኛም ሆነ የበታች ሥፍራ የለም ማለት ነው።

አመለካከቱ በቀጥታ የሚያንጸባርቀው የኢትዮያን ማህበራዊ ግንዛቤ ነው። ቋሚ መደቦች አሉ፤ ነገር ግን ግለሰቦች በትውልድ የሚወርሱት ሥፍራ የለም። በተለይም ከፍተኛ ቦታዎች ከታች በሚመጡ ግለሰቦች ይነጠቃሉ። ይህ ከአንድ መደብ ወደ ሌላ መደብ የመሸጋገር ችሎታ ኢትዮጵያውያን ዕድል ብለውታል። ዕድል የሚገልጸው የኢትዮጵያን ማህበራዊ ኑሮ ተንቀሳቃሽነት ነው።

ከበታች ወደ በላይ ማህበራዊ ሥፍራ መሸጋገር ዕድገት እንደመሆኑ መጠን ዕድል ከማለት ይልቅ ለምን ኢትዮጵያውያን ችሎታ አላሉት ብለን ብንጠይቅ መልሱ ቀላል ነው። ችሎታውን የሚለግሰው እግዜር በመሆኑ በእርሱ መመረጥን ይጠይቃል። ከእግዜር የሚደርስንን ለማሰብ የምንችለው እንደ ስጦታ ወይም ዕጣ እንጂ እንደሚገባን እስካልሆነ ድረስ ትክክለኛው አስተሳሰብ ዕድል የሚለው ነው።

የዕድል ጽንሰሐሳብ ከኢትዮጵያዊ ጊዜ ግንዛቤ ጋር የተቆራኘ መሆኑ ግልጽ ነው። የጊዜ መፈራረቅ ዕድል ከፋች ነው። የተለያዩና በበታችና በበላይ የተከፋፈሉ ማህበራዊ መቀመጫያዎች አሉ። ነገር ግን ግለሰቦች በተራ እንጂ በቋሚነት የሚይዟቸው አይደሉም። የፈረቃ ሕግ የወጣውን ስለሚያወርድ ግትር ማህበራዊ አቋም እንዳይኖር ያደርጋል። ስለሆነም በታች የነበረው ግልስብ ከላይ ያለውን የሚተካበትን ሂደት ያመቻቻል።

ልክ እንደ አውሮፓ ቋሚ የመኳንንትና የንጉሥ ዘር ለመመስርት አለመቻሉ የኢትዮጵያ ረጅም ታሪክ ይመስክራል። በንጉሥ ብንጀምር፤ ሥልጣኑን በእራሱ ቤተሰብ ውሰጥ ለማስቀረት የቻለ የኢትዮጵያ ንጉሥ የለም። ይህ ማለት መቼም የንጉሥ ልጅ ሥልጣን አልወረሰም ማለት አይደለም። መንገሥ በዘር የወሰደው ልዩ መብት ሳይሆን ተቀናቃኞቹን ድል በማድረግ የተቀናጀው ሥልጣን ነው። ድሉም የሚያበሥረው ዕድሉን፤ ማለት በእግዜር የተመረጠ መሆኑን ነው። በዚህ የተነሳ በ ኢትዮጵያ እንድ ተዎድሮስ የተባለ የኮሶ ሻጭ ልጅ ሊነግሥ ችሏል።

ብዙ ጥናቶች እደሚያመለከቱት፤ እንደ አውሮፓ በገበሬውና በመኳንንቱ መካከል ግትር ልዩነት በኢትዮጵያ ውስጥ አልነበረም። ግለሰቦችን የሚለያቸው በዕድላቸው የተለያየ ስፍራ መያዛቸው እንጂ የትውልድ ዘራቸው አይደለም። ገበሬው በዕጣው ገባሪ ሆነ እንጂ የበታች ሰው አልነበርም። በመሆኑም ዕድሌ ተቀይሮ ያንዱን ከፍተኛ ቦታ አገኛለሁ እያለ ሳያቋርጥ ይመኛል።

powerful. By giving a false autonomy to the self and things, arrogance produces a metaphysical confusion by shrouding God's rulership.

TIME AND FATE

At this juncture, it is necessary to point out Ethiopia's uniqueness. Even if all premodern views claimed that time is cyclical, such views mostly focused on natural phenomena. However, Ethiopians, by applying this thought to the social, have said that the cyclicality of time is seen in society too. Not only have they claimed that individuals' social place is not permanent, but they also have gone as far as to say it is subject to reversal. As Kebede Mikael's poem says, the wealthy is replaced by the poor; the weak becomes powerful. And when the rich becomes poor, the poor becomes wealthy. In a society that is divided into fixed classes, it is surprising to claim that there is no permanent rule and social position. To say that people's social status is reversible is to say that there is no high or low position that is held permanently.

This view directly reflects Ethiopia's understanding of society. While there are permanent classes, there is no position that individuals inherit by birth. Higher positions, especially, are taken up by individuals who come from lower positions. Ethiopians have called this ability to move from one class to another "luck." Luck reveals Ethiopia's social mobility.

Since transferring from lower to higher social positions is advancement, we may ask why, instead of calling it luck, Ethiopians did not call it talent. The answer is simple. Talent requires being chosen by God, since it is bestowed by Him. Since we can think of what we receive from God only as a gift or allotment, and not as something we deserve, the right view is the one that speaks of luck.

It is clear that the concept of fate is interlinked with the Ethiopian conception of time. The cyclicality of time opens doors for opportunities. There are varying higher and lower social positions. However, these positions are held by individuals not permanently, but in turn. Because the law of rotation demotes those who have been promoted, permanent positions do not exist. Thus, the opportunity for a person in a lower position to replace someone in a higher position is made available.

The impossibility of having permanent lines of gentry and kingship, as in Europe, is proven by Ethiopia's long history. If we start with the king, no Ethiopian king was able to keep power in his family line. This does not mean that no son of a king has ever inherited the throne. Rather, ascent to the throne was not so much a special right as an outcome of victory over competitors. His victory revealed his destiny, that is, the fact that he was chosen by God. Because of this, in Ethiopia, a son of a *kosso* seller, as Tewodros was, could become king.†

As many studies show, in Ethiopia, there was not a rigid separation between peasantry and gentry as there was in Europe. What created difference between individuals was their holding a position as a result of individual

እዚህ ላይ ነው በኃይለ ሥላሴ ዘመን ከባድ ከባሕል ውጪ የሆነ አሠራር መጀመሩን የምናየው። ንጉሡ የራሳቸውን ቤተሰብ ልዩ በማድረግ ሥልጣን በአልጋ ወራሽነት ለልጃቸው እንዲተላለፍ ደነገጉ። ድንጋጌው የጊዜን ተፈራራቂነት በመሻር ሥልጣንን ለተወሰነ ቤተሰብ በቋሚነት የሰጠ ነው። የሰሎሞን ዘር የሚለውን በኃይለ ሥላሴ ዘር በመተርጎም ለአገሪቱ ባዕድ የሆነ ሥልጣንን የማውረስ ልዩ መብት የፈጠረ ነው። በቅድመ ኃይለ ሥላሴ ዘመን የኢትዮጵያ አንድነት ስሜት አንዱ ምንጭ ይኸው ለዋናው ዙፋን የተለያዩ ክፍሎች የነበራቸው እኩል መብት ነበር።

ከፈረቃዊ ወደ ግባዊ ጊዜ

የኢትዮጵያን የጊዜ ግንዛቤ በፈረቃዊ አመለካከት መወሰን ስህተት ይሆናል። የክርስቲያን ሃይማኖት ተከታይ የሆኑ ኢትዮጵያውያን እንደ ማንኛውም ክርስቲያናዊ ባህል ጊዜ ወደ አንድ ግብ እንደሚያመራ ያምናሉ። የእስልምና ሃይማኖት ተከታይ ኢትዮጵያውያንም የጊዜን ግባዊነት ይቀበላሉ። ፈረቃ ወደ ፊት የማይሄድ፤ አዲስ ለውጥና መሻሻል የማያሳይ ድግምግሞሽ ነው። ሂደት ግባዊ ሲሆን በአንድ አቅጣጫ ከመጓዙም በላይ የሚያከናውነው ዓላማ አለው።

እግዜር ዓለምን ሲፈጥር አብሮ ሂደቱን ቀይሷል። ዓለም መጀመሪያ እንዳለው ሁሉ መጨረሻም ይኖረዋል። መጨረሻውም በክርስቶስ ዳግም ምጽዓት ይፈጸማል። በመሆኑም የጊዜና የታሪክ ሂደት የሚደጋገም ብቻ ሳይሆን ወደ ፍጻሜም የሚያመራ ነው። ፍጻሜውም ወደ የተሟላ ኑሮ ደርጃ የሚያሸጋግር እንጂ የመኖር ማለቂያ አይደለም።

እዚህ ላይ ነው የኢትዮጵያውያን አመለካከት ከሌሎች አፍሪካውያን በግልጽ የሚለየው። እንደ አፍሪካዊው ፈላስፋ ጆን ምቢቲ አባባል የአፍሪካውያን የጊዜ ግንዛቤ ከአውሮፓዊው የተለየ ነው። አውሮፓውያን ጊዜ ሶስት ማዕዘናት አሉት ይላሉ፡፡ እነሱም ያለፈው፤ አሁን ያለውና መጪው ናቸው። ለአፍሪካዊውን ግን "ጊዜ በረጅም ያለፈ፤ አሁንና መጪነት እስከ ማጣት የሚደርስ የሁለታዊ ማዕዘን ክስተት ነው።"[8] ክርስቲያናዊ አመለካከት ኢትዮጵያውያን፤ ልክ እንደ አውሮፓውያን፤ መጪውንና ወደ እጅግ የበለጠ ኑሮ የሚያሸጋግረውን ፍጻሜ የሚጠባበቅ የጊዜ ግንዛቤ እንዲኖራቸው አድርጓል። የጊዜን ጠባይ በሶስት ማዕዘናት በማየታቸውም ለኢትዮጵያውያን ጊዜ ግባዊ ክስተት ሆኗል።

ልንክድ የማንችለው ፈረቃዊ ግንዛቤ ከግባዊ ግንዛቤ ጋር እንደማይጣጣም ነው። የጊዜ ሂደት እንዴት በአንደነት ፈረቃዊም ግባዊም ሊሆን ይችላል? ፈረቃ በራሱ የሚገለባበጥ ግበቢስ ሂደት ከመሆኑ ሌላ የእግዜርን ዘወትር ጣልቃገቢነት አይጠይቅም። ለእንዲህ ያለ ተመላላሽና አቅጣጫ የሌለው ሂደት ግብ ማስቀመጥ በእርግጥም ተቃራኒ አነጋገር ይመስላል። ለዚህም ነው ይህን ዓለም ከንቱ በማድርግ ከበደ ሚካኤል "የዚህ ዓለም ነገር ምንም የለው መላ" ያለው።[9]

በፈረቃዊና በግባዊ ሂደት መካከል የሚታየው አለመጣጣም ለኢትዮጵያውያን ግን እውን አይደለም። በጥሞና ብናስበው፤ ተፈራራቂ ሂደት ላይ ግብ ሲታከል የሚሰጠን የፈረቃው በድንገት መቋረጥን ነው። ይህም ማለት እግዜር የጀመረውን ሂደት በገዛ ፈቃዱ በድንገት ያቆማል ማለት ነው። አውሮፓውያን እንደሚሉት ጊዜ የሚቆመው የተሻለ ሁኔታ ስለተፈጠረ አይደለም። እግዜር በቃ ስለሚል ብቻ ነው። የፈረቃው ሁሌም መቀጠል የሚያመለክተው

fate, rather than because of bloodline. The farmer or peasant, because of his fate, became a payer of duties, but that did not make him a lower person. He therefore unceasingly wished that someday his fate would change and that he would gain someone's higher position.

It is here that we see the beginning of a radical shift from tradition during Haile Selassie's reign. Assigning a special status to his family, the king proclaimed that power would go to his son as the sole heir to the throne. This declaration abolished the cyclicality of time and gave power to a particular family permanently. By equating Solomon's genealogy with Selassie's, it created a special right of transmission of power that was alien to the country. One of the sources of the pre–Haile Selassie sentiment of Ethiopian unity was the equal right of different regions to accede to the throne.

FROM CYCLICAL TIME TO TELEOLOGICAL TIME

To reduce Ethiopia's understanding of time to cyclicality would be a mistake. Like any Christian people, Ethiopians believe that time moves toward a single goal. Followers of Islam in Ethiopia accept the goal-oriented nature of time as well. Cyclicality is a repetition that does not move forward or show change and improvement. A goal-oriented process not only moves in one direction but also has a purpose to accomplish.

When God created the world, He also planned its process. Just as the world has a beginning, it also has an end. The end will arrive with the second coming of Christ. Thus, not only is the process of time and history not repetitive, but it also heads toward an end. The end is not the end of life but rather its transition to a higher form.

This is where the Ethiopian outlook is different from other African outlooks. According to John Mbiti, the African's conception of time is different from that of the European. Europeans say time has three dimensions. These are: past, present, and future. But for Africans, "time is a two-dimensional phenomenon, with a long *past*, a *present* and virtually no *future*."[8] Just as in the case of Europeans, Christianity has enabled Ethiopians to have a conception of time that anticipates the coming and the transition to a greatly superior life. Since they saw the three-dimensional nature of time, time for Ethiopians became a teleological occurrence.

It is undeniable that the cyclical conception does not agree with the teleological conception. How could the trajectory of time be cyclical and teleological at the same time? In addition to being a goalless process that turns on its own, cyclicality does not require the intervention of God. Indeed, to give a goal to an oscillating and directionless process appears to be contradictory. This is why Kebede Mikael expressed the vanity of the world by saying: "The nature of this world is unpredictable."[9]

The opposition between cyclical and teleological process is, however, not real for Ethiopians. If we think deeply about it, what results from the insertion of a goal into a cyclical process is its sudden interruption. This

ሰዎች በራሳቸው ፍላጎትና ጥረት የሚደርሱበት የተሻሻለ ሁኔታ መቼም እንደማይኖር ነው። የሚሠሩትን ሁሉ መልሰው ስለሚያበላሹ፤ በገዛ ጥረታቸው ከፈረቃ ሕግ መቼም አይላቀቁም።

በመሆኑም የጊዜ መጨረሻ የእግዜርን ፍጹም ሥልጣን ገላጭ ነው። በራሱ ፈቃድ የትም የማይደርሰውን ድግምግሞሽ እግዜር ሲያቆም ብቻ ነው ሰዎች ከፈረቃ የጸዳ ቋሚ ወይም ዘለዓለማዊ ኑሮ የሚኖራቸው። ሕይወት የማይለዋወጥ፤ ውጣ ውረድ የሌለው የሚሆነው፤ ሰዎች የእግዜርን ዘለዓለማዊ ፍቅር ሲያገኙ ብቻ ነው። ስለሆነም የጊዜ መጨረሻ ከፈረቃዊ ኑሮ መላቀቅ ወይም መዳን ማለት ነው።

የክብረ ነገሥትን ልዩና ትልቅ መልዕክት የምናገኘው እዚህ ላይ ነው። እሱም ነገሮች ሁሉ በድግምግሞሽ ሕግ ሲገዙ ኢትዮጵያ ብቻ የተለየ ዕጣ ወይም ዕድል አላት የሚል ነው። አነጋገሩ ኢትዮጵያን ከውጣ ውረድ ደንብ በማግለል በመጨርሻ ጠላቶቿን በሙሉ አሸንፋ ብቻዋን ትቀራለች ይላል። በሌላ አባባል፤ ነገሥታት ሁሉ በተራ ሲነሱና ሲወድቁ ኢትዮጵያ ከፈረቃዊ ጊዜ በመላቀቅ በድል ጸንታ "እስከ ዓለም ፍጻሜ ድረስ ትኖራለች።"[10]

ክብረ ነገሥት ይህን እምነት የሚያፈልቀው መጽሐፍ ቅዱስ ውስጥ ከሰፈረው የዳዊት መዝሙር በመነሳት ነው። "ኢትዮጵያ እጆችዋን ወደ እግዚአብሔር ትዘረጋለች"[11] የሚለው የዳዊት ትንቢት እንደ ክብረ ነገሥት አባባል የሚያመለክተው ኢትዮጵያ በኦርቶዶክስ ሃይማኖት ጸንታ በድል አድራጊነት እስከ ጊዜ ፍጻሜ፤ ማለትም እስከ ክርስቶስ መምጫ ደረስ እንደምትቆይ ነው። ምንም ሊያጠፉት እንደማይችል ሲገልጽም፤ ሃሳዊ መሲህ በሚመጣበት ጊዜ እንኳን አትጠፉም ወይ ተብሎ ሲጠየቅ፤ የክብረ ነገሥት መልስ በፍጹም አትጠፉም ነው። ምክንያቱም "ዳዊት 'ኢትዮጵያ እጆቿን ወደ እግዚአብሄር ትዘረጋለች' ሲል ትንቢት አልተናገረም" ወይ?[12]

እርግጥ ነው፤ ኢትዮጵያም የምትወደቅባቸው ጊዜያቶች ይኖራሉ። ነገር ግን መቼም ቢሆን ወድቃ አትቀርም። የምትውድቀውም በገዛ ጥፋትዋ ስለሆነ ውድቀቷ የእግዜር ቅጣት ይሆናል። ለምሳሌ የጣሊያንን ወረራ እንደ አምላካዊ ቁጣ በመተርጎም ከበደ ሚካኤል እንዲህ ብሏል።

እግዜር አዞት ሕዝቡን አምስት ዓመት ቀጣ፤
ትእዛዙን ፈጽሞ በቃህ ሲለው ወጣ።[13]

እግዜር እራሱ የወሰነውን የውድመት መጨረሻ ለምን ኢትዮጵያ ላይ ያፈርሳል? ለዚህ ጥያቄ መልስ የሚሰጥ አሁንም ክብረ ነገሥት ነው። እስራኤላውያን ክርስትናን ባለመቀበላቸው ኢትዮጵያ እስራኤልን በመተካት የአምላክ ምርጥ አገር ሆናለች። ሹመቱም ኢትዮጵያን ከፈረቃ ሕግ በመከለል ልዩ ዕድል ይሰጣታል። ምርጥ ለሆነች አገር እግዜር ልዩ እንክብካቤ ያደርጋል ማለት ተገቢ ነው። እግዜር ኢትዮጵያን የታቦት ባለቤት በማድረግ ልዩ ሥፍራ እንደሰጣት ክብረ ነገሥት ሲያረጋግጥ እንዲህ ይላል፤ "እግዚአብሄር ለኢትዮጵያ ንጉስ እንደዚህ ያለ ክብርና ግርማን አደርገ። ስለ እግዚአብሄር ታቦተ ህግ ስለ ሰማያዊቷ ጽዮንም ከምድር ነገስታት ሁሉ ከፍ ከፍ አደረገው። እግዚአብሄር መንፈሳዊት ፈቃዱን እንድንፈጽም ያብቃን።"[14] አነጋገሩ የኢትዮጵያ ልዩ ሥፍራ የመነጨው ከአምለክ ፈቃድ መሆኑን በግልጽ ያስቀምጣል።

means that God will suddenly stop, by His own will, the cyclical process that He started. Time does not stop because a better situation is created, as the Europeans say. It will stop because God says, "Enough." The continuation of cyclicality shows that humans will never reach a better situation by their own effort. Since humans destroy what they have built, they can never escape, by their own efforts, from the law of cyclicality.

Thus, the end of time reveals God's absolute power. Only when God stops the directionless repetition of time will humans have a fixed or eternal life that is free of cyclicality. Life becomes unchanging and free from ups and downs only when humans receive God's eternal love. Thus, the end of time signifies freedom from cyclical life, that is, it signifies salvation.

We find here the special and important message of the *Kebra Negast*. This message is that, while all things are ruled by the law of repetition, only Ethiopia has a special fate. This message removes Ethiopia from the norm of ups and downs by stating that she will vanquish all her enemies and remain the last one standing. To put it another way, while kings rise and fall by turn, Ethiopia, because she has been delivered from cyclical time, will remain victorious and "will live until the end of time."[10]

The *Kebra Negast* derives this belief from the part of the Bible dealing with the Psalms of David. According to the *Kebra Negast,* David's prophecy, "Ethiopia shall stretch her hands unto God," indicates that Ethiopia, staying faithful to the Orthodox religion, will remain victorious to the end, that is, until the coming of Christ.[11] Nothing can destroy Ethiopia; even when asked whether Ethiopia will not disappear when the false prophet comes, *Kebra Negast*'s answer is "absolutely not." For, "has not David prophesied that Ethiopia shall stretch forth her hands unto God?"[12]

True, there will be times when Ethiopia falls down. However, Ethiopia shall never remain fallen. When she falls, it is her own fault; as such, her fall is God's punishment. For example, interpreting the Italian invasion as God's anger, Kebede Mikael said:

> God ordered the punishment of the people for five years
> Accomplishing His order, it [Italy] left when God said enough[13]

Why would God break with His plan of total destruction by excluding Ethiopia? Once again, the *Kebra Negast* provides the answer. Since the Israelites did not accept Christianity, Ethiopia replaced Israel and became God's chosen country. This election protects Ethiopia from the laws of cyclical time by giving her a special destiny. It is appropriate to maintain that God provides special care for His chosen country. Confirming that God gave Ethiopia a special place by making her the keeper of the Ark, the *Kebra Negast* says: "God confers such honor and grace on the Ethiopian king. Due to God's Ark and the heavenly Zion, He raised him higher than all the kings of the world. May God help us fulfill His spiritual will."[14] This statement clearly shows that Ethiopia's special place came from God's will.

የከብረ ነገሥት አባባል የሚያሳየው ኢትዮጵያ የራሷ የሆነ የታሪክ ንድፈሐሳብ እንደነበራት ነው። ታሪኩም የተቀመረው ኢትዮጵያን እምብርት አገር በማድረግ ሁሉም ነገር፤ የሌሎች አገሮች ታሪክ ጭምር፤ ወደ እሷ ድል አድራጊነት እንደሚያመራ በማስቀመጥ ነው። የዓለም ታሪክ በኢትዮጵያ ድል አድራጊነት መደምደም የልዩ ዕድል ባለቤት መሆኗን ያረጋግጣል። አሁን እንደሆነው የሌሎች አገሮች ታሪክ ተከታይ መሆኗ ቀርቶ ሌሎች አገሮች በእሷ ታሪክ ይመሩ ነበር ማለት ነው። የከብረ ነገሥት ትልቁ መልዕክት ኢትዮጵያን የታሪክ መሪ ኃይል ማድረጉ ነበር።

ኢትዮጵያና ዘመናዊነት

የኢትዮጵያ የታሪክ ባለቤትነት ዘመናዊ ሥልጣኔ ከገባ ጀምሮ ማብቃቱ አይካድም። የታሪክ መሪነቷን በምዕራባዊ አገሮች ከተቀማች ጀምሮ፤ በተለይ ምዕራባዊ ትምህርት በቀመሱ ኢትዮጵውያን ዘንድ ኢትዮጵያ የምትታየው እንድ ኋላቀር አገር ነው። እንዲህም በመታየቷ የምዕራባዊ አገሮች ተከታይና ቀጂ ሆናለች። ተከታይነቷ በምጣኔ ሀብትና በቴክኖሎጂ መስክ ብቻ ሳይሆን በባህልም ጭምር ነው።

ይህ እንዴት ሆነ ቢባል መልሱን የሚሰጠን የአውሮፓውያን ትምህርት ካለምንም ገደብ የመለቀቅ ሁኔታ ነው። ትምህርቱ የተመሰረተበት የታሪክ ንድፈሐሳብ የአውሮፓውያን አመለካከት፤ ፋይዳና ማህበራዊ ሥርዓት ተቀዳሚ በማድረግ አውሮፓዊ ያልሆኑ ባህሎችና አሠራሮችን ሁሉ ኋላቀር ያደርጋል። ከዚህም አልፎ ሌሎች አገሮች ሊሠለጥኑ የሚችሉት አውሮፓን በአርአያነት ሲከተሉ ብቻ ነው ይላል፡፡ በመሆኑም ኢትዮጵውያን ዘመናዊ የሚሆኑት ከራሳቸው ታሪክና ባህል ወጥተው በምዕራባዊነት ሲጠመቁ ብቻ ነው።

ው ታላቁ ፈላስፋ ሄገል እንዳለው፡ "የዓለም ታሪክ የሚጓዘው ከምስራቅ ወደ ምዕራብ ነው፤ ምክንያቱም አውሮፓ የመጨረሻ የታሪክ ግብ ነች።"[15] ይህንን የታሪክ አቅጣጫ ኢትዮጵውያን ስለተቀበሉት መጪውን ማሰብ የቻሉት ኢትዮጵያዊነትን በማሻሻልና በማሳደግ ሳይሆን ወደ ምዕራባዊነት በመቀየር ነው። የአውሮፓ ትምህርት ዋና ውጤት ለራስ ታሪክና ባህል ባይተዋር መሆን ነው።

በዘመናዊ ትምህርት ከባድ ተጽዕኖ የተነካ ኢትዮጵውያን ለእነሱ የሚበጀውን የጊዜ ተፈራራቂ ጠባይን ወደ ጎን አደረጉት። ጥቅሙ የት ነው ብለን ብንጠይቅ መልሱ አያስቸግርም። ፈረቃዊ ጊዜ የሚለው ሁሉም ጊዜው ይመጣል፤ ማንም አገር ታሪክን በቋሚነት አይመራም ነው። የተነሳ ሁሉ ይወድቃል፤ የወደቀም ይነሳል። ገናናነት ሁሌም ጊዜያዊ ነው። በመሆኑም፤ የታሪክ መሪነትን በፈረቃ እንጂ ማንም በቋሚነት አይዘውም።

ለዚህም ይመስላል ኢትዮጵያውያን የምዕራባዊ ሥልጣኔን መጀመሪያ ሲሰይሙት "ዘመናዊ ሥልጣኔ" ያሉት። ዘመናዊ ሲሉ ጊዜ ያመጣውና ኃላፊ ማለታቸው ነበር፡፡ ይህን ሲሉ ደግሞ ኋለቅር አይደለንም፤ ጊዜ ባመጣሽ ሥልጣኔ ለጊዜው ተገፋን እንጂ ማለታቸው ነበር። የአውሮፓ አሁን ገናናነት በውድቀት ይተካልና አውሮፓን ማየት መከተል እንዳለብን ደንብ ሳይሆን እንደ ተቀናቃኝ ነው። በእርግጥ ከተቀናቃኝ ብዙ መማር አለብን፤ ትምህርቱን የምንወስደው ግን እሱን ለመምሰል ሳይሆን እራሳችንን ለአዲስ ለውጥና ሁኔታ አላምደን እሱን ለመብለጥ ነው።

What the *Kebra Negast*'s statement shows is that Ethiopia had her own theory of history. By making Ethiopia the center of the world, the historical scheme was designed in such a way that all things, including other countries' histories, march toward the realization of her victory. That world history was to conclude with Ethiopia's victory proves that she had a special destiny. This means that, unlike the present situation making Ethiopia the follower of other countries' histories, other countries used to be led by her history. The greatest message of the *Kebra Negast* is that it makes Ethiopia history's leading force.

ETHIOPIA AND MODERNITY

It cannot be denied that Ethiopia's ownership of history has ended since the coming of modernity. Ever since her leadership in history was snatched away by Western countries, Ethiopia has been seen as a backward country, especially by Ethiopians who have tasted Western education. Because of this perception, she has become the follower and copier of Western countries. She has become a follower not only in the fields of economics and technology but also in that of culture.

If it is asked how this happened, the answer lies in the situation that allowed European education to spread unhindered. The theory of history upon which this education was based privileges the European viewpoint, values, and social order, thereby defining non-European cultures and ways of doing things as backward. In addition, it declares that other countries can becomes civilized only when they follow Europeans as their example. Accordingly, Ethiopians become modern only when, abandoning their history and culture, they convert to Westernism.

As the great German philosopher Hegel said: "The History of the World travels from East to West, for Europe is absolutely the end of History."[15] Since Ethiopians have accepted this trajectory of history, they have come to think about the future not in terms of improving and cultivating Ethiopianism, but in terms of converting to Westernism. The main result of European education is to be alienated from one's history and culture.

Because of the heavy influence of modern education, Ethiopians have put aside the cyclical nature of time, which had been beneficial to them. If we ask what its benefit is, the answer is not difficult. What cyclical time tells us is that everybody's time will come; no country will permanently lead history. All those who were up will fall and those who were down will rise. Greatness is always temporary. Thus, leadership of history is held by turn; no one holds it permanently.

It seems that is why Ethiopians, when they first named Western civilization, called it "modern civilization." By "modern," they meant something that time brings, that is, and something that is transient. In so saying, they implied that they were not backward; rather, they were temporarily pushed back by a civilization that time brought. Since Europe's current prominence will be replaced by downfall, we should see Europe not as a model to follow but as an opponent. To be sure, we should learn a lot from an opponent;

ዘመናዊነትና ተሐድሶ

የታሪክን መመላለስ ኢትዮጵያውያን አቆይተው ቢሆን ኖሮ እራሳቸውን ኋላቀርና የሌሎ አገሮች ታሪክ ተከታይ አድርገው ከማሰብ ባመለጡ ነበር ብለናል። የምዕራባዊ ታሪክ አቀራረጽ የሚያስተምረው አውሮፓን መከተልና መቅዳት በመሆኑ ራስን መቻልንና የፈጠራ ችሎታን ማዳበር አያበረታታም። ተደጋጋሚ የጊዜ ግንዛቤ ግን በአንድ መሥመር የሚሄድ ባለመሆኑ መንተትን ሳይሆን ተራ መጠበቅን ነው የሚያስተምርው። ለተነሳ ሁሉ መውደቅ አይቀሬ ነው ስለሚል ለሁሉ የመነሳት ዕድል ይሰጣል።

ይህም በታሪክ የተመሰከረ እውነታ ነው። አውሮፓ ኋላቀር በነበረበት ጊዜ የኤጊፒያና የአፍሪካ ሕዝቦች ከፍተኛ ሥልጣኔዎችን አሳይተዋል። ዘመናዊ ታሪክን ብንወስድ የአውሮፓ ፍጹም ኃይል በአሜሪካን ገናናነት ተዳከሟል። የዘመናዊ ጃፓንና ቻይና አካሄድ መልሶ የኤጊፒያን የበላይነትን የሚያመቻች ይመስላል።

አንድ አገር ተራ የሚያገኘው ደግሞ ሌላውን ተከትሎ ምንነቱን ሲያጣ አይደለም። የራሱን ባሕርያት በማደስ መሻሻል ሲያሳይ ብቻ ነው፤ ምክንያቱም የሌላ ቅጂ ሆኖ እስከቀረበ ድረስ የሚጫወተው አዲስና የላቀ ሚና አይኖረውም። ዋናው የያዘውን ሥፍራ የበታች የሆነው ቅጂው ሊነጥቅ አይችልም። ተንታች ልዩነትን ካላመነጨ መቼም ቢሆን ጎታች አይሆንም።

እራስን ማሻሻል ሌላን መቅዳት ሳይሆን እራስን ማደስ ነው። ይህም የሚሆነው ወደ ኋላ፤ ወደ ራስ ሥልጣኔ ምንጭ በመመልስ ነው። ሂደቱ ዳግም ትውልድ የሚባለውን የለውጥ አቅጣጫ ያመጣል። ወደ ኋላ የሚኬደው የድሮውን፤ ያለፈውን ለመመልስ አይደለም። ወደ ራስ ታሪክ ምንጭ መመለስ መንፈሳዊ ቅስቀሳ ከመስጠቱም በላይ የተጣራ አመለካከት ያስገኛል።

በግልጽ እንደሚታየው ዘመናዊነትን እንደ ዕድሳት ለማየት በመጀመሪያ ደረጃ ከአውሮፓ በአንድ መሥመርና አቅጣጫ ከሚሄደው የታሪክ ግንዛቤ መላቀቅ ይጠይቃል። መተካት ያለበትም የጊዜን መደጋገም በሚያስተምረው አመለካከት ነው። በአንድ አቅጣጫ መሄድ ቀርቶ ጊዜ የሚደጋገም ከሆነ የመታደስን ሁኔታ ይፈጥራል። የጠፋ መንገደኛ ወደ መነሻው ለመመልስ ይጥራል እንጂ በያዘው ስህተት ዝም ብሎ አይቀጥልም። አቅጣጫ የጠፋው ግለሰብ ወይም ሕብረተሰብም መፍትሄ የሚያገኘው ወደ ታሪኩ መነሻ ሲመለስና መሠረቱን መልሶ ሲጨብጥ ነው። እንዲህ በመመለሱ ደግሞ ከመንከራተት መላቀቁ ብቻ ሳይሆን እንደገና ይታደሳል፤ ይወለዳል።

ይህ የሚያሳየው የድግምግሞሽ ምስጢር መታደስ መሆኑን ነው። ሕይወት እራሱን የሚያድስው ወደ ኋላ በመመለስ አይደለም ወይ? ያደገው የሚታደስው እንደገና ሕጻን በመሆን ነው። ተፈጥሯዊ ነገሮች ሁሉ የሚታደሱት በአንድ የማይቀለብስ አቅጣጫ ከመሄድ ይልቅ የመደጋገም ጠባይ ስላላቸው ነው። የተበላሸው እንደገና ይጠራል። የደከመው እንደገና ጉልበት ያገኛል። የታጨደው መልሶ ይበቅላል። የታወቀው ሲሻር እውቀት ይታደሳል።

ሥልጣኔዎች የሚወድቁት በየጊዜው በሚያከማቿቸው ስህተቶችና መጥፎና ጎታች ልምዶች በመሆኑ ከራስ ታሪክ መሥመር ሳይወጣ የሥልጣኔ ጽዳት ማድረግ የሚቻለው ወደ ምንጩ በመመለስ ነው። የመመለሱ ሂደት ትክክለኛውን መሠርት እንደገና ያስቀምጣል፤ እስካሁን

however, we learn not to look like our opponent but to adapt ourselves to a novel situation of change so as to supersede him.

MODERNITY AND RENEWAL

We said before that if Ethiopians had kept the thought of the repetition of history, they would have escaped from thinking of themselves as backward and as followers of other countries' histories. Since Western history is designed to teach people to follow and copy Europe, it does not encourage independence and the cultivation of creativity. The concept of cyclical time, since it does not travel in a single direction, teaches one not to be pulled but to wait one's turn. Since it says that whatever is up must fall down, it gives everybody a chance to rise.

This is a truth that is proven by history. When Europe was backward, the peoples of Asia and Africa displayed high civilizations. If we take modern history, Europe's absolute power has been weakened by America's might. The trend of modern Japan and China seems to prepare the restoration of Asia's dominance.

A country does not get its turn if it loses its identity by following another country. It does so only when it shows improvement by renewing its characteristics. Evidently, as long as it presents itself as a copy of another, it will not have a new and better role to play. The place occupied by the model cannot be appropriated by its copy. Unless the one being pulled brings difference, it can never become the one who pulls.

Self-improvement is not copying another: it is renewing oneself. This happens by going back, that is, by going to the source of one's own civilization. This movement will bring a change of direction, which is known as "renaissance." To go back is not to bring back the old and the past. To return to one's source of history not only provides spiritual awakening but also begets a clear perspective.

Clearly, in order to see modernity as renewal, it is necessary, as a first step, to break with Europe's understanding of history, which travels in a single line and direction. What we need in its place is the perspective that teaches the repetition of time. If, instead of going in one direction, time is cyclical, a situation conducive to renewal is created. A lost traveler attempts to return to his point of departure; he does not continue on the same mistaken path. A lost individual or society finds its path when it returns to its historical beginnings and grasps its foundation. To return in this manner not only saves from it wandering but also produces renewal and rebirth.

This reveals that the secret of repetition is renewal. Does not life renew itself by going back? The adult is renewed by becoming a child again. All natural things are renewed because, rather than going in one irreversible direction, they have a repetitive character. In this way, that which is damaged is recreated. The weak regain strength. That which is reaped will grow again. When the known becomes obsolete, knowledge is renewed.

Since civilizations fall because of the mistakes and depraved habits that they accumulate over time, the way to purify one's civilization without abandoning its proper historical trajectory is by returning to its source. This

የተያዘውን የተሳሳተ አቅጣጪያ ያርማል። ወደ ኃላ መመልስ ማጽዳትንና ለዳግም ትልቅነት መዘጋጀት ያስከትላል። በዚህ አባባል ዘመናዊነት ዳግመትውልድ ይሆን ማለት ነው።

ለዚህ አመለካከት ጥሩ ምሳሌ ጃፓን ናት። የዘመናዊነትን ጉዞ ጃፓን የጀመረችው አውሮፓን በመከተል ሳይሆን ወደ እራሷ ታሪክ ምንጭ በመመለስ ነው። ይህ ሂደት ነው የሜኢጂን ሥልጣን የመለስና የንጉሡን መለኮታዊ መልክ ያደሰ። መመለሱ የዘመናዊነት ጥረትን በንጉሡ የተደገፈ ስላደረገ የሚያስፈልጉት ማህበራዊና የምርት ዘዴ ለውጦች በንጉሡ ፈቃድ ስም በቀላሉ ሊከናወኑ ችለዋል። የዘመናዊነት ሂደት ባሕላዊ የሆነውን በንጉሡ መለኮታዊ መለያ በመባረኩ ሂደቱ ሰፊ ተቀባይነት ከማግኘቱ ሌላ ከፍተኛ የማስፈጸምና የመፈጸም ጉጉት በጃፓኖች ዘንድ ፈጥሯል።

አውሮፓውያንም የዘመናዊነት ሂደትን መጀመራቸውን ያበሰሩት ወደ ሥልጣኔያቸው ምንጭ በመመለስ ነው። ረጅምና ጨለማ ከነበረው የፊውዳል ሥርዓት ለመላቀቅ የቻሉት ወደ ጥንት ግሪክና ላቲን ሥልጣኔውች በመመልከት ነው። ይህንንም የለውጥ አቅጣጫ "ዳግማዊ ውልደት" ብለውታል። እንዲሁም በሃይማኖት በኩል የፕሮቴስታንት እንቅስቃሴ የጀመረው እውን ወደ ሆነው ክርስቲያን እምነት እንመልስ በማለት ነው። ያለው እምነት የተሳሳተና በመጥፎ ልምዶች የተበከለ በመሆኑ ወደ ምንጩ በመሄድ መታደስ አለበት የሚለውን ሂደት ነው አውሮፓውያን በቀጥታ "ተሐድሶ" ያሉት።

ኢትዮጵያ ውስጥ የተቀየሰው ሂደት ግን እንደገና መወለድ ሳይሆን ከራስ ምንነትና ታሪክ በመውጣት ሌሎች አገሮችን ተከተል የሚል ነው። በኃይል ሥላሴ ዘመን ኢትዮጵያ የአውሮፓን ትምህርት ካለ ገድብ በመቀበል ምዕራብ አገሮችን ተከተለች። የዚህ ትምህርት ውጤት የሆነው ዘመናዊ ትምህርት የቀመሰው ትውልድና የደርግ መንግሥት ደግሞ የምሥራቁ፤ ማለትም የሶሺያሊስት ዓላማ ብቻ ይበጃል በማለት፤ ወደባስ ስህተት አገሪቱን ጨመሯት። የምዕራባዊ ታሪክ ንድፈሓስብን ከመውረስ ይልቅ ኢትዮጵያዊ የሆነውን የጊዜ ተፈራራቂነት ተከትለን ቢሆን ኖሮ የዘመናዊነትን ችግሮች ወደ ኋላ፤ ወደ ምንጫችን በመመልስ ልንፈታቸው በሞከርን ነበር። ዘመናዊነት ዕድሳት እንጂ ከራስ መውጣት ባልሆን ነበር።

ከሁሉም በላይ ድግምግሞሻዊ የጊዜ አመለካከት የፉክክርን ስሜት ያዳብራል። እንደ ምዕራባዊው ግንዛቤ ጊዜ በአንድ መሥመር ብቻ ስለማይሄድ አንድን መሪ ሌላውን ተከታይ አያደርግም። ይልቁንም ሁሉ ነገር ይደጋገማል ስለሚል ከመነሻው መፎካከርን ያመቻቻል። አሁን መሪ የሆነው ወዳቂ ነው ስለሚል ተራ ጠብቆ የመተካትን ስሜት ያመነጫል። የሚለው ተከተል ሳይሆን ለመተካት ተዘጋኧ፤ ዕድልህን አመቻች ነው። ምዕራባውያን እኛን ብትከተሉ ለሁሉ የሚበጅና የሚበቃ ዓላማና ብልጽግና አለን እያሉ ሲሰብኩ ፈረቃዊ አመለካከት ግን ሁሉንም የሚያስደስት ሁኔታ ስለሌለ የታሪክን ሂደት ማየት ያለብን እንደ "ሻሞ" ጨዋታ ነው ይላል።

የኃይል ሥላሴን ሥርዓት የገለበጠው እንቅስቃሴ እራሱን የተመለከተው እንደ ተሐድሶ ሳይሆን እንደ አብዮት ነው። የተፈለገውም ሥርነቀል ለውጥ እንጂ ዕድሳት አልነበረም። ለምን ሥርነቀል ለውጥ ተፈለገ ብለን ብንጠይቅ መልሱን የሚሰጠን የነበረው ዓላማ ኢትዮጵያዊነት ማልማት ሳይሆን አርአያ ናቸው በተባሉ አገሮች አንጻር እትዮጵያን መቅረጽ መሆኑን ስናጤን ነው። ተሐድሶ ለማሰብ በእራስ ምንነትና ታሪክ ውስጥ መቆየት ይጠይቃል። ስርነቀል ለውጥ ለመመኘት ግን ለእራስ ባዕድ መሆንና የሌል አገር ተንታች ሆኖ መቅረብ ያሻል። ይህን አመለካከት የሚቀርጸው ከዘመናዊ ትምህርት የሚወሰደው የአውሮፓ የጊዜና የታሪክ አመለካከት መሆኑ ግልጽ ነው።

return reinstitutes the correct foundation; it corrects the mistaken direction that has previously been pursued. Return results in purification and preparation for renewed greatness. This suggests that modernity just is renaissance.

A good example of this is Japan. Japan started her path to modernity not by following Europe, but by returning to the source of her own history. It was this movement that allowed for the Meiji Restoration and the renewal of the emperor's position as a divine figure. Since the return signified that the attempt to modernize had the emperor's sanction, it facilitated the implementation of necessary social and economic changes in the name of the emperor. Because modernization was approved by the traditional belief in the divine nature of the emperor, it not only gained wide acceptance but also created great eagerness among the Japanese for its realization.

Europeans also announced the beginning of their modernization by returning to the source of their civilization. They were able to break with the long and dark era of feudalism by turning to ancient Greek and Roman civilization. They called this change of direction "renaissance." Likewise, on the religious front, the Protestant movement started on the ground that it had become necessary to return to the true faith. Since the existing faith had become tainted with bad and incorrect habits, Europeans called the movement to go back to the source so as to renew it the "Reformation."

But the movement that was initiated in Ethiopia advocated, not rebirth, but the desertion of selfhood and history by following other countries. During Haile Selassie's time, by accepting European education without any limits, Ethiopia followed Western countries. The results of this education, that is, the generation that tasted modern education and the Derg regime, claimed that only the Eastern, or socialist, goal was good, thereby putting the country in a worse situation. If, instead of inheriting the Western theory of history, we had followed the Ethiopian conception of cyclical time, we would have attempted to solve the problems of modernity by going back to our source. Modernity would have been renewal rather than denial of self.

More than anything else, the repetitive concept of time encourages the feeling of competition. Unlike the Western conception, it does not move in a single line, and so does not allow for one to be a leader and the other to be a follower. Rather, since it says that everything repeats, repetitive time encourages competition from the beginning. Since it says that the one who is a leader now will fall, it invites one to wait one's turn. It does not say, become a follower, but be ready to fill in, prepare your destiny. While the Europeans preach that, if you follow us, we offer comprehensive goals and prosperity for all, the cyclical view says that since there is no situation that can make everybody happy, we must see the movement of history as an up-for-grabs game.

The movement that overthrew Haile Selassie's rule saw itself not as renewal but as revolution. What they wanted was uprooting change rather than renewal. If we ask why uprooting change was sought, the answer is found in realizing that the goal was not to develop Ethiopia but to shape Ethiopia in accord with model countries. Obviously, what shaped this view is the European view of time and history taken from modern education.

አንድ አገር ሊበለጽግ የሚችለው የራሱ ታሪክ ባለቤት ሲሆን ነው። የራሱ ታሪክ ባለቤት አንድ አገር ለመሆን የሚችለው ደግሞ በጊዜ ውስጥ እራሱን በማየት ለመኖሩ ሉዓላዊ የሆነ ትርጓሜ ሲሰጥ ነው። የዚህ ጽሁፍ አጀማመር እንዳመለከተው፤ ጊዜ የኑባሬ ተርጓሚ ከሆነ በሌላ አገሮች ታሪክ የሚኖር ሕዝብ ለእራሱ ፍችና ዓላማ የሌለው ሕዝብ ነው። ዓላማ ከሌለው ደግሞ ዘመናዊነትን ሊያራምድ አይችልም። የሚችለው የሌላ አገር ዘመናዊነት ጥገኛ ወይም ተለጣፊ መሆን ነው። የራስን የጊዜ ግንዛቤ ማጣት የራስን ዓላማ መነጠቅ ማለት ነው። የራሱን አቅጣጫ የጠፋው ሕዝብ ዘመናዊነትን ቢያጨመላልቅ ሊገርመን አይገባም።

NOTES

1. ማርቲን ሃይደገር፤ ቤዚክ ራይቲንግ (ሳንፍራሲስኮ፤ ሃርፐር ኤንድ ሮው፤ ፐብሊሽር፤ 1977) ገጽ 61። ትርጉም ከጸሐፊው።

2. ሃንሪ በርግሶን፤ ዕቭረ (ፓሪስ፤ፐረስ ዩኒቨሲቴር ደ ፍራንስ፣ 1970) ገጽ 534። ትርጉም ከጸሓፊ።

3. ፓርመኒዲዝ፤ ዘፐሪሶክራቲክስ (ኒውዮርክ፤ አደሲ ፐሬስ፤ 1966) ገጽ 97። ትርጉም ከጸሓፊ።

4. በዚህ ጽሁፍ ውስጥ ኢትዮጵያና ኢትዮጵያውያን የሚለው አጠራር የሚመልከተው ቀድም ሐበሻ ተብሎ የሚታወቀውን በአመዛኙ ኦርቶዶክስ ክርስቲያን የሆነውን የኢትዮጵያን ሰሜን ክፍል ነው። ሆኖም ምንም እንኳን የደቡብ ክፍል አመለካከቱን ባያመነጭም በሰሜኑ ባሕል መዝመትና መሰራጨት የተነሳ አመለካከቱ ጥቅል ኢትዮጵያን የሚወክል ሆኗል።

5. ክብረ ነገስት፣ ተርጓሚ ስርግው ገላው (አዲስ አበባ፤ ንግድ ማተሚያ ቤት፤ 1994) ገጽ 59።

6. እዛው ገጽ 60-61።

7. ከበደ ሚካኤል፤ የቅኔ አዝማራ (አዲስ አበባ፤ ብርሃንና ሰላም ማተሚያ፡ 1946) ገጽ 97-99።

8. ጆን ምቢቲ፤ አፍሪቃን ሪሊጂን ኤንድ ፊሎዞፊ (ኒውዮርክ፤ ፍሬዴሪክ ፐራገር፤ 1975) ገጽ 17። ትርጉም ከጸሓፊ።

9. ከበደ፤ የቅኔ አዝማራ፤ ገጽ 99።

10. ክብረ ነገስት፣ ገጽ 146.

11. መጽሐፍ ቅዱስ፤ "መዝሙረ ዳዊት" (አዲስ አበባ፤ ብርሃንና ሰላም ማተሚያ ቤት፣ 1980) ገጽ 460.

12. ክብረ ነገስት፤ ገጽ 146

13. ከበደ፤ የቅኔ አዝማራ፤ ገጽ 35።

14. ክብረ ነገስት፤ ገጽ 149።

15. ጂ.ዊ. ኤፍኄ. ሄግል፣ ዘ ፊሎዞፊ ኦፍ ሂስትሪ (ኒውዮርክ፤ ዶቨር ፐብሊኬሽን፤ 1956) ገጽ 103። ትርጉም ከጸሓፊ።

A country prospers when it becomes the owner of its own history. A country becomes the owner of its history when it sees itself through time and gives an autonomous meaning to its existence. As pointed out at the beginning of this essay, if time is the interpreter of being, a people who lives by other countries' histories is a people without its own meaning and goal. Having no goal of its own, such a people cannot promote modernity. The only thing possible is for it is to become a dependent or a vassal of other countries' modernity. Losing one's own conception of time is to be robbed of one's own goal. We should not be surprised if a people who has lost its direction mucks up modernity.

NOTES

1. Martin Heidegger, *Basic Writings,* ed. David Farrell Krell (San Francisco: HarperCollins, 1977), 61.

2. Henri Bergson, *Creative Evolution* (New York: The Modern Library, 1944), 53.

3. "The Eleatic School," in *The Presocratics,* ed. Philip Wheelwright (New York; The Odyssey Press, 1966), 97.

4. In this paper, the terms *Ethiopia* and *Ethiopians* refer to the mostly Orthodox Christian northern part of Ethiopia, previously known as "Habesha." However, even if this view does not originate in the southern part of Ethiopia, the deployment and dissemination of northern culture has made it representative of all of Ethiopia.

5. *Kebra Negast,* trans. Sergew Gelaw (Addis Ababa: Commercial Printing Press: 1994), 59.

6. Ibid., 60–61.

7. Kebede Mikael, *Yeqiné Azmara* (Addis Ababa: Birhanena Selam Printing Press, 1946), 97–99.

8. John Mbiti, *African Religions and Philosophy* (New York: Frederick A. Praeger, 1975), 17.

9. Mikael, 99.

10. *Kebra Negast,* 146.

11. Psalms 68:13.

12. *Kebra Negast,* 146.

13. Mikael, 35.

14. *Kebra Negast,* 149.

15. G. W. F. Hegel, *The Philosophy of History,* trans. J. Sibree (New York: Dover Publications, 1956), 103.

*Compiled early in the fourteenth century, the *Kebra Negast* is considered Ethiopia's most important literary work. Translated as the "Glory of the Kings," the book relates, among other things, the Solomonic descent of Ethiopian kings.

†Emperor Tewodros ruled Ethiopia from 1855 to 1868. Besides being the first emperor who seriously sought to unify and modernize Ethiopia, his other distinguishing feature was that his mother was so impoverished that she was selling *kosso,* which is a native herbal remedy against intestinal worms, mostly originating from the eating of raw meat.

Ngero ok Rias:

Kaka Puonj mar Ngero Chalo, Kendo Kaka Ngero Opogore gi Pimo Wach

D.A. Masolo

WACH M'OTELO

E i andike ma biro luwo hulo wach-ni wabiro temo nyiso kama: Ni kit ngero nyiso ni ngero en pimo kaka gik-moko, kata paro, chalo gi wedegi e piny. Ni ng'ano ma goyo ngero ok tem hulo kata dimo kaka gik-moko chalo. Omiyo ka oyudore ni nitie pogruok e kind gik-moko kata e kind weche to gi kaka ngero wacho, ok nyal wach ni jalo ma ogoyo ngero oriaso, to nikech ok ochuno ni ngero odimre gi kaka kit piny chalo. Ma e ma omiyo wawacho ni ngero ok rias.

CHUNY WACH

Dhok ka dhok nitie gi ngeche m'opogore-opogore. Ngeche-gi duto nyiso gigo ma oganda ka oganda paro ni oting'o puonj madongo ma ji onego ng'e. To kaka asenyiso e wach motelo, ngeche gin kit weche ma ok nyal lokore ka luwore gi puonj-no ma oganda dwaro chiwo, to gin mana weche ma ipimo-go kaka kit gik-moko, kata kit paro, chalo. Gimiyo jalo ma igoyo-ni ngero-no yudo winjo kata ng'eyo matut kuom tim kata timbe mag dhano ei piny.

Mana kaka ogendni ma moko, wan bende kaka joLuo wantiere gi ngeche ma wagoyo mondo wapuonj-go tiend weche kata ng'eyo m'opogore opogore. Jogo matindo, kata jogo ma odongo e pinje ma bor gi piny oganda-wa ma ok wach-ye dhowa, ok ong'eyo ngeche mang'eny, kata ok ging'eyo tiend ngeche, to nikech ok giyud puonj ma o-a kuom jogo madongo kaka nene timore e kinde machon. Ka luwore gi dongo kata dak e-pinje ma oko, kata ka luwore gi sumo wat mar kend gi dak gi jogo ma ok gin joLuo, jowa matindo mang'eny dhi ka wi-gi wil gi wacho dhowa, to ahinya to wi-gi wil gi kit dhok matut machalo kaka ngeche. Mani miyo ka dwarore mondo jogo ma podi dongo mondo gipuonjre dhoLuo to gi weche duto ma nyiso kit Luo ka-achiel gi timbegi, mana kaka Ker mar Luo m'osenindo chon Paulo

A Proverb Never Lies

On the Nature of Proverbs and How They Differ from Propositions

D. A. Masolo, *Louisville University*
Translated by Stephen Omondi Owino, *Kenyatta University*

INTRODUCTION

In what follows, we will try to show that unlike propositions, proverbs are not claims about the world. Rather, they indicate general impressions about the world which may or may not be true in their specific circumstances. For this reason, anyone who uses a proverb to describe a situation does not assume to be saying anything specific about such a *descriptur,* and so cannot be held accountable for any discrepancy between the meaning of the proverb and the referential circumstance to which it is applied. Proverbs are neither true nor false.

THE TEXT

Every language has various proverbs. All these proverbs illustrate what the community feels are the main teachings that its members ought to know. But as I have indicated in the introduction, proverbs are kinds of expressions whose meanings do not vary according to the circumstances that the speakers are talking about, but are rather expressions to indicate the people's general impressions, experiences, and thoughts. Proverbs enable the person to whom they are told to acquire deeper understanding of human conduct in life.

We Luo people, just like other communities and peoples, have our proverbs, which we employ to teach and explain various matters. The young, or people who do not speak our language, often do not know many of our proverbs or their true meanings because they no longer learn from the old people as it was in the traditional setting. As a consequence of living in foreign lands, or of establishing relationships with people of non-Luo origins, usually through interethnic marriages, most of our youth are increasingly forgetting our language and above all, the more specialized aspects of the language, such as its proverbs. This demands that the young be instructed in the Luo language and other expressions that teach and symbolize the customs and practices of the community, just as the late Luo elder, Paul Mbuya Akoko, recommended

Mbuya Akoko nene ondiko e kitape ma ong'ere sidang', kendo m'iluongo ni *Luo Kitgi Gi Timbegi.*[1] Jo thum, jo wer, jo-telo ma-chon, ka-achiel gi ji madongo ma nee pimo sigend Luo nee hinyo bedo jogo ma nene ong'eyo dhoLuo maber kendo matut. Jogi nene ong'eyo ngeche mag Luo ahinya, kendo nene ginyalo goyo mbaka gi ngeche ma ji matindo ok ne nyal winjo mbak-gi duto. Kaka wasewacho, Ker Paulo Mbuya nee en achiel kuom jogo manee ong'eyo dhoLuo matut ahinya, kendo nene ohero wuoyo gi ngeche. Jalo machielo nee en jathum kendo ja Sigana ma nyocha ong'ere ahinya e piny Luo, Daniel Owino Misiani. Jali nene ohero wer gi ngeche ka opimo-go weche mag siasa, kendo ka onyiso-go timbe maricho mag jogo manee omonore gi oganda mar Luo.

Ng'eng' ngeche oting'o paro kata rieko ma ji osepimo ka luwore gi gigo ma gise-neno kendo ginono mos kuom kinde m'ogwaro. Rieko-gi bedo puonj ma oganda oyie ni nyalo geng'o dhoch kata kiragi moko ma nyalo ketho dak kata winjruok e kind ji. Omiyo idwaro ni ji ong'e ngeche kendo mondo ging'e puonj-go ma ngeche oting'o. Nyaka nene joLuo wacho-ga ni *Nyathi kata ng'ato ang'ata ma ok winj puonj wuotho-ga gi chieth e piere.* Mano bende en ngero, kendo onyiso ni puonj gi rieko ema loso dhano, mana kaka *teko ema dago le e thim.* To kendo bende, joLuo wacho ni ji duto onego winj puonj, nikeche onge ng'ato ma ohingo puonj. Mani miyo ka joLuo goyo ngero moro ni *Rabet kipuonj*, tiende ni nitie ji moko ma paro ni gidongo koro gihingo puonj, to mani en miriambo, to nikech, kaka kendo giwacho, *Kata Fulu oro-ga Mamba.*

Obed duong' mar telo, kata duong' mar mbas, kata mar anyuola, onge ng'ato ma ong'eyo duto. *Ng'ato ong'eyo to ng'ato kia*, tiende ni ji duto oriwo ng'eyo kata fuwo. Mani ema nyiso ni en gin maber mondo ji matindo omi ji madongo luor, kaka giwacho ni *Luor Lwar*, to mani ok nyis ni ji m'otegno onego cha jogo matindo. *Nyathi kaka opuonje ekaka odongo*, kata ni *Nyathi timo mana ma oseneno*, nyiso ni jogo ma dongo onego chiw puonj gi ranyisi mabeyo ni nyithindo ma a chien, to bende *Nyathi ma i-oro ema yieng'-ga*, kata *ema pielo chieth maduong'*, nyiso ni nyathi ma timo luor ema yudo gweth to kendo dongo maber.

TIENGE MAG NGERO

Ngeche nitie tienge mang'eny; moko yot winjo, to moko bedo tiend-gi dwarore doyo mos-mos eka fueny-gi winjre maler. Kendo pile, ngeche hinyo bedo weche ma ong'ad ma ok hul ligendni-ge duto. Nitie ngeche ma puonjo kaka kit dhano obet, e timbe-gi, kata i chal mar-gi kaka anyuola. Mani miyo ka ji oneno chal mar tim e kind nyithindo ariyo ma gin wede to penjo kama: "*maru ni en mar kodhi?*" Ngeche ma puonjo kaka ji riwo kido mar tim kata mar chal mar del, kata kaka ji pogore gi kit-gi chalo gi ngero ma wacho ni

in his famous book *Luo Kitgi Gi Timbegi* "Luo Customs and Practices"].[1] Poets, musicians, leaders, and the elders who used to narrate the history of the Luo often were people with deep knowledge and command of the Luo language. They had a vast knowledge of the Luo proverbs, which they could employ in their conversations to an extent that sometimes uninitiated young people could barely understand their discussions. As we mentioned already, Mr. Paul Mbuya was one of those people who had a deep mastery of the Luo language and liked to use proverbs. Another notable one was the renowned Luo musician-cum-storyteller, Daniel Owino Misiani, who preferred to use proverbs in his songs to make political commentary and to recount the ill motives of other people and communities who were inimical to the Luo.

Most proverbs contain impressions, reflections, and knowledge of the people accumulated over a long period of time. The wisdom of the proverbs is constitutive of the knowledge that the community deems vital for averting disasters and disharmony in the community. Therefore, it is necessary for individuals to know the proverbs and the teachings they embody. Since time immemorial, the Luo have had the saying, *A child who does not follow advice walks with feces stuck in his anus*. This is a proverb that means that learning and wit is what makes and adapts a human being, whereas *strength sustains animals in the forest*. They also say that everyone should strive to learn because no one is superior to knowledge. This prompted the Luo to add another saying: *The big one is not taught,* which means that there are individuals who feel that they are too old to learn or too big to be taught; this is wrong because, as another proverb explains, *The small fish also sends the big ones*.

There is nobody who knows it all on the basis of superiority in status, age, or lineage. *One both knows and does not know,* which means that all of us are simultaneously both knowledgeable and ignorant, or that we are not all ignorant of the same thing. *Respect grey hair* is another proverb that teaches that it is advisable for the young to respect the old, but it does not imply that the old should disrespect the young. *A child grows according to how he has been taught,* or *A child imitates what he has seen,* shows that the elders should teach the young by setting good examples. Besides, the proverbial saying that *A child who runs errands is the one who gets well-fed,* or *is the one who defecates big feces,* indicate that a respectful child receives blessings and grows up well.

TYPES OF PROVERBS

There are various types of proverbs; some are simple and easy to understand while others are complex, thus requiring reflection in order to decipher their meanings. Commonly, proverbs are short sayings that do not completely explain their applications. There are proverbs that teach about the nature of human beings, their conduct and communal customs. This is why when the Luo notice a similarity in the conduct of two related children, they ask: "*Does it derive from blood?*" Proverbs that teach how people resemble each other in character

Awendo ok we yiere, kata ni *Nyathi thuol en thuol*, nikech anyuola ema miyo dhano chal mare, kendo anyuola e kama nyathi puonjoree timbe ma odongo-go. Ka nyathi owuok ei anyuola ma bondo chamo, to en bende onyalo bedo rabondo; to ka owuok ei anyuola ma iyidee, to en bende onyalo bedo jajuok kata jayido.

Kendo bende, joLuo puonjo ni dhano ok rom kende, ji duto dwaro wede-gi, kata ji mamoko eka gidag kaka dhano. Mani miyo ka joLuo goyo ngero niya: *Lwedo achiel ok lwokre kende*, kata ni *Ruoth ok yier-re kende*, kata ni *Jawuoro ochuto ring'o gi pien*, kata ni *Jadak kende en ng'a m'oyuma m'iwuoro*, tiende ni o-onge wich kuot. Jadak kende chalo nyathi matin ma ok odewo kaka ji moko biro kawe kaluwore gi timbe-ne. Kendo joLuo wacho ni ng'ano ma timbe-ne nyiso ni ok oluoro oganda niya: *Wang'i tek ka wang' jajuok*. Mani nyiso ni dhano kite en dak gi jowetene, dak ei oganda. Jajuok en ng'ano ma ok dew ji ma moko, ema omiyo joLuo wacho ni *Jajuok yido k'owad-gi to kore to oling'*. To dak ei oganda kanyo ema kiragi, dhoch kata dhawo wuok-ye bende. Mani omiyo nitie ngeche ma puonjo ni timo ber ok en gi konchiel kende. Ber nyaka wuog kuom ji duto: *Tawo ma itokee ema itoko-nie*, kata *Wang' ma ithiedho ema gawi*, kata *Wat iriwo gi osiep*, kata ni *Waduu ma ichiemo-go e tawo achiel ema negi*.

Aye kendo bende, joLuo nitie gi ngeche ma puonjo ni tim dhano ema loso dak, omiyo ber dhano ipimo kuom timbe, ok kido mar del. Mani miyo ka joLuo goyo ngeche kama: *Jaber jahula*; kata *Chwo lore gi timbe-gi*, kata *Ber ok cham*; kata *Ber imedo di-riyo*. Magi duto gin ngeche ma joLuo goyo mondo opuonj ji olos chuny-gi kendo gibed ji mabeyo ma timo gigo ma kelo kwe, gi mor, to gi dongruok.

Ngeche ma yot

Ngeche mayot gin mago ma ipuonjo-go ji duto weche gi rieko ma konyo dongo gi dak maber. Achiel kuom ngeche mayot chalo kaka ngero ma wacho kama: *ja rikini ja muod nyoyo gi kuoyo*. Tiend ngero-ni nyiso ni ber mondo dhano kik rikni e timbegi kata e weche-gi, to nikech rikni gi weche kata gi timo gin-moro nyalo kelo both kata masira ma dak ne obedee ka dinee ng'ano oparo wechene kata timne mokuongo. Ngero-ni iwache ni nyathi, kata ng'ato ang'ata ka oreto timo gin-moro ma mit oketho. Ei oganda nitie jogo ma nitie gi kido mar rikni, nikech ok girit ma gipar maber motelo ka podi ok giwacho

or physically or even how they differ in these respects include *A guinea fowl does not abandon its feathers,* or *A snake begets a snake,* because the family is what endows one with one's characteristics and is also the locus where the child learns the rules of conduct that he or she grows up with. For example, if a child is born of a lineage of baldheads, he might become baldheaded too; and likewise if he comes from a lineage of wizards, he too might be one.

The Luo teach also that no human being is self-sufficient. Everybody needs others, whether relatives or not, in order to live like human beings. That is why they have sayings such as: *A hand does not wash itself,* or *A chief does not elect himself,* or *A glutton eats meat with skin on it,* or *One who lives alone acts weird,* because he has no shame. One who lives alone is like a small child who does not care how others will perceive him or her on account of his or her conduct. The Luo would tell one who does not respect others: *You are as daring as a wizard.* This illustrates that an individual's character derives from living with others. A wizard is a person who does not care about others and that is why the Luo describe or refer to that person with the proverb *A wizard is one who does mischief at his brother's home while his home is quiet.* However, it is also recognized that disasters, epidemics, and conflicts come from living together in a community. That is why there are proverbs that counsel that benevolence is reciprocal and should be imperative for every member of the community: *The plate you serve others with is the same one you are served with,* or *The eye you treat soon stares at you,* or *Friendship spices kinship,* or *The one you eat with from the same plate is the one who kills you.*

Besides, the Luo have proverbs that teach that a harmonious community derives from good human conduct, and hence that the goodness of a person is measured by their acts and not by the beauty of their looks. That is why they say: *The beautiful are not flawless*; or that *Men are contrasted by their acts*; or that *Beauty is not edible*; or yet again, that *Beauty should be doubled,* meaning that corporeal beauty by itself does not account for a person's goodness; it must be accompanied by the beauty of character. All these sayings are employed by the Luo to teach people to carefully cultivate their habits so as to become good people who are able to bring about peace, happiness, and development.

Simple Proverbs

Simple proverbs are those that are used to teach everybody about matters and ways that would help them to develop and live well. One of the simple proverbs is: *A hasty person eats nyoyo* [mixed maize and beans] *with sand.* It means that it is better to be slow and thoughtful in deeds and words, because being hasty with words or works can lead to mistakes or disasters that would have been avoidable if only one had been a bit thoughtful before acting. This proverb is told to a child who hastily carries out a task but ends up messing things up. In society, there are some individuals who have the habit of hurrying

kata gitimo gin-moro. Rieko-ni wuok kuom kit Luo machon ka nene podi ji toko nyoyo ei odheru kata adita ma omuon gi wuoch dhiang', kendo nikech mano, kata nikeche kan moro nee both moro matin otimore kuom daro cham, nee lowo moro nyalo dong' e cham. Omiyo ka nee ji muodo nyoyo, nee chuno mondo ng'ato non maber ka podi ok oketo chiemo e-dhoge. Tiende niya: onego ji par maber ka podi ok giwacho kata gitimo ginmoro, to nikeche rikni nyalo kelo dhoch, kata kiragi, kata sigu kuom oganda. To nitiere kinde moko ma rikni nyalo bedo gin maber. Rikni nyalo kelo ni ng'ato hawi mar telo yudo ginmoro. Mani miyo ka joLuo wacho bende niya: *Jarikni ok deny*. Jo-Alego wache niya: *Mrikni k'deny*. Tiend ngeche ariyo-gi nyiso ni nyaka ng'ato ng'e ka manade ma rikni ber, kendo ka manade ma rikni en bam.

Ngero machielo ma yot en kama: *Ng'ato ma ogombo chuny bang'o bet yude-ga*. Ngero-ni ipuonje ni ji mondo giwinj ogaye kata puonj mag ji madongo. Jogo ma ok winj puonj mar ji ma-dongo bet yudo-ga chandruok, kata *yudo-ga ma ok olwer*, kaka jo piny machon nene opuonjo, to ma nitie podi wacho-ga kamano. Ng'ato ka podi tin to dwaro ni owinj ogaye kata puonj mag ji madongo eka en bende onyalo yudo rieko ma taye e ngima-ne.

Inind diere, inind tung' bende en ngero moro ma yot, kendo opuonjo niya: chando nyalo yudo ng'ato angata e ngima-ne ma onge chano, to nikech onge ng'ano ma ong'eyo ma nyalo ng'eyo kaka ndalo ma podi biro nyalo bedo. Jo moko wacho ngero-ni kama: *piny agonda*, kata jogo ma nitie-go, kata ma ni-gi hawi, kik gi-cha jogo ma onge-go. Magi gin ngeche ma puonjo ji mondo gibed jogo ma onge sunga gi acheye kuom jogo ma onge gweth kata nyalo mar bedo gi mwandu, nikech mwandu gin gik makadho. Kendo giwacho ni *dhier ok kuong'ruok*, to mana nikech gigo ma asewacho-go, nikech ji wachogi kaka ngeche m'opogore, to tiend-gi to bet en achiel.

Kendo ngero machielo ma chalo gi mago en kama: *Fuwo ok ng'iew*. Nikech jalo ma ofuwo en ng'ato ma onge rieko, o-onge gin-moro; tiende ni en nono, to nono ok ng'iew. Ng'ato ok dhi e chiro ng'iewo nono kata ng'iewo dhier. Ng'ato ma dwaro nono to bet gi piere ma ok otimo gin-moro. Mani opogore gi wang' e ohala, to nikeche jalo ma owang' e ohala en jalo ma otemo yuto to ohala ema ogoye adhong', kaka ji moko wacho. Ka ng'ato dwaro goyo ngero ni jalo ma otamore winjo puonj to onyise kama: *fuwo ok ng'iew Owada, chodh-ni go*.

Ithanyori ka yap ng'at-achiel, kata *Ithanyori k'agwata, kendo kata Othanyore ka od nyawanga* duto gin ngero achiel, kendo en ngero m'oriere, kendo winje yot. En ngero ma nyiso ni ng'ato onge gigo ma opando, ahinya to ka owacho duto ma ni e dende; omiyo ji duto winje kendo ging'eyo kore. To jalo ma kore tek ng'eyo to igoyo-ne ngero niya: *Igori kwangla*.

up with everything, even when careful reflection and analysis is called for. This wisdom comes from the old practice of the Luo when people used to serve food in and eat from a traditionally woven tray called an *odheru* or a basket, both of which were plastered with cow dung. And precisely because of the fact of being plastered with cow dung or because during the separation and preparation of the beans and maize, grains of sand could remain or drop into the mixture, it was necessary that when eating *nyoyo,* one needed to be very careful before putting it into the mouth. The lesson to be learned is that life is generally complex, as is often seen in the details of thought. Hence, judiciousness is encouraged as a virtue to be exercised by all. People ought to think through matters before their pronouncements or deeds. But there are instances when haste can be benign or a virtue that leads to success, whereas laxity leads to failure. The call, therefore, is for people to be of measured judgment even for determining benign haste and distinguishing it from the faulty or vicious kind.

Another simple proverb is: *Whosoever wishes to eat liver finally gets it.* This one teaches that people should pay attention to the counsel of the elders. Those who ignore such counsel are likely to get into trouble or as the saying of the ancients goes, those who ignore the advice of the elders *encounter untrimmed, bushy hedges,* meaning that they are likely to run into trouble in life because they lack learning on how to make discernments crucial to navigating one's way through life. When one is young, one should listen to the elders so as to acquire knowledge to guide one in life.

*One time you sleep in the middle and yet another time, on the edge of the bed** is another simple proverb and teaches that problems can come upon anybody anytime because no one knows or can reliably predict what the future will hold for them. Others alternatively use the saying *The course of life meanders,* which means that the rich should not despise the poor. These are instances of proverbs that urge people not to despise the poor because fortune can be merely transitory. Another proverb that says the same thing is *Poverty is not a curse.* This shows that various proverbs may have the same meaning or teaching.

Another proverb that has the same meaning is: *Ignorance costs nothing.* Since a fool lacks knowledge, he has nothing, and one does not buy nothingness. Nobody goes to the market to buy nothingness, or ignorance, or poverty. Whoever wants nothing only has to sit down and do absolutely nothing. This is different from making losses in business because, by virtue of the nature of the occupation, a trader always tries to succeed but only unintentionally may incur losses. So, if one wants to use a proverb to mock someone who does not want to listen to advice he says: *Ignorance costs nothing my brother, so take as much as you wish.*

You are as shallow as one man's well, or *You are as shallow as a calabash,* or *He is as shallow as an eagle's nest* are instances of one and the same proverb, which is simple and easy to understand. They are told to someone who is not discreet. On the contrary, one who is excessively secretive is told the proverb: *You are extremely twisted and intertwined.*

Ngeche machalo gi mago ma wapimo-go igoyo e dier mbaka, kata ichogo-go jalo ma ipako, kata ma idwaro ni mondo oyud puonj kuom tim ma otimo kata kido marach ma onyiso e tim kata wuoyo-ne.

Ngeche ma tek

Kuom ranyisi, achiel kuom ngeche matiend-gi tek chalo kama: *Dhano ombasa.* Mani nyiso niya: *dhano en ombasa,* kata ni *dhano chalo ombasa.* Mondo ng'ato ong'e tiend ngero-ni, dwaro ni m'okuongo onego ong'e tiend *ombasa.*

Ombasa en alawa kata olando ma hinyo tii (twi) e mbuga kata e pap, kendo olawore machieg-ni gi lowo; oboke ne chalo gi lum kuom kido, to gidongo ma romo gi lwet nyathi matin. Onyuolo kodhi ma dongo ma opadore, kendo kano nya-iye kaka oganda, to ka osetegono, to kothe loko kido koro chalo ma rateng' kata rabuor ma riwo. Ka osetwo to pado mar kothe-no muoch to kiro kothe kata nya-iye mabor. Pile nyithindo pono ombasa kendo bulo nikech omit chamo chalo njugu.

Koro, tiende ang'o wacho ni *Dhano chalo ombasa*? Mani en ngero ma puonjo niya: mana kaka ombasa en apidhe ma kite en landore nikech omuoch mit oke kothe kuonde maboyo, dhano bende kite en landruok e piny ka okeyo kothe. Nyaka nene chakruok piny, joLuo gin oganda ma osebedo ka gilandore. Mani miyo jowa gin jogo ma dar kendo weyo gund-ni ka gidhi goyo mier manyien kendo ka gidhi dak kuonde machielo ma gipeyo, kata kuonde ma gin-tiere gi osiepe. Mani e-ma miyo bende ka joLuo pogo kind jopiny gi jodak.

Kendo joLuo goyo ngero moro niya: *Gima ok one jabedo miriambo.* Mani en puonj maduong' ahinya ma nyiso kaka joLuo nene pimo wach ma inyalo kawo kaka adiera ma ji nyaloyie-go. Wach ma ji yie en wach mar jalo ma oneno gin-moro gi wang'e, ok wach mar jalo ma owinjo awinja. Mani miyo-ga ka ogo bura piny to ipenjo jogo duto ma theno jo-yalo ka gin bende ging'eyo weche-go. Ng'eyo en neno, ok en winjo awinja; koro eka jetend bura wacho kama: "par maber, nikeche gin ma ok one jabedo miriambo; ineno gi wang'i, koso iwinjo awinja"?

To paro maduong' ma ne wadwaro pimo en kama: ni ka ng'ato owacho ni *dhano ombasa,* kata dhano en ombasa, ok onyiso ni en, kata jogo duto ma ong'eyo kendo tiyo gi ngero-no paro ni dhano en apidhe moro ma tii (twi) e lowo ma chalo gi cham kata gi oboke moro kata yath. Jogo duto ma wacho dhowa ong'eyo ni dhano opogore gi apidhe ma tii e lowo, kendo bende opogore gi le ma moko. Omiyo wach ni dhano en ombasa ok en hulo, kata dimo wach kata ng'eyo ni dhano en apidhe. Kendo bende, wach ni ok

Proverbs such as the ones we have discussed above are used in the course of informal conversations, or to commend someone, or to politely reprimand and teach someone who has erred in deed or words.

Complex Proverbs

An example of complex proverbs can be the following: *Humans are ombasa* [a kind of a plant]. This shows that *a human is an ombasa* or that *humans are like the ombasa.* In order to know the meaning of this proverb, it is imperative to know the characteristic of the *ombasa* plant that makes it apt for the proverb.

The *ombasa* is a plant that spreads on the ground or the field. It does not grow upward. Its leaves are green in color but broad enough to be the size of the palm of an infant's hand. Its pods are big and flat, enclosing bean-like seeds. When it matures, its seeds turn black or dark brown. When it dries, the pod explodes and disperses the seeds far and wide. Usually, young boys and girls pick the seeds to roast because they taste like peanuts when roasted.

What, then, does it mean to say that *Humans are like the ombasa*? This is a proverb that teaches that just as the *ombasa* is a plant that spreads its seeds by explosion and dispersion, humans too transmit their traits by spreading their "seeds" far and wide. Also, humans have spread across the globe through migrations to distant frontiers. From time immemorial, the Luo have been a community that has been spreading and expanding its territories by the spread of the population to new lands. These migrations usually lead to abandoned homesteads as new ones are erected, or as the Luo conquer new lands or settle where they have friends. This also explains why the Luo make a clear distinction between natives and immigrants in any settlement.

The Luo have another saying that *Whatever is not eye-witnessed is often a lie.* This is a very significant teaching which indicates how the Luo used to discriminate between what is worthy of belief and what is to subject to skepticism. What is believable is that which has been witnessed firsthand by the reporter and not merely hearsay. For this reason, when there is a court case, witnesses are asked if they "know" the issues under dispute, or if they have only heard about them. One knows only those matters that one has witnessed firsthand, while the rest remains hearsay. So the judges would insist: "Try to remember well because whatever is not eye-witnessed often is not precise; did you see it or merely hear of it?"

The main thought we want to express is that by using the *ombasa* proverb as explained above, the speaker does not imply that a person is literally a kind of plant that spreads on the ground like an *ombasa*. Everyone competent in our language knows that a person is different from a plant that spreads on the ground and is even different from other animals. So, the saying is not a proposition or a judgment that a person is a plant. Moreover, this expression cannot be clearly understood unless it is well explained to the hearer. This means that to say it is not like saying that *Omondi is a grandson to Lady Theodora.* The latter can be true or false. The difference lies in the verb "to be." As I indicated before, proverbs are commonly short phrases whose

bed maler ni ji duto ka podi ok opime kata olere ne-gi. Tiende niya, wacho ni dhano ombasa ok chal gi wacho ni *Omondi en nyakwar Mama Theodora*. Wach m'ogik-ni nyalo bedo adier, kata onyalo ma ok odimore. Pogruok bedo kuom wach matin nono ma en rahulo "*en*." Kaka asepimo e wach mokadho, ngeche hinyo bedo weche ma ong'ad, kendo ok wache kaka gigo ma ji wacho e wuoyo ma pile. Kuom ngeche mang'eny, pogruok-no bedee nikech giko ngero ok en hulo kata temo dimo adiera moro. Mani miyo ka wawacho, bang' paro matutu, niya: ngero ok rias, tiende ni ngero ok wach miriambo, to mana nikech giko mare ok en wacho adier. To kata kamano, ngeche duto temo chiwo paro ma opimore gi gigo duto ma osetimore, kata ma ji oseneno. Ngero ma chalo *dhano ombasa* timo puonj ni jogo duto ma paro matut e wach-no nikech gisepimo sigand oganda. Ngero machielo machalo gi ma en *Dhano winyo*. JoLuo goyo ngero ni ka ginyiso ni ng'eyo kor ji tek, nikech thoth ji ohero kano weche e chuny-gi, kendo ginyalo loko pach-gi kata e winjruok kata muma ma giseloso gi ng'ato machielo. Mani miyo ka joLuo wacho bende ni *Dhano osiep chunye*. Ng'eyo chuny dhano tek, mana kaka ng'eyo chuny winyo tek, to nikeche chopo machiegni kode tek. Omiyo dhano bende nyalo bedo kodi machiegni gi dende, to chunye, kata pache to bedo dong' mabor mana kaka chuny winyo. Gino ma ng'ato ong'eyo e chunye, en kende ema ong'eyo, to nikeche opando wachno mit koro opondo e chunye. Ng'ato nono ok nyal ng'eye. To kata ka oyango wach-no, to en kende ema ong'eyo adiera mar gin ma oyango-no. Mani miyo ka joLuo kawo gigo duto ma ji wacho nyaka giwegi gifueny tiende-gi koda adiera mar weche-go. To bende dwarore mondo ji odim wach ka giwacho adiera maler kinde duto.

Fueny mar tiend ngeche-go nyiso kaka jopiny madongo nene ni gi tiegruok kuom weche mag paro. Nene giparo matut kendo nene gipimo ahinya weche mafulo kit piny, kata kit dhano ka-achiel gi kit pache bende. To bende, ngeche-gi nyiso kaka tiend ngero en paro kata rieko mafulo winjo kata puonj m'opondo. Mano ema miyo ka ng'ato kia wach moro to openjo mondo nyise ngech wach-no. Jogo ma nono tiend weche gin jogo ma ong'eyo ngeche, kendo ginyalo nono tiend wach mit nyaka ging'e ngeche kata ngech-ene ka gin mathoth. To mano bende ema omiyo jalo ma osepuonjore gin-moro matut kendo nyalo fuenyo tiende ni jogo ma podi kia koro iluongo ni Ngire, tiende ni olony gi wach-no maler kendo matut sidang', kendo ohingo dhano mathoth kuom ng'eyo tienge m'opogore opogore mag wachno.

Pile, inyalo winjo ka ng'ato penjo niya: "to dhano nyalo bedo winyo nade? Dhano opogore gi gigo ma fuyo e wi muya, kendo opogore gi le ma moko." Yalo weche ema kelo puonj kendo tugo wi weche ma kor-gi tek. To nyiso ni jalo ma wacho ni "Dhano ok en winyo" en jalo ma kia tiend ngero-no. En oparo mana ni ngero-no temo dimo chal e kind dhano to gi

constituent words are not literal but rather figurative. For most proverbs, the difference derives from the fact that the function of a proverb is not to express a proposition. This is why we say after reflection that a proverb never lies, meaning that a proverb has no truth-value, as it cannot be either true or false, simply because its function is not to state the truth. Nevertheless, all proverbs attempt to express impressions built over time through observations and experiences of the people. A saying such as *Humans are like the ombasa* has something to teach those who reflect deeply on its meaning and the history of the community. Another proverb that is like this one is one which says that *Humans are like birds*. The Luo use it to indicate that it is difficult to understand humans well because the majority of them keep secrets and, besides, they can always change their minds, even to the point of breaking their promises and commitments. This tendency also prompts the Luo to say that *A person's best friend is his or her own mind or consciousness*. Without their own truthful revelation, knowing what is in the mind or heart of an individual is impossible. Even in the instance of truthfulness, only they hold the secret of what is the case. So, a person may be close to you physically while his mind or heart drifts and flies away just like a bird. The proverb teaches that knowledge of our own minds is always firsthand knowledge, and is the first among others. Additionally, knowledge by introspection is not only immediate but is also open only to self-examination and not to the skepticism of others. That is why it is important to be truthful.

Grasping the meaning of these proverbs reveals how the older generation was advanced in knowledge of human psychology. They reflected deeply on the nature of the world, and especially on the nature of human beings together with their mind. Besides, these proverbs show that the meaning of a proverb is a profound and hidden thought. That is why when someone does not know the meaning of a word, they ask for its meaning. Those who seek to clarify the meaning of words are the ones who acquire mastery of proverbs and concepts and can analyze words until they grasp their meanings. That is also why someone who has acquired considerable knowledge in a given field and who can teach those who do not know yet is referred to as a doctor or a professor, which means that he has very vast knowledge in the area and he or she is superior to most people in the knowledge of meanings and interpretations in that field.

At times, one may hear someone pose the question: "How can a person be a bird? A human being is different from flying things and other animals as well." Discussion is the best way to learn and grasp the meaning of difficult words and phrases. But whoever retorts that "a person is not a bird" clearly does not understand the meaning of the proverb. He is mistaken in thinking that the proverb is stating a factual similarity between humans and birds, as if humans fly with wings like birds, or as if birds speak like humans. The speaker would respond to such a person by saying: "No, I only gave a proverb." This shows that proverbs are mere indications about what people have observed and reflected on regarding the nature of the world or human beings. A proverb never lies, because it is an opinion that does not have just

winy, ka gin dhano dum gi buombe ka winyo, kata ka gin winyo bende wacho gi dhoge. To ja-go ngero to duoke ni "Ooyo, an agoyo mana ngero." Mani nyiso ni kata bedo ni ngeche gin pim kuom gigo ma ji oseneno kendo gise-paro kuom kit piny kata kit dhano, ngero ok rias, nikech ngero en pach dhano ma ok wach ginmoro achiel. Mani miyo ka ng'ato o-oro nyathi mondo otim-ne ginmoro, kata oloone yo moro, nyathi no ok nyal biro bandhe niya: "Nee i-ora, koro miya ginmoro acham ayieng'," kata ni "nyoro i-ora to ok aneno ka apielo thieth maduong'"; kae to wuon ote kwere niya: Mano en mana ngero, chieng' moro in-iyieng', cha-achaya." Kendo nyathi-no ok nyal dhawo ni nee jaduong' owuonde. Duto ok timre kaka ngero wacho. Ngero en paro, kendo omiyo ji timo paro matut e rieko ma ngero puonjo.

Ranyis machielo en kama: ngero ma wacho ni *Awendo ok we yiere* pimo nyuolruok mar awendo winyo to gi kaka dhano luwo timbe kata kido mar del mar anyuola-ne. To mani ok onyiso ni dhano bende chalo gi anyuola-ne pim-pim kaka awendo chalo gi wedene. To chutho chutho, kata awendni wege ok chal kaka ji paro-no. To m'oloyo, ji ong'eyo maber ni gigo ma nyuolore hinyo riwo kido m'ogwaro ka owuok ei anyuola. To kendo bende, kuom kido mar tim to dhano hinyo luwo gigo ma gineno ka jogo ma gidak godo timo. Omiyo ngero-no en mana yor nyiso ni dhano kawo kite ka owuok kuom oganda-ne, to kendo jogo ma onyuol e-ot achiel ok luw oganda-gi machal. Ja-thum moro ma wuod Luo puonjo ji gi wer ni "ji opogore. . . . kata kwodho bee, ji opogoree; to kata ng'wenyo kuon bende ji opogoree."

To wawuondre ni wuon ote-cha nee owacho ni yathi ni "tim-na tij-ni, to ka itieko, to abiro miyi chiemo mit ichiem iyieng," to bang'e ka nyathi-no osetieko tij-no to jaduong' koro nyise ni chiemo onge. Mani bedo miriambo kata aram, to nikech jaduong' nee ochiwo singo; tiende ni nee owacho maler, kata opimo gino ma obiro timo bang'e ka nyathi-no otieko tich. Ka ok otimo kamano to en ja richo nikech ok orito singo. To nyathi ok nyal mako sisa ngang' gi jalo ma ogoyo mana ngero kode. Mani en pogruok maduong' ahinya. Wacho ginmoro opogore gi goyo ngero. Ng'ato ma ogoyo ngero ok makne richo ka ok otimore kaka ngero pimo, kendo ok pake ka otimore kaka ngero ma nee ogoyo nyiso. Tiende en kama: Ngero ok wuo kuom jal ma ogone-no, kendo ngero ok en singo e kind jagoye gi jal ma ogone-no.

To kata kamano, nitiere ngeche moko ma chalo adiera, kaka ngeche mag pak, kata ngeche ma iluongo-go ng'ato ma ose-ne timbene. Nying mar *Apong' Kor* en ngero, to kendo en nying mar pak bende, to imiye jalo ma timbene obaro ji e kor gweng', kata jalo ma ji o-ol gi timbene, koro ji wacho ni "timbene opong'o kor ji e gweng'"; ochalo ja maundu. Mani nyiso ni chutho chutho *Apong' Kor* ok en ngero. En pak ma ji luongore-go kata

one meaning. Nor are proverbs case-specific. That is the reason why when a child is sent to run errands or given a task to accomplish, he or she cannot come back to demand to be given something to eat to his or her fill or ask why he did not defecate a lot. The sender would say to the child: "Do not worry, it was merely a saying, one day you will be satisfied." The child would also not complain that the sender lied. Whatever a proverb says does not necessarily obtain. Proverbs are not propositions, and most obviously, they are not empirical statements. A proverb is a thought that leads others to think deeply about its teachings.

Another example to illustrate the distinction between a proverb and a proposition is the one that says, *A guinea fowl does not abandon its feathers*. It compares the inheritance of the feather coloring of the guinea fowl with the fact that human beings take after the habits and traits of the family. It does not mean at all that humans resemble their parents or relatives in all respects, as the guinea fowl resembles its kind. Actually, even the guinea fowl do not resemble each other in all respects as people tend to think. Most importantly, people know that things that reproduce tend to have many family resemblances without being identical with each other. Moreover, with regard to habits and character, human beings tend to be influenced by what they have observed from the community in which they grow. So a proverb is merely a way of indicating that humans inherit their habits from their communities while not excluding the fact that those who belong to the same family may not necessarily have the same characteristics. A certain Luo musician teaches this point by singing: "People are different . . . even in their manner of farting . . . even in their manner of *ng'wenyo kuon*."†

But let us assume that the sender tells the child, "Do for me this job and at the end I will give you food to your fill," yet at the completion of the task, he tells the child that there is no food. This then becomes a lie or conman-ship because the sender made a promise, meaning that he stated clearly what he would do at the completion of the task. If he fails to fulfill the promise then he is guilty, because he has not honored the promise. But the child cannot keep a grudge against the one who merely gave a proverb. This is a very fundamental difference. Stating a fact is different from giving a proverb. Whoever uses a proverb is not blamed even if the circumstances do not agree with the proverb; at the same time, he is not praised if circumstances correspond to the proverb. The point is this: a proverb does not refer to the hearer to any specific state of affairs, nor does it create an agreement between the speaker and the hearer.

Nevertheless, there are some proverbs that have shades of truth, for example, praise-proverbs or proverbs used to refer to or to describe someone whose deeds have been noted. A name such as *chest-congester* is a proverb and a praise-name at the same time and it is given to someone who is notorious for being a nuisance to those who interact with him or her, which prompts people to say that his or her conduct is upsetting in the village; he is a social misfit. This actually shows that *chest-congester* is not really a proverb because it states an assessment of the character of specific

giyo-go osiepe-ge kar thum kata kar tuke ma moko. Kata kamano nitie ji moko ma kawe kaka ngero.

NOTES

1. Mani en kitabu ma jaduong' Paulo Mbuya nene ondiko e higa mar 1938 to jo-go Chapa mar Equatorial Publishers ogole e higa-no; kendo oseyudo meto mar 6 e higa 1969.

individuals and thus bears some claim to fact. It can also be a praise-name among close friends who take pride in such traits. Usually, it is used with a tinge of sarcasm, or only jokingly, as no one takes pride in being a social misfit within their community. Nevertheless, there are those who take it as a proverb.

NOTES

1. This is Mr. Paul Mbuya's book written in 1938 and published by Equatorial Publishers in 1969, which has been reissued in six editions since then.

*This proverb comes from the fact that people, especially young ones, could share a bed. It was possible for even four people to sleep on the same bed. It means that one day one could be in the midst of others or at the extremities. Being in the middle was considered more comfortable than at the extremities because there was less risk of falling off the bed to the floor or less chances of having your covers pulled off by the rest.

†*Kuon* is the staple food of the Luo. It is made out of maize or cassava or sorghum flour or a mixture of these. It is thick in texture. It is usually eaten together with various dishes such as fish, vegetables, meat, etc. Traditionally it is eaten from the plate with bare hands. No cutlery is used. *Ng'wenyo* is the infinitive form of the verb which describes the act of picking it up from the plate with the hands.

Ang'o Man e Nying'?

Okange Ang'wen Mag Nyinge e Oganda Luo

F. Ochieng'-Odhiambo

WACH MOKWONGO

Piny ka piny bedo gi timbegi koda chikegi ma jokanyo luwo mondo eka omigi gi bed e kanyachiel. Piny ma ket ni onge chike koda timbe, kata piny ma jokanyo ok dew chikegi koda timbegi en piny mokethore, en piny machalo libamba kendo en piny ma ok nyal bedo gi huma maber e nyim thoth pinje ma moko. Ma en nikech chike koda timbe ema kelo chanruok maber to resruok bende bedo e piny, kendo gin ema gi miyo dongruok bedoe. Chike koda timbe ma oganda piny ka piny luwo thoth, kendo moko kuomgi pogore ka luwore gi pinje, to kata kamano gin ema gitayo pinje. Hie hie, pogruok pinje luwore gi pogruok ma nitiere e chikegi, timbegi koda buchegi bende. E obokeni, chike ma omakowa ma wadwaro lose gin chike mosekungo Joluo e chako nyinge ma giluongore kodo. Chike koda kido mag nyinge Joluo chal ka pogore gi mag pinje ma moko. Ma ema omiyo Joluo, kata jodhoudi ma moko molony gi kido nyinge Joluo koda chikegi mag chako nyinge, kata ka gin e pinje ma oko to ginyalo pogo kendo fwenyo Jaluo nikech nyinge. Kata ka oboke kata oset moro loso kuom Jaluo to ginyalo ng'eyo ni mano en Jaluo ka luwore gi nyinge.

Kiwacho adiera, kanyachiel mar oganda Luo ti dhi ka dok chien. Wach achiel gi ma omiyo ma timore en nikech ng'eny Joluo mantiere ndalogi ok omako matek kata ok gi dew chikegi koda timbegi, to ma en gi ma lich kendo miwuoro nikech okethо chanruok malong'o e oganda Luo. Yawa moko mag Luo dhi ka luwo timbe gi chike mag pinje ma moko sinawuoya. Yawagi dhi ka mako gi tekregi te weche mathoth mag pinje ma moko nyaka kata kaka gichakore nyinge. Moloyo to githoro luwo chike mag jorachare. Nikech luwo timbe gi kido jorachare, nyinge ma moko ma kindeni Joluo chakore kendo luongorego kata pakorego ok gin ranyis malong'o kendo madiera kuom jogo miluongo gi nyingego. Obokeni ondik mondo kik chike gi kido mag Joluo e chako nyinge lal, kendo maduong' moloyo en ni oganda mag pinje ma moko mondo ong'e kit Luo gi kaka gichakore nyinge. Ma eka piny Luo di po ka omedo bedo gi huma maber e nyim dhoudi gi pinje ma moko.

What's in a Name?

Four Levels of Naming among the Luo People

F. Ochieng'-Odhiambo, *University of the West Indies, Cave Hill*
Translated by Oriare Nyarwath, *University of Nairobi*

INTRODUCTION

Every community has its practices and customs that members follow in order to live in unity. Any community that does not have customs and practices, or whose customs and practices are ignored by members, is a ruined community; it is alienated and it cannot earn respect from other communities. Customs and practices bring order and benefit to a community and consequently prosperity. In truth, differences between communities emanate from differences between their respective customs, practices, and organizations. In this paper, we would like to address those customs that have preserved the Luo people with regard to naming and the names they use. Customs and traditions of naming among the Luo are perhaps different from those of other communities. For that reason, the Luo or people from other communities who are conversant with the naming traditions and customs of the Luo are able to recognize and differentiate a Luo even in a foreign land merely by name. Even from a newspaper or magazine, such a person would know a Luo simply by name.

However, a matter that is disturbing and of grave concern these days is that the customs, practices, and organizations of the Luo seem to be on the verge of disappearance. Some Luos tend to follow foreign practices and customs mindlessly. Such people wholeheartedly hold to a lot of foreign things, including the names they give themselves. Mostly, they tend to follow the customs of white people. As a result of following the practices and traditions of white people, some names that the Luo use these days and by which they are called, or the ones by which they refer to themselves during self-praise, are not proper and correct reflections on the people by whom they are called. This paper is written in order to preserve the customs and traditions of naming among the Luo, but more importantly, for those who are not Luo to understand the Luo traditions and customs of naming. Perhaps this would earn the Luo community more respect from other people and communities.

AWENDO OK ONEGO E YIEGE

WE kinde ma sani, adiera en ni pinje mathoth mag yawa ma joratenge dhi ka wito timbegi koda buchegi. Pinje makamagi thoro luwo timbe gi kido mag jorachare, jo ma gidendo ni jonanga. Wamedo wacho ni paroni korang matut, chutho chutho en ni onge piny manyalo bedo gi dongruok malong'o ma adimba ka jokanyo owito timbegi mabor to timbe gi kit welo ema gimako gi tekregi. Ma ema omiyo Joswahili ni gi ngero ma wachoni "*Mwacha mila ni mtumwa.*" Ngeche en ni ng'ano ma owito chike gi timbe anyuola en kaka jatich. Ma ema omiyo nyaka puo bug Paul Mbuya[1] miluongo ni *Luo Kitgi gi Timbegi*. E bugno Mbuya ochoko kanyachiel kido, timbe, gi buche mag Luo. To kata wapuoyo bug Mbuya kama, diber ndi ka olok bugno e dhok ma moko. Mbuya ne ondiko bugni mokwongo e higa 1938 to nyaka seche ma andiko obokeni ok apar ka bugeno oselok e dho jorachare. To ma ok en wach maber nikech ng'eny rowere Luo ma ndalogi, nikech sombgi, olony gi dho jorachare; thoth gi ok ong'eyo somo kata wacho dholuo malong'o, omiyo ok apar ka thoth Joluo ma sani osesomo bugni. Jodongo mag Luo molony gi dho jorachare onego ti matek kendo ma piyo mondo gilok bugni e dho jorachare eka roweregi dipo ka osome ka ayeto omi gilony kata ging'e kido koda timbe mag Luo.[2]

Puonjruok maduong' e bug Mbuya en ni:

> Onego jopiny ket chikegi gi timbegi mabeyo ka mise (misingi) mokwongo; eka giger buche gi timbe welo e wi mise ma giseradho . . . Piny madewo buche gi timbe mabeyo e piny madongo motegno; kendo welo dewo pinyno, gi ji modakie. Ng'ato mariek pile odewo buche, gi timbe mabeyo, kendo otimogi.[3]

E piny ma sani thothwa ok luw puonj mar Mbuya, to kata tiend ngero mar Joswahili mornwa amora. Ng'enywa thoro rikni luwo timbe gi kit jorachare nono. Ma en nikech ka chakre e ndalo mokadho ma ne jorachare ohango donjo e pinje mag joratenge, ne gikelo puonjruok mar akwede kendo achaye ma ne ok adiera dawe. Ne gipuonjo ni joratenge ne gin ji modok chien; ni ne gin ji ma onge kendo kia weche dongruok. Ka ma bam ne omedo betie ne en ni kwerewa moko ma ne nitiere ndalogo ne okawo wechego ma ne jorachare keyo kaka adiera, moloyo to kwerewa ma Injili ne obarogo yoo. Omiyo e kinde ma sani yawa mathoth ogeno kendo gilamo ndi dak ka jorachare e yore duto te; giwito mabor gimoro amora ma luwore gi timbe kata weche Joluo.

Nikech huma ma ok adiera ni chike gi timbe jorachare beyo moloyo mag Joluo, chike gi timbe Joluo dhi ka lal chutho. Kaka ranyis, thoth rowere Luo ma sani mokikore gi jodongo moko bende ok olony kata gi kaka Joluo chakore nyinge. Otho ni moko kuomgi ni nying' en nying', pachgi en ni nying' en mana gi ma ng'ato yie ni "an tiere" kata ni "an" ka oluonge godo to tiend kata ngech nyingno to ok ging'eyo. Nitiere rowere mathoth ma kia tiende nyingegi mag Luo. Aseyudo rowere moko ma iluongo ni "Okaka" to

A GUINEA FOWL SHOULD NOT ABANDON ITS FEATHERS

In these present times, it is a fact that many communities of black people tend to be losing their traditional practices and forms of organizations. Such communities mostly follow the practices and traditions of white people; the people to whom they fondly refer as the "people of clothes." We would like to emphasize that if this behavior were to be critically examined, then there would be no doubt that no community can have proper and genuine progress if it abandons its practices and, instead, only embraces wholeheartedly foreign practices and traditions. For this reason, the Swahili people have a saying: "*Mwacha mila ni mtumwa.*" This means that whoever abandons his/her culture is a slave. In this regard, Paul Mbuya's[1] book *Luo Kitgi gi Timbegi* ["Luo Customs and Practices"] is commendable. In this book, Mbuya puts together the traditions, practices, and organizations of the Luo.[2]

The most important lesson from Mbuya's book is:

> A community should first put their good customs and practices as the foundation upon which thereafter they build foreign organizations and practices. . . . It is the land whose good organizations and practices are valued by its inhabitants which progresses; and foreigners respect that land and its people. A wise person always values good organizations and practices, and follows them.[3]

Most of us today do not follow the advice of Mbuya, and even the meaning of the Swahili saying is just a hollow sound to us. Most of us rashly embrace the practices and traditions of white people for no good reason. This is as a result of a false teaching introduced by white people when they first arrived in the lands of black people. They used to teach that black people were backward and they neither had nor knew of progress. But the situation was made worse by some of our grandparents at that time who believed such false teachings; especially those grandparents who were taken away by Christianity. As a result, many of our people these days very much believe and adore virtually every aspect of European lifestyle; they have completely discarded everything to do with the practices or teachings of the Luo.

Due to the false belief that the customs and practices of white people are better than those of the Luo, the customs and practices of the Luo are on the verge of disappearing for good. For instance, most young as well as some old Luos are not conversant with how the Luo give themselves names. To most of them, a name is just a name, and they think that it is just a word to which one responds, "Here I am," or, "Me"* when called out, yet they do not know the meaning of the name. There are so many young people who do not know the meaning of their Luo names. I know some young men called "Okaka" and others called "Okach," yet they do not know why they

moko ni "Okach," to ok ging'eyo gi ma omiyo ochakgi nyingego. Kendo e ndalo ma sani nitiere Joluo mathoth ma iluongo gi nyinge ma ok oluwore gi kaka Joluo chako yawagi nyinge. Ji makamago thoro neno nying' mana ka gi ma itiyogo mar pogo jal achiel kuom jomoko mana kaka nying' mar "mawembe" en mar pogo gigo miluongo ni mawembe kuom gik moko duto te ma nitiere e piny, to kara nying mar "mawembe" onge tiende. Ngeche en ni onge tudruok e kind nying mar "mawembe" koda gigo ma iluongo ni mawembe. Ka luwore gi paroni, gigo duto miluongo ni mawembe ne inyalo luongo ni "machunga" to weche ne dodhi adhiya mayom nono ma onge pek moro. To ka luwore gi chike ma Joluo chako yawagi nyinge ma ok timre; "Ochieng'" to nobed mana Ochieng' nikech "Ochieng'" ni gi tiende, en ranyis mar ng'ano ma iluongo ni Ochieng'.

Jaluo gitiende ok nyal neno gima omiyo Jaluo onego chakore nyinge jorachare kata jokristo wat gin mana nyinge mag yie. Ma en nikech nyinge welo ok nyis gin moro malong'o kuom Jaluono mayie koluong nyingno. Jonyuol ma kindegi ma chako nyithindgi nyinge mag jorachare kata mag jokristo, thoro chako nyithindgi nyinge ma gin giwegi ema gihero. Iyudo kata ka jonyuol moko, nikech gihero nyinge ma moko sidang', chako nyithindgi nyinge kata ka pod nyithindo ni e iye minegi. Samoro bende inyalo yudo ni kata ka min ot pod ka omako ich to en kanyachiel gi wuon ot giseyiero nying' maber nigi ma gi rito chako nyathi ma nigi yud ka wuon osimbo oyie. Kaka wananyis bang'e, chanro machalo kama orochre, ok gilure gi kit Luo gi timbegi da. Chike gi timbe Luo dwaro ni nying' obed ranyis; nying' onego wachie wach moro machuop kuom jalno ma iluongo gi nyingno. Omiyo nyathi onego chak nying' mana ka osenyuole, ok ka pod en e ich kata ka min ot pod ka omako ich dawe.

Jaramogi Oginga Odinga en achiel kuom jogo ma ne ok oyie giwach ni jarateng' ichako nying' jarachar, kendo ne okwedo chik mar jokristo ma miyo nyithind joratenge nyinge jokristo e seche ma itisogi. Oginga Odinga ne ong'ado bura ni nyinge mag jorachare ne ok nyal bedo ranyis malong'o ka luwore gi chike Joluo nikech ok gi ler gin moro malong'o kuom nyithind Luo miluongo ginyingego.[4] Ma ema ne omiyo bang'e ka osebedo maduong' ne owito mabor nyinge jokristo ma ne ochake kane en pod rawera; ne oweyo tiyo gi nyinge jokristo ma ne iluonge kodo ni Obadiah Adonijah.[5] Wuod Kenya ma anyuola Jokuyu majandiko mong'ere e piny gima, Ngugi wa Thiong'o, bende ne oweyo tiyo gi nying' jokristo ma ne omiye ni James. Kata mana achiel kuom joratenge mariek man gi huma maber e piny ngima ma wuod Joghana miluongo ni Kwasi Wiredu, bende ne owito nying' jokristo mane iluongego ni John. Kar John ne ochako tiyo gi nying' ma luwore gi chike chako nyinge mag anyuolane ni Kwasi. Ka luwore gi ng'eruok koda luor ma piny omiyo ji adekgi, joratenge onego par ahinya wach mar tiyo gi nyinge welo. Ji adek ma okwan gi ok gin kendgi dawe, nitiere ji mang'eny ma moko.

were given such names. Moreover, these days there are many Luos who have names that do not conform to how the Luo name their people. Such people tend to view a name as intended solely for differentiating one person from others just as the name "mango" serves to differentiate a mango from everything else in the world, but it does not have a meaning. According to this view, the things referred to as "mango" could as well have been referred to as "orange" without any problem. However, according to the custom of how the Luo name people, that would not do; "Ochieng'" just has to be Ochieng' because it has a meaning, it signifies the person called Ochieng'.

A strict Luo does not see any good reason why a Luo should be given a white person's or Christian name except perhaps as a name to which one merely responds when called out. This is because foreign names do not give any important information about the person by whom they are called. Parents who give their children the names of white people or Christian names these days mostly give them the names they themselves like. Some parents like certain names so much that they would give their children such names even before they are born. In certain cases, some couples would even choose a name for a child long before conception; just in case they were to be blessed with one. Such arrangements, as will be explained later, do not conform to Luo tradition and practices. The Luo customs and practices require that a name be a signifier; a name has to express something about the person called by it. For that reason, a child should be given a name after birth, not when still in the womb or before conception.

Jaramogi Oginga Odinga is one of those who did not believe that a black person should be given a white person's name, and he rejected the Christian practice of giving black children Christian names at baptism. Oginga Odinga decided that, according to Luo customs, white people's names could not be proper since they do not give any important information about the Luo children called by them.[4] For this reason, when he became an adult, he discarded the Christian name he had been given while he was a child; he stopped using his Christian name Obadiah Adonijah.[5] A son of Kenya and a Kikuyu writer of international reputation, Ngũgĩ wa Thiong'o, also discarded the Christian name James that he had been given. Even one of the brilliant black scholars from Ghana who is respected all over the world, Kwasi Wiredu, discarded his Christian name John. Instead of John, he started using the name Kwasi in accordance with the naming customs of his people. In the light of the fame and respect that these three people have earned in the world, black people should carefully think about their use of foreign names. There are many more people who have discarded the use of foreign names other than the three mentioned.

Puonjruok kuom weche ma osewach nyaka sani en ni oganda joratenge onego par ahinya kuom wach mar tiyo gi chike koda timbe jorachare kaka mise. Ma e tiend ngech Joluo ma wacho ni awendo ok we yiege—nikech ka oweyo yiege to berne ni dipo ka orumo nyamonge nono. Nying' ok onego yier ayiera maonge chanro kata, kaka Joluo moko ma ndalogi nyalo wacho ni, abaramach. Nying' onego yier ka luwore gi kido kata kaka ne onyuol ng'ano miluongo gi nyingno. E seche ma iyiero nying' tekre onego ket mondo nying' obed ranyis malong'o mar ng'ano ma ibiro luong gi nyingno. Ngeche en ni nying' gi ng'ano onego bed e achiel ma kata ka jal machielo kowinjo ka iluongo ng'ano to jalno onego ng'e gin moro kuom ng'ano ka luwore gi nyingno. Nying' ok onego bed ni tiende kata ngeche ok fweny kata ok wach gin moro kuom ng'ano ma iluongo godo nyingno. Nying' ok onego bed kaka maua ma iyiero ayiera ka luwore gi hero ng'ano kata jonyuol. Obokeni temo nyiso yore kaka Joluo ne chakore nyinge. Wafwenyo yore ang'wen ma Joluo luwo ka gi chakore nyinge. Ngeche en ni kido koda chike ma Joluo chakore nyinge inyalo pog e okange ang'wen. E yore kata okange ang'wengi paro Joluo ok ne ni nying' en mana gi ma ka oluong to ng'ato yie, kata ni en mana gi ma itiyogo kuom pogo jalni kuom jalcha, ooyo.

OKANG' MOKWONGO: NYINGE MICHAKO NYATHI KA POD YOM

Nyinge ma Joluo chakore godo kaluwore gi okang' mokwongo gin nyinge michako ka e ka onyuol nyathi kata ka nyathi pod yom. Ma pogore gi nyinge mani e okange ma moko. E okang' mar ariyo, nyathi inyalo chak nying' kata ka pod en e ich. Nyinge ma iluongo ng'ato ka luwore gi okang' mar adek kata okang' mar ang'wen gin nyinge ma ithoro tiyo kodo bang'e ka ng'ato osebedo maduong'. Ka luwore gi okang' mokwongo, nyithindo ma eka onyuol ithoro miyo nyinge ka luwore gi ka ma wang' chieng' nitiere e seche ma onyuolgi (gonyango, godiechieng', godhiambo, gi weche ma kamago); kata ka luwore gi seche mag otieno ma onyuolgi (ka otieno nyako, chuny dier otieno); kata ka luwore gi kaka onyuolgi (ka oumore, ka wino odhogore kuome, ka guoguo oume, gi weche ma kamago); kata ka luwore gi ka ma onyuolgi (e agola, e tok ot, oko e pap, e tie yath, e tie bondo, e yoo, gi weche ma moko makamago); kata ka luwore gi ndalo ma jogweng' odich e puodho e kinde ma onyuolgi (ka gichwoyo, ka gidoyo, ka gikeyo, ka gikomo); kata ka luworegi kaka piny chalo e kinde ma onyuolgi (ka en ndalo bonyo, ka en ndalo kech, ka piny otimo luoch, ka en kinde lweny, ka en kinde ma pi omodho piny, ka en ndalo ma dede ng'eny, gi weche ma kamago).

The lesson from what has been said so far is that black people should rethink using the customs and practices of white people as the foundation of their life. This is the meaning of the Luo saying that a guinea fowl should not discard its feathers—because if that happens then it loses its beauty too. A name should not just be chosen without any order, or in any old way—as some Luos would say these days. A name should be chosen according to tradition or the circumstances of birth of the person called by it. When choosing a name, effort should be directed toward making a name a proper signifier for the person called by it. This means that a name should signify the person to whom it refers such that, when the name is called out, it expresses some information about the person to whom it refers. A name should neither be meaningless nor express nothing about the person by whom it is called. A name should not be like a flower that is chosen according to the liking of a person or parents. This paper is an attempt to show various ways by which the Luo give themselves names. We identify four ways which the Luo follow in giving names. In other words, the Luo naming traditions and customs can be divided into four categories or levels. In all the four ways or categories, the Luo never simply thinks of a name as something to which a person responds when called out, or for differentiating one person from the other. That is not the case.

THE FIRST LEVEL: NAMES GIVEN TO INFANTS

The first-level names are given when a child is born or in infancy. In this way, the first-level names are different from those of the other levels. At the second level, a child may be given a name even during pregnancy. The third or fourth-level names are mostly acquired later after childhood. At the first level, children are mostly given names according to when they are born, such as the position of the sun at birth (morning, midday, evening, and such like); the time of birth at night (early night, midnight); how they were born (facing down, entangled by the umbilical cord, covered in amniotic membrane, etc.); where they are born (under the eaves of a house, behind a house, in a field, under a tree, under a cactus tree, by the path/ road, etc.); engagement with agricultural activities (planting, weeding, harvesting, sowing); or the general situation in the land (locust invasion, famine, overcast day, time of war, time of floods, grasshopper invasion, etc.).

Ka ma wang' chieng' nitiere, kit otieno, kaka nyathi owuok e ich, ka ma onyuolie nyathi, kaka jogweng' odich e puodho, gi kaka piny chalo ok gin yore duto te ma oganda Luo luwo e chako nyithindo nyinge. Inyalo chako nyathi nying' ng'ato moro maduong' mosenindo, nying' ng'ato moro maduong' marahuma e gweng' kata nying' ng'ato maduong' ma okadho e piny kinde monyuol nyathino,[6] gi weche ma moko machalo kamano. Jaluo ok thor chako nyathi nying' ng'ato ma jajuok kata nying' ng'ato ma timbene richo. Ka po ni ochak nyathi nying' jajuok kata ng'ato ma timbene richo, to mano bedo mana ka wat luworegi nyinge michako nyathi e okang' mar ariyo ma wabiro lose bang'e. Nying' ng'ato ma timbene richo ichako nyathi mana ka jonyuol nyathi oleko kuome ni chake nyathino to ka gidagi chake to onego nyathino.

Nyinge (moko) ma ichako nyithindo ka luwore gi seche ma ne onyuolgi, ndalo ma ne onyuolgi, gik ma ne timore kinyuologi, kata ka ma ne onyuolgi gin kama: Nyathi ma wuoi monyuol ka wuon ne osenindo to jal machielo osetero min kendo jalno e monyuol gi min, Joluo chake ni Ochola. To ka en nyathi ma nyako gichake ni Achola.[7] Tiende nikech en nyathi chola. Nyathi monyuol kamano, monyuol gi chi liel, ma ochak ni Ochola kata Achola, gibolone del nikech en nyathi lowo, chola. Kuom nyithindo monyuol rude, nyathi ma okwongo wuok (nyathi ma owuok piyo) gichake ni Opiyo ka en wuoi to Apiyo ka en nyako. Nyathi ma owuok bang'e (ma pod odong' chien) ichako ni Odongo ka en wuoi to Adongo ka en nyako. Nyathi ma onyuol bang' rude ichako ni Okello ka en wuoi kata Akello ka en nyako nikech en akend rut. Nyithindo moko ichako kama:

- Nyathi monyuol ka biero ema otelo ichako ni Obiero ka en wuoi to Abiero ka en nyako.
- Nyathi monyuol e tie bondo ichako ni Obondo ka en wuoi to Abondo ka en nyako.
- Nyathi monyuol achiel kende ichako ni Obong'o ka en wuoi to Abong'o ka en nyako.
- Nyathi monyuol ndalo bonyo iluongo ni Obonyo ka en wuoi to Abonyo ka en nyako.
- Nyathi monyuol ka liel ni e dala iluongo ni Obura ka en wuoi to Abura ka en nyako.
- Nyathi monyuol odiechieng' iluongo ni Ochieng' ka en wuoi to Achieng' ka en nyako.
- Nyathi monyuol ka ichwoyo ichako ni Ochwoyo ka en wuoi to Achwoyo ka en nyako.
- Nyathi monyuol ndalo dede ichako ni Odede ka en wuoi to Adede ka en nyako.

The position of the sun, the situation at night, how the child comes out during delivery, where a child is delivered, agricultural activities in which people are engaged, and the general situation in the land are not the only ways that determine how children are named among the Luo. A child can be named after a dead adult person, a great person in the community, or a great person who passes by the community at the time a child is born,[6] and such other things.

The Luo seldom name a child after a witch/wizard or an evil person. If a child is named after such a person then it is perhaps in accordance with the second-level naming about which we explain later. However, a child can only be named after a bad person when the person appears to any of the parents in a dream and demands that a child be named after him or her, or else the child dies.

The following names are given to children depending on how they were born, when they were born, what happened when they were born, and where they were born. A child born after the death of the father, sired by a surrogate husband ("through a sort of levirate"),† is named Ochola if a boy, but Achola if a girl.[7] This is because the child belongs to mourning. Such a child, because he/she is born to the wife of the grave,§ would have a strip of skin of a domestic animal tied around the waist because it is a child of the soil, a child of mourning. Of twins, the one who is born first (faster to come out) is named Opiyo if a boy, but Apiyo if a girl; the last to be born of the twins (the one that remained behind) is named Odongo if a boy, and Adongo if a girl. A child born after twins is named Okelo/Okello if a boy, but Akelo/Akello if a girl; this is because he or she is brought by the twins, that is, comes after the twins. Other names are given as follows:

- If at birth the placenta comes out before the child, the child is given the names Obiero if a boy, and Abiero if a girl.
- A child born under a cactus tree is named Obondo if a boy, and Abondo if a girl.
- Born single or only child is given the name Obong'o if a boy, and Abong'o if a girl.
- A child born during locust invasion is named Obonyo if a boy, or Abonyo if a girl.
- A child born when there is a funeral in the home is named Obura if a boy, and Abura if a girl.
- A child born at midday is given the name Ochieng' if a boy, but Achieng' if a girl.
- A child born during planting season (planting by broadcasting) is named Ochwoyo if a boy, and Achwoyo if a girl.

- Nyathi monyuol e tiend dero ichako ni Odero ka en wuoi to Adero ka en nyako.
- Nyathi monyuol seche mag odhiambo iluongo ni Odhiambo ka en wuoi to Adhiambo ka en nyako.
- Nyathi monyuol ka tiende ema okuongo wuok iluongo ni Odhoch ka en wuoi to Adhoch ka en nyako.
- Nyathi monyuol e dipo iluongo ni Odipo ka en wuoi to Adipo ka en nyako.
- Nyathi monyuol ka idoyo ichako ni Odoyo ka en wuoi to Adoyo ka en nyako.
- Nyathi monyuol e duol ichako ni Oduol ka en wuoi to Aduol ka en nyako.
- Nyathi monyuol chuny dierotieno (odiewuor) ichako ni Oduor/Owuor ka en wuoi to Aduor/Awuor ka en nyako.
- Nyathi monyuol e agola iluongo ni Ogola ka en wuoi to Agola ka en nyako.
- Nyathi monyuol e tok ot iluongo ni Ogutu ka en wuoi to Agutu ka en nyako.
- Nyathi monyuol ka wuon ne otho to oweyo e ich kata ka wuon/min otho kapodi oyom iluongo ni Ojwang' ka en wuoi to Ajwang' ka en nyako.[8]
- Nyathi monyuol e tie okaka ichako ni Okaka ka en wuoi to Akaka ka en nyako.
- Nyathi monyuol ndalo kech ichako ni Okech ka en wuoi to Akech ka en nyako.
- Nyathi monyuol ka ikeyo ichako ni Okeyo ka en wuoi to Akeyo ka en nyako.
- Nyathi monyuol okinyi iluongo ni Okinyi/Odikiny ka en wuoi to Akinyi/Adikiny ka en nyako.
- Nyathi monyuol ndalo koko iluongo ni Okoko ka en wuoi to Akoko ka en nyako.
- Nyathi monyuol ka kong'o nie dala iluongo ni Okong'o ka en wuoi to Akong'o ka en nyako.
- Nyathi monyuol ka koth chwe kata kinde koth ichako ni Okoth ka en wuoi to Akoth ka en nyako.

- A child born during grasshopper invasion is given the name Odede if a boy, but Adede if a girl.
- A child born in the shade of/next to a granary is named Odero if a boy, and Adero if a girl.
- A child born in the evening is given the name Odhiambo if a boy, but Adhiambo if a girl.
- A child born with the legs coming out first is named Odhoch if a boy, and Adhoch if a girl.
- A child born in an open space within the homestead is given the name Odipo if a boy, but Adipo if a girl.
- A child born during the first weeding season is named Odoyo if a boy, and Adoyo if a girl.
- A child born in the private quarter of the male head of a home or in the livestock barn is given the name Oduol if a boy, and Aduol if a girl.
- A child born at midnight is named Oduor/Owuor if a boy, but Aduor/Awuor if a girl.
- A child born in the space around the house under the eaves is given the name Ogola if a boy, and Agola if a girl.
- A child born at the back of a house is named Ogutu if a boy, but Agutu if a girl.
- A child whose father died while still in the womb or one of whose parents dies when still an infant is given the name Ojwang' if a boy, and Ajwang' if a girl.[8]
- A child born next to a cactus plant is named Okaka if a boy, but Akaka if a girl.
- A child born during famine is named Okech if a boy, and Akech if a girl.
- A child born during harvesting is given the name Okeyo if a boy, but Akeyo if a girl.
- A child born in the morning is named Okinyi/Odikiny if a boy, and Akinyi/Adikiny if a girl.
- A child born during conflict is given the name Okoko if a boy, but Akoko if a girl.
- A child born when beer is being drunk in the home is named Okong'o if a boy, and Akong'o if a girl.

- Nyathi monyuol ka guoguo oumo ichako ni Okuku ka en wuoi to Akuku ka en nyako.
- Nyathi monyuol e kulo ichako ni Okulo ka en wuoi to Akulo ka en nyako.
- Nyathi monyuol kamin omako ich to podi ka oneno dwe chakore ndalo mane onyuolo nyathi moteloni ma koro onyuolo iluongo ni Okumu ka en wuoi to Akumu ka en nyako.
- Nyathi monyuol bang' nyathi motho iluongo ni Oloo ka en wuoi to Aloo ka en nyako.
- Nyathi monyuol e luanda iluongo ni Oluanda ka en wuoi to Aluanda ka en nyako.
- Nyathi monyuol ka piny otimo luoch ichako ni Oluoch ka en wuoi to Aluoch ka en nyako.
- Nyathi monyuol ka iludo ichako ni Oludo ka en wuoi to Aludo ka en nyako.
- Nyathi monyuol e lum ichako ni Olum ka en wuoi to Alum ka en nyako.
- Nyathi monyuol ndalo lweny iluongo ni Olweny ka en wuoi to Alweny ka en nyako.
- Nyathi monyuol osirawende iluongo ni Omondi/Omolo ka en wuoi to Amondi/Amolo ka en nyako.[9]
- Nyathi monyuol seche mag onyango iluongo ni Onyango ka en wuoi to Anyango ka en nyako.
- Nyathi monyuol oko e pap ichako ni Ooko ka en wuoi to Aoko ka en nyako.
- Nyathi monyuol ka ikomo ichako ni Oomo ka en wuoi to Aomo ka en nyako.
- Nyathi monyuol ndalo oro ichako ni Ooro ka en wuoi to Nyaoro ka en nyako.
- Nyathi monyuol ka i min chwer iluongo ni Opondi ka en wuoi to Apondi ka en nyako.
- Nyathi monyuol to i min ne tin mang'enyji ne ok ong'eyo ni oyach iluongo ni Opondo ka en wuoi to Apondo ka en nyako.

- A child born when it is raining or rainy season is named Okoth if a boy, but Akoth if a girl.
- A child born with a caul is given the name Okuku if a boy, and Akuku if a girl.
- A child born when the mother has gone to fetch water is named Okulo if a boy, but Akulo if a girl.
- A child conceived before the mother experiences menstruation after the previous birth is given the name Okumu if a boy, and Akumu if a girl.
- A child born after the death of the one before is named Oloo if a boy, but Aloo if a girl.
- A child born on a rock is named Oluanda if a boy, and Aluanda if a girl.
- A child born during an overcast day is given the name Oluoch if a boy, but Aluoch if a girl.
- A child born during the second weeding is named Oludo if a boy, and Aludo if a girl.
- A child born on grass is given the name Olum if a boy, but Alum if a girl.
- A child born during war is named Olweny if a boy, and Alweny if a girl.
- A child born early in the morning is named Omondi/Omolo if a boy, but Amondi/Amolo if a girl.[9]
- A child born during mid morning is given the name Onyango if a boy, and Anyango if a girl.
- A child born in the open place or field is named Ooko if a boy, and Aoko if a girl.
- A child born during planting season (planting by putting seeds under the soil) is given the name Oomo if a boy, but Aomo if a girl.
- A child born during dry season is named Ooro if a boy, and Nyaoro if a girl.
- A child born after a difficult pregnancy period during which the mother used to bleed is named Opondi if a boy, but Apondi if a girl.
- A child born though the mother's womb was so small such that most people never realized that she was expectant is given the name Opondo if a boy, and Apondo if a girl.

- Nyathi monyuol ka ji osin iluongo ni Osino ka en wuoi to Asino ka en nyako.
- Nyathi monyuol ka otieno pod nyako ichako ni Otieno ka en wuoi to Atieno ka en nyako.
- Nyathi monyuol ka oumore ichako ni Ouma ka en wuoi to Auma ka en nyako.
- Nyathi monyuol ka wino odhogore kuome ichako ni Owino ka en wuoi to Awino ka en nyako.
- Nyathi monyuol bang' nyithindo motho mang'eny to iparo ni jochiende emanego, min wite ka osewinjore gi ng'ato mabiro kwanye mapidhe mabor kod dala majachien no nitie iluongo ni Owiti/Omamo ka en wuoi to Awiti/Amamo ka en nyako.
- Nyathi monyuol e tie yath iluongo ni Oyath ka en wuoi to Ayath ka en nyako.
- Nyathi monyuol e yoo iluongo ni Oyoo ka en wuoi to Ayoo ka en nyako.[10]

OKANG MAR ARIYO: NYINGE LEK GI JUOGI

Oganda Luo machon ne ni gi jodongo ma ne olony gi timbe koda kit Luo ma ne tayogi e yalo buche mag kuo, achaya, laro lowo, wang'o ot, nek, terruok, wang' teko, gi weche ma moko ma ne nyalo himo pinygi. Jodongo machon ne okwedo matek weche gi timbe maricho, ma ema omiyo Joluo ne ok nyal chako nyathi nying' jajuok kata ng'ato ma timbene richo. Ma ne nyalo mana timore ka po ni jonyuol nyathi oleko kuome ni chake nyathino to ka gidagi chake to onego nyathino. Ma e yoo kende ma inyalo chako nyathi nying' jajuok, jakuo kata ng'ato ma ne timbene richo. Jaluo thoro chako nyithindo nyinge ma oleki.

Nyinge ma oleki gin nyinge ma ichako nyithindo bang' ka osechakgi nyinge ma luwore gi kit ndalo monyuolgi kata kaka onyuolgi. Bang'e ka osechak nyathi nying' ma luore gi okang' mokwongo, watne moro ma ne osenindo ma korka wuon kata dan nyathi nyalo biro ni achiel kuomgi e lek ni odwaro ni ochake nyathino. Seche moko bende kata ka wuon nyathi osechake nying' mokwongo to pod nyathi yuak aduwa, mano ngeche ni nitiere watne moro ma ne osenindo ma dwaro ni obe chake nyathino to wuon kata min nyathi ok ong'eyo ni en ng'ano. Ka ma otimore to wuon nyathi kamoro

- A child born during times of sadness is named Osino if a boy, and Asino if a girl.
- A child born at night is given the name Otieno if a boy, and Atieno if a girl.
- A child born facing down is named Ouma if a boy, but Auma if a girl.
- A child born entangled by an umbilical cord is named Owino if a boy, and Awino if a girl.
- A child born after all those born before died and hence is thought likely to die like the ones before would symbolically be thrown away as a sign of hopelessness. It was believed that if the child were kept at home then the very evil spirits that killed the previous ones would kill him/her. Therefore, the mother would take the child away from home and put him/her somewhere, after a prior arrangement with someone who would come by the spot and pretend to have found an abandoned child. Such a child is named Owiti/Omamo ("thrown away") if a boy, but Awiti/Amamo if a girl.
- A child born under a tree is given the name Oyath if a boy, and Ayath if a girl.
- A child born at the roadside is named Oyoo if a boy, but Ayoo if a girl.[10]

THE SECOND LEVEL: NAMES FROM DREAMS AND ANCESTRAL NAMES

The Luo of long ago had elders knowledgeable in their practices and traditions, which guided them in settling disputes over theft, contempt, land, setting a house on fire, killing, adultery, disrespect, and such other things that may afflict their land. Since Luo elders of long ago strongly disapproved of bad talk and behavior, a child could not be named after a wizard/witch or a bad person. However, a child could be named after such a person if the person appeared to any of the parents in a dream and demanded that the child be named after him/her, or else he/she would kill the child. That is the only condition under which a child could be named after a wizard/witch, thief, or a bad person. The Luo often give children names received from dreams.

Names from dreams are given to children after they have been named according to the situation at the time of their birth or how they were born. After a child has been named according to the first level, some dead relative of the child's father or dead grandmother of the child may appear to any of the parents in a dream demanding that the child be named after him/her.

achiel gi min ot luongo nyinge mag wedegi mosenindo to nying' moluong ka ayeto nyathi oweyo yuak e nying' michake, mano iwacho ni e nying' ma omoko. To ka jonyuol ok nyal fwenyo nying' ma moko mano chunogi ni mondo gi ter nyathino e ajuoga gi bel e ondong'. Bel ma gidhi godono en mondo oyaw wang' ajuoga eka one gagi malong'o.

Seche moko ka dhako omako ich to ng'atno mosenindo nyalo kelo lek ni nyathi mani e ichno onego chake. Ka ma otimore to ichako nyathino nying' ng'at mosenindono kata ka podi nyathino ni e ich. Nikech nyinge michako nyithindo mag lek kata mag juogi, nyathi ma wuoi seche moko ichako nying' ng'a ma dhako kaka Achieng', Anyango, Atieno, gi ma moko. Kata seche moko nyathi ma nyako ichako nying' ng'a ma dichwo kaka Owino, Ouma, Odongo, gi ma moko. E oganda Luo nying' wuoi pile chakore gi "O" to nying' nyako chakore gi "A." To kata kamano nitiere nyinge ma moko ma chakore gi "M" kaka Masolo, Marunga, Miruka, gi ma moko; "N" kaka Nyawade, Nyarwath, Nyikal, gi ma moko; "W" kaka Wanyande, Wagude, Waga, gi ma moko; "R" kaka Rabala, Raila, Rang'inya, gi ma moko. Nyinge machal ka magi ket pogo tek e kind yowuoi gi nyiri, to kata kamano thoth nyingegi thoro bedo nyinge chwo.

Nyinge ma oleki kata nyinge juok thoro bedo nyinge kwere gi daye ma ne osenindo, wede ma moko mosenindo be samoro jokel lek ni ochak nyithindo nyingegi. Kaka wasewacho, seche moko ka osenyuol nyathi, nyathino nyalo yuak ayuaka nyaka achiel kuom kwere kata daye kata wede moro amora ma ne osenindo bi ni achiel kuom jonyuol e lek to ka nying' kwarono, dayono kata watno oluong sa ma jonyuol goyo mbak lekno to nyathino ling. Kamano otimore to nyathino ichako nying' kwarono, dayono kata watno. Seche ma moko kwaro, dayo kata wat ok kel lek ni jonyuol dawe. Kama e wach to jonyuol koro chako kwano akwana nyinge wede mosenindo. Nying' ma wat okwan ayeto nyathi oling' e nying' michake. To ka nyathino pod medo yuak kata ka osekwan nyinge modhuro mano nyiso ni pod kofweny nying'. Ma koro chuno jonyuol ni nyaka giter nyathi ka ajuoga nikech en onyalo neno gagi malong'o. Seche moko nying' kwaro, dayo kata wat ma dwaro ni ochake nyathi bedo ma yot fwenyo ma ok chun jonyuol ni mondo olek kata ter nyathi ka ajuoga. Nying' samoro nyalo moko nyamonge nono seche ma jonyuol ochako luongo nyinge wedegi mosenindo sama nyathi ochako yuak.

Joluo omako matek wach mar chako nyithindo nyinge kwere, daye gi wede ma osenindo nikech ging'eyo ni kido ma moko mar jogo nyaka nyisre e nyithindo ma ochakgi. Kido gi timbe mag nyithindogo thoro bedo kaka kit kwere, daye gi wede ma ochakgi ne chalo. Seche moko be, mbelni ma

Sometimes when a father has given a child a name according to the first level but the child continues to cry very much, it means there is some dead relative as yet unknown to the parents who would like the child also to be named after him/her. If that happens, then the father, perhaps together with the mother, would call out the names of dead relatives and the one at whose call the child stops crying would be given to the child. That, they say, is the name the child has caught. But if the parents cannot detect the desired name, then they will have to take the child to the diviner to unravel the desired name; carrying along with them some millet grains in a small basket. The millet is meant to open the eye of the diviner so that the divination will be successful—so that the diviner can see the cowry shells properly.

In certain cases, a pregnant woman might dream of a dead relative asking that the child in the womb be named after him or her. If this happens, then the child will be given such a name even while still in the womb. As a result of giving children names from dreams or ancestral names, a male child may be given a woman's name such as Achieng', Anyango, Atieno, and others. And also in some instances a female child may be given a man's name such as Owino, Ouma, Odongo, and others. Among the Luo, a boy's name usually begins with "O" while a girl's name begins with "A." However, there are some names that begin with "M" like Masolo, Marunga, Miruka, and others; "N" such as Nyawade, Nyarwath, Nyikal, and others; "W" like Wanyande, Wagude, Waga, and others; "R" such as Rabala, Raila, Rang'inya, and others. With such names, differentiating the male from female ones is difficult; nevertheless, most of them tend to be masculine.

Names from dreams or ancestral names are mostly of dead grandparents, though sometimes some other dead relatives also appear in dreams wanting children to be named after them. As we have stated, sometimes a child will cry very much until some dead grandparent or relative appears to one of the parents in a dream, and at the mention of that person's name by the parent as they talk about the dream, the child stops crying. In such a case, the child would be named after that grandparent or relative. But sometimes neither a dead grandparent nor a dead relative appears to either of the parents in a dream. If that is the case, the parents would then just call out the names of their dead relatives. The name at whose mention the child stops crying would then be given to the child. But if the child continues crying despite calling out the several names, that means the desired name has not been identified. The parents would then be forced to take the child to a diviner who can rightly detect the desired name. Sometimes detecting the right name of the dead grandparent or relative is easy and the parents do not have to get it from a dream or diviner. A child may immediately catch a name and stop crying as soon as the parents begin calling out the names of dead relatives.

The Luo attach great importance to naming children after grandfathers, grandmothers, and relatives who died, because they know that some of their character traits manifest in the children named after them. The character and behavior of such children tend to resemble those of the people after whom

ne ni e ring're mag kwerego, dayego kata wedego nyalo nyisre e del mag nyithindo ma ochakgi. Pach Jaluo ok en ni gik ma chon kata gik ma osekalo ni gin gik ma onge tich ma ji onego werego. Gineno ngima mag ji ma pod nitiere ka omakore gi ngima mag wedegi ma osenindo. Kendo gineno ngima oganda Luo ma sani ka otudore giweche ma chon. Jaluo ong'eyo ni weche gi gik ma chon ma osekalo jaduogoga to nyisore e ngima ma sani. Ma ema omiyo mita ka nyathi ochak nying' wuon min (kwaro) to anyuola miye luoro ma ne gimiyo wuon min kinde ma ne pod ka onindo. Kit Jaluo en ni anyuola nyathi nyaka mi nyathino luor ka luwore gi nying' ng'a ma ochake.

Ka luwore gi okang' mar ariyo ma Joluo chakore nyinge, jo moko (moloyo to jorachare) nyalo paro ni mita ka Joluo paroni ka ng'ato kosenindo to ninyuole kendo; ni nyathi ma onyuolni en ng'at achiel cha ma ne osenindo higni mokalo. Adiera en ni ok en kamano. Jaluo ong'eyo maler ni kwere, daye gi wede mosenindo ok gin nyithindo ma ochakgi, en mana ni nitiere tudruok e kind kwere (daye gi wede) mosenindo kod nyithindo ma ochakgi. Nikech wich samoro jawil, nyithindo ma ochak kwere gi daye ma ne osenindo e rapar, to kendo moloyo ahinya gin e yoo achiel ma kwere, daye gi wede nyisore ni podi gidewo to kendo gin e kanyachiel gi jogi ma pod ngima.

OKANG' MAR ADEK: NYINGE MAG RANYIS ANYUOLA

Okang' mar adek mag nyinge e oganda Luo en ranyis mar wede mar ng'ano ma iluongo gi nyingego. Pogruok kuom nyinge ma nitiere e okang'ni gi ma nitiere e okang' mar ariyo en ni nyinge ma nitiere e okang' mar ariyo gin nyinge lek kata juok, gin nyinge mag wede ma ne osenindo to nyinge ma nitiere e okang' mar adek thoro bedo nyinge mag wede ma pod ngima.[11] Hie hie, nyinge ma nitiere e okang' mar adek gin nyinge ma nyiso wat ma nitiere e kind ji ariyo. Ka luwore gi okang'ni, to kendo nikech ng'eny wede, Jaluo bedo gi nyinge mathoth. Inyalo luong ng'ato gi nying wuon, min, kwaro, dayo, nerane, wayane, wuode, nyare, owadgi, nyamin, jaode, gi ma moko. Ranyisi en ni ka wuon ng'ato iluongo ni Odhiambo, jalno bedo kiluongo ni wuod Odhiambo; ka nerane iluongo ni Onyango, jalno bedo okew Onyango; ka dane en Abila, to iluongo jalno ni nyakwar Abila, gi ma kamago. Wach ma duong' e okang' mar adekni en ni wat ma nitiere e kind ng'a ma iluongo gi nyingno koda wuon nyingno nyaka ful. Ka wat ma nitiere ok oful, to mano en tich ma nono. Ka nying' wuora en Odhiambo, ok inyal luonga ni "Odhiambo," inyalo mana luonga ni wuod Odhiambo. En achuna ni nyaka ketie "wuod" ka pod ka owach kata ndiko "Odhiambo," mano e chik.

they are named. Sometimes even the same body marks of the grandfathers, grandmothers, or relatives would show on the children named after them. The Luo do not believe that their traditions are worthless and should be discarded. They see a bond between the life of the living and the dead relatives. And they also see a link between their present life and their old traditions. A Luo knows that the old teachings and traditions always reemerge and manifest themselves in contemporary life. This perhaps is the reason why if a child is named after a maternal grandfather, the kindred of the child would accord that child respect that corresponds to the respect they accorded the grandfather while he lived. According to the Luo traditions, the kindred have to accord that child respect commensurate to the name of the person after whom the child is named.

Because of the second-level naming, some people (especially white people), might think that the Luo believe in the reincarnation of the dead; that the child born is the reincarnation of the same person who died many years ago. That is not true. The Luo know very well that the dead grandfathers, grandmothers, and relatives are not the children after whom they are named, but that there is a connection between the grandparents and the children named after them. But since people sometimes forget, children are the memory through whom the dead grandparents and relatives after whom they are named are remembered, but more importantly, they are the means through which the dead grandparents and relatives are shown to be still concerned and together with their kindred who are still physically alive.

THE THIRD LEVEL: NAMES THAT SHOW KINSHIP

The third-level names of the Luo indicate the relatives by whose names a person is called. The difference between the third-level and second-level names is that the second-level names are from dreams or ancestral names—they are names of dead relatives while the third-level names are mostly of living relatives.[11] In fact, the names at the third level show kinship relation between two people. At this level, because relatives are many, a Luo tends to have several names. A person can be called by the name of the father, mother, grandfather, grandmother, uncle, aunt, son, daughter, brother, sister, spouse, and others. For instance, if one's father is called Odhiambo, that person would be called son of Odhiambo; if his uncle is called Onyango, that person is called nephew of Onyango (*okew* Onyango);** if his grandmother is called Abila, that person is called grandchild of Abila, etc. The most important thing at this level is that the nature of the relationship between the person called by a name and the one after whom the person is named has to be stated. If the nature of the relationship is not stated, then it is a useless undertaking. If my father's name is Odhiambo then I cannot be called Odhiambo; I can only be called son of Odhiambo. It is a must that "son of" be prefixed to "Odhiambo" whether in oral or written conversation; that is the rule.

Chikni pogore gi chik mar jorachare e kaka gichakore nyinge ma giluongo ni *surnames* kata *family names*. Ka luwore gi kido koda timbe mag jorachare, iyudo ni jo ot kata anyuola thoro tiyo gi nying' achiel kanyakla. Iyudo ka kwaro, wuoro, yowuoi koda nyikuayo bende duto te iluongo gi nying' achiel. E kit Luo gi timbegi ma ok timre, ranyis mar wat nyaka medie ka po ni ng'ato dwaro tiyogi nying' jal machielo.[12] Ka dipo ni wuoro nigi nying' machalo gi mar wuode moro, mano tin nobed ka luwore gi yore michako nyithindo e okang' mar achiel kata mar ariyo. Kamoro en nikech ne onyuolgi e seche machal to ndalo ema opogore. Inyalo yudo ni ne onyuolgi e seche ma gonyango ma ka luwore gi okang' mokwongo ochakgi ni Onyango. Samoro be inyalo yudo ni wuoro ochak ni Onyango nikech ne onyuole e seche mag onyango, to wuode bende ochak ni Onyango ka luwore gi okang' mar ariyo. Ma nyiso ni jonyuol gi nyithindgi moko samoro nyalo bedo gi nyinge machal to pogruok bedo e okang'. Wach maduong' e ranyis ariyogi en ni kata ka wuoro gi wuode nigi nyinge machal, nyingego gin nyingegi. Nying wuoro en mare, to nying' wuode be en mare ka luore gi okange mane ochakgigo nyingego—ok en ni jal achiel tiyogi nying' jal moro.

Yo ma jorachare tiyogi "*Mrs*" wat ka pimore gi okang' mar adek nikech onyiso wat ma nitiere e kind ng'at mayie ka oluong nying' kod ng'a mayie ka "*Mrs*" ochomgi nyingno. Kaka ranyisi, "Mrs Odhiambo" nyiso wat ma nitiere e kind ng'ano ma iluongo ni Odhiambo gi jalno mayie ka ochom "Mrs" gi "Odhiambo." Ka olok "Mrs Odhiambo" e dholuo to en "chi Odhiambo." Kata kamano, pogruok ma nitiere e kind kaka jorachare tiyo koda "Mrs Odhiambo" gi "chi Odhiambo" mar Joluo en ni jorachare mako matek nying' mar "Odhiambo" moloyo "Mrs."[13] Omiyo seche moko ginyalo luongo mikayi mana ni Odhiambo to giweyo "Mrs" thenge. Ka luwore gi kido Joluo ma ok timre, nyaka "chi" bedie; ok nyal luong chi Odhiambo mana ni Odhiambo nikech nitiere pogruok mabor e kind chi Odhiambo gi Odhiambo. "Odhiambo" en ranyis mar dichwo ma ne onyuol e seche mag odhiambo, "chi Odhiambo" en ranyis mar dhako ma jaode iluongo ni Odhiambo. Omiyo ok en kare luongo chi Odhiambo ni Odhiambo mana kaka ok en kare luongo Odhiambo ni chi Odhiambo. Ka ng'ato seche moko dwaro luongo ng'a ma dichwo ginying chiege mano chune ni nyaka oluong wat ma nitiere kaka ni "jaod Akinyi" kata "chwor Akinyi." Mano e kaka okang' mar adek obedo.

Pogruok moro kendo ma nitiere e kind okang' mar adek gi kido mar jorachare en kama: E oganda Luo okang'ni ok en mana mar nyiso wat ma nitiere, e ie kanyo bende nitiere nying'. Kaka waseneno, ka ochom wat mar "chi" ginying' mar "Odhiambo" to chomono "chi Odhiambo" bedo nying'

This rule differs from the way white people use surnames or family names. According to the traditions and practices of white people, the whole family or kindred would use the same name. One finds that the grandfather, father, sons, and grandchildren are called by the same name. In the Luo tradition and practices, this would not happen; the nature of the relationship between the kindred has to be added if one is called by somebody else's name.[12] For instance, if a father and a son share a name, it would be due to the customs of naming according to either the first or second level. Perhaps both were born at the same time but different days. For instance, if both were born in the mid morning, then they would be given the name Onyango. At other times, the father could have been named Onyango because he was born in the mid morning, while the son could have been also named Onyango but in accordance with the second-level naming. This shows that parents and their children may have the same names due to different levels of naming. The important point in the two examples is that even if the father and the son share a name, each one of them has his own name. The father has his own name just as the son depending on how the name was acquired—it is not a case of one person using the other person's name.

The way white people use "Mrs." perhaps corresponds to the third-level naming of the Luo in the sense that it shows a relationship between the one who uses a name and the one who responds to the name when "Mrs." is attached to the name. For instance, "Mrs. Odhiambo" expresses a relationship between the person called Odhiambo and the person who responds when "Mrs." is attached to "Odhiambo." When translated into Luo language "Mrs. Odhiambo" means "*chi Odhiambo*" (the wife of Odhiambo). However, the difference between how white people use "Mrs. Odhiambo" and how the Luo use "*chi* Odhiambo" is that white people take more seriously the name "Odhiambo" than "Mrs."[13] As a consequence, they may simply refer to Mrs. Odhiambo as Odhiambo leaving out "Mrs." But according to the Luo tradition, this would not happen, as "wife" must be added; the wife of Odhiambo cannot just be called Odhiambo because there is a big difference between the wife of Odhiambo and Odhiambo. "Odhiambo" signified a man who was born in the evening, "wife of Odhiambo" signifies a woman whose husband is called Odhiambo. For that reason, it is wrong to refer to the wife of Odhiambo as Odhiambo just as it is wrong to refer to Odhiambo as the wife of Odhiambo. But if one would like to call a man by referring to his wife's name then the relationship between the two must be made explicit such as "spouse of Akinyi" ("*jaod* Akinyi")†† or "husband of Akinyi" ("*chwor* Akinyi"). That is how the third level of Luo naming is.

Another difference that exists between the third-level naming of the Luo and the tradition of white people is that the third-level naming among the Luo does not only show the kind of relationship that obtains between people, but in itself it is also a name. As we have already explained, joining a relationship "wife" to a name "Odhiambo" becomes "wife of Odhiambo," which is a name to which one responds, "Here I am" when called out. But

ng'ato ma ka oluong to jalno yie ni "an tiere." Ka luwore gi kit jorachare chomono ok en nying' dawe, en mana mar nyiso wat. Jorachare ok nyal luongo ng'ato mana kaka ni "wuon George" kata ni "okew Peter." Githoro tiyo gi "nyingegi" mana ka gidwaro ni jo moko ong'e ng'ato malong'o. Kaka, ka ng'ato ae wacho gin moro kuom John Brown to ng'at machielo ok olony kod John Brown, ng'ano nyalo medo ni John Brown ma wuod Stanley kata ma nyakwar Henry. Gi maduong' en ni "wuod Stanley" kata "nyakwar Henry" ok ne ni gin nyinge John Brown. E okang' mar adek mar Joluo, "wuod Stanley" koda "nyakwar Henry" ikawo kaka nyinge ma moko mag John Brown. Inyalo wach ni e oganda jorachare, "wuod Stanley" kata "nyakwar Henry" chalo mana kaka ng'ato nyalo pogo dhok ariyo ka owacho ni achiel en rabuor to moro en dibo. Kuom Joluo ka ng'ato oluong ni "wuon Ochieng'" mano ok en mana mar poge gi, kata kuom, jo moko—mano bende ikawo ni en nying' jalno.

Okang' mar adek mar nyinge luwore gi dak kanyachiel mar Joluo. Joluo ok ne ng'ato mana kaka achiel kuom oganda, to moloyo, gineno oganda kaka rasir kendo okumba dhano; oganda ema orito dhano. Omiyo dhano onego luorore kendo ti kanyakla e achiel. Oganda ma jokanyo ok ni e achiel to kendo ok gi luorore, en oganda ma onge huma maber kendo dongruok ok nyal bedoe. Ngeche en ni kuom Joluo, dhano bedo mana dhano nikech oganda to ka ok kamano dhano bedo mana dhano-a-dhana; long'o mar oganda e long'o dhano.Omiyo kido mar ng'ato omakore gi kido mar oganda; kidone ok nyal pog gi kido mag wedene ma nitiere koda wedene ma osenindo. Ma ema omiyo Joluo omako okang' mar adek (koda okang' mar ariyo) mar nyinge matek. Nyinge ma nitiere e okange ariyogi medo kanyachiel kuom oganda Luo.

Kido mar ng'ato ok omakore gi kido oganda (anyuola) kende, kidone makore bende gi kido mar gweng'; gi kido mar ka ma anyuola opon. Timbe Joluo en ni kata tich ema otero ng'ato mabor kapango to ok one kuro ka dala, oneno kuro kaka ka ma owendo. Ka ma anyuola ng'ato nitiere en ranyis ng'ato ma Joluo omako sidang' kendo matek. Ma ema omiyo e okang' mar adek, Joluo seche moko thoro tiyo bende gi ka ma anyuola ng'ato odakie. Ma nyalo bedo nying' mar dhoot, gweng', kata pacho mar ka ma anyuola ng'ato nitiere. Jalno inyalo luong ni Jakondiek, nyar Ukwala, wuod Alego Kaugagi, wuod Oremo, wuod nam, gi ma moko. Nyinge machal kamagi ok gin mana ranyis mar ka ma ng'ato oae, ooyo. Moloyo, ngechgi en ni ng'ato ok en mana wuod kata nyar wuon gi min monyuole, en wuod kata nyar oganda.[14]

according to the tradition of white people, the joining of the relationship "wife" to the name "Odhiambo" does not constitute a name; it only shows a relationship. White people cannot, for instance, just call a person "father of George" or "nephew of Peter." They often use such "names" only for clarification. For instance, if one were making a reference to John Brown, but there is some other person who does not know John Brown, then one can clarify that John Brown is the son of Stanley or grandson of Henry. What is more important here is that "son of Stanley" or "grandson of Henry" is not a name of John Brown. However, according to the third level of Luo naming, "son of Stanley" and "grandson of Henry" are considered other names of John Brown. It can be said that according to white people, "son of Stanley" or "grandson of Henry" is used in a way similar to when someone differentiates two cows by stating that one is brown and the other is white. But for the Luo, calling some person "father of Ochieng'" is not just for differentiating that person from others—it is also a name.

The third level of naming relates to the living together of the Luo. The Luo people do not just see a human person as one among many, but more importantly, they see the community as a support and shield for an individual; it is the community that takes care of the well-being of an individual. For that reason, there should be respect among people and they should work together as a community. A community in which members are not united and do not have mutual respect has no good reputation and cannot have progress. This means, according to the Luo, a person acquires substance because of the community or else a person lacks in substance; the well-being and worth of an individual is a function of the well-being of a community. For that reason, a person's character is therefore linked to the character of the community; it cannot be detached from the character of relatives both alive and dead. This explains why the Luo treat the third and second levels of naming with great importance. The names in these two levels reinforce the unity and togetherness of the Luo community.

An individual's character is not only connected with the character of the community (kindred), but also with their territory and where one's kindred grew up. The tradition of the Luo is that any place away from their territory or a faraway town where one works is never considered as one's home; one would always see such places as foreign lands. According to the Luo, the territory where one's kindred live signifies that person, and this is a belief they hold dearly and take seriously. For that reason the third-level names sometimes also refer to where one's kindred live. It can be the name of one's clan, territory, or village. A person may therefore be called *Jakondiek* (a man from Kondiek), *nyar Ukwala* (daughter of or a lady from Ukwala), *wuod Alego Kaugagi* (son of or a man from Alego Kaugagi), *wuod Oremo* (son of or a man from Oremo), *wuod nam* (son of or a man from the lake), and such like. Names such as these not only indicate where one is from, but more importantly, they mean that a person is not only the son or daughter of their parents, but also the son or daughter of the community.[14]

OKANG' MAR ANG'WEN: NYINGE PAKRUOK

Okang' mar ang'wen oting'o nyinge pakruok kata nyinge nyadhi. Nyinge pakruok chalo kaka ngeche. Kaka nyinge ma ni e okang' ma moko, nyinge pakruok gin nyinge mar ranyis ng'ano ma iluongo kata ma pakore, to pogruokgi gi nyinge ma ni e okange ma moko en ni gin seche moko ng'ato nyaka par matut eka onyalo fwenyo kata neno tiendgi. Ng'ato ma pod ka ofwenyo tiend nying' pakruok, nying'no biro mor-ne-amora. Nying' mar pakruok chalo ka ngero, ng'ato ok ne-a-neya tiendgi nyalhodia. Thoth nyinge pakruok gin nyinge mor ma nyalo miyo ng'ato nyier matek ka ng'ano ong'eyo kata sa ma ofwenyo ngechgi. Omiyo Joluo hinyo tiyo gi nyinge pakruok seche nyadhi. Nyinge pakruok chalo kaka tugo gi weche. Joluo thoro pakore gi nyinge manyien mondo eka ji ma nitiere kanyo ma winjo nyingego ochak mi wigi tich mar fwenyo ngech nyingego.[15] E fwenyo ngech nyingno nyaka jogo ma nitiere ng'e gik moko mathoth ma luwore gi ng'at mipako kata ng'at ma pakoreno. E pakruok, kaka itiyo gi weche pogore gi kaka itiyo kodgi e loso ma pile. Nyinge pakruok chalo kaka sigende mak mana ni gichuok. Ng'ano ma pakore kata ng'at ma pako nyawadgi chalo kaka dayo ma goyo sigana ni nyikwayo e siwindhe, mak mana ni sigand jal ma pakore kata jal ma pako wechene ok thoth. Omiyo e ganda Luo, nyinge pakruok ok gin weche-a-wecha dawe. Jandiko moro ma jarachar ne owachoni tim mar pako gi miyo nying' pandoga weche, to kata kamano en kaka sigana ma miyogi ng'eyo kido mar jokanyo.[16] Gima jandikoni owacho en adiera moloyo kuom Joluo.

Nyinge pakruok bende chalogi mnaye. Tiend mnaye manyien ok bed mayot ng'eyo. Mnaye manyien ma ng'eyo tiende yot ok en mnaye maber nikech jalno ma ogoye ok bi yudo gik mang'eny.[17] Mnaye maber en ma fwenyo tiende tek, en mnaye ma miyo ji paro matut eka gifweny tiende. Moloyo bende, mnaye maber en mnaye ma ka otamo ji fwenyo tiende to bang'e ka onyis gi tiende eka koro gineno ngeche (tiende) nyamonge nono. Mnaye ma kata ka osenyis ji tiende to pod ok gi ne tudruok malong'o e kind mnayeno gi tiende, mano ok mnaye maber. Mano mnaye ma ok mi ji mor. Ma nyiso ni mnaye maber nyaka bed matek kendo mayot; matek ni mondo eka tiende kik ng'ere ma piyo, to mayot ni mondo seche ma tiend mnayeno onyis eka ji koro neno ngeche nyamonge. Nying' pakruok maber chalo kaka mnaye maber, ok en gin ma iwinjo to achiel ka chiel iseng'eyo tiende. Ng'a ma ong'eyo pakore kata pakoji, en ng'a ma ong'eyo loso; en ng'a ma riek. Thothgi bende thoro bedo ji mong'eyo lungo wach nikech ber achiel mar nyinge pakruok, mana kaka mar mnaye maber, en mar miyo ji mor. Ma wat ema omiyo nitiere tudruok e kind rieko gi lungo wach. Ng'eny jodongo mariek ong'eyo lungo wach.

Ka luwore gi weche ma wasewacho, inyalo wach ni nyinge pakruok gin nyinge ma ng'ano ma pakore dwaro nyiso kidone e yoo ma ok ratiro. E nyingegi ng'ato nyiso kite ka luwore gi kido kata weche mag ji ma moko, kata kit gik moko kaka le. E lero nyinge pakruok mag Jaluo, jandiko kendo japuonj ma Moi University e dala mar Eldoret, Peter Amuka, ne otiyo tich

THE FOURTH LEVEL: PRAISE NAMES

The fourth level consists of names for praise or virtue boasting. Praise names are like proverbs. Like the names in the other levels, praise names signify the person who is being praised or self-praising; however, unlike the names in the other levels, one has sometimes to think very hard in order to detect or get their meanings. To a person who has not gotten the meaning of a praise name, the name is simply a hollow sound. The praise names are like proverbs in the sense that one does not just easily see their meanings. Praise names are used during moments of joy and can cause great laughter in a person who understands their meanings or discovers their meanings. For that reason, the Luo mostly use praise names during virtue boasting. They are like a game of words. The Luo often use new praise names in order to make those who hear them think hard about their meanings.[15] In order to get the meaning of a praise name, the people present have to know a lot of things about the character of the person being praised or praising oneself. In praise names, words are used differently from their ordinary usage. Praise names are like stories except that they are short. One who is praising another or self-praising is comparable to a grandmother who is telling a story to her grandchildren in her hut, except that the story in a praise name is short. For the Luo therefore, praise names are not just mere words. A white author once wrote that though the act of praising and naming conceals things, it is nonetheless a story that gives information about a member.[16] The position expressed by that author is true, but moreso among the Luo.

Praise names are also like a riddle. The meaning of a new riddle is not easy to get. A new riddle whose meaning is easy to get is not a good one because whoever tells the riddle would not earn many things.[17] A good riddle is one whose meaning is difficult to get and therefore makes people think hard to get the meaning. But more important, a good riddle must be such that when people are told the meaning after they have failed to get it, they are able to easily understand the meaning. A riddle is not good when even after people have been given the meaning, they still fail to see a proper connection between the riddle and its given meaning. Such a riddle does not give people joy. This implies that a good riddle must be difficult and easy at the same time; difficult to get its meaning, but easy to see the connection between it and its meaning after the meaning is given. A good praise name is like a good riddle; its meaning is not gotten straight away once one hears it. Whoever knows how to praise other people, or praise himself/herself is a person who knows how to talk; one who is intelligent. Most such people have great sense of humor since part of the beauty of a praise name, just like a good riddle, is that it can make people happy. This is perhaps why there is a connection between wisdom and humor. Most wise elders have a sense of humor.

From what we have explained it can be said that praise names are intended to indirectly convey certain character traits. In the names, one's character is revealed through the character of other people or some other things such as animals. In explaining the praise names among the Luo, Peter Amuka,

malong'o ma ipuoyo. E obokeni wadwaro tiyo gi nyinge pakruok moko ma otiyo kodo e oboke ma ne ondiko e dho jorachare, obokeno iluongo ni "The Play of Deconstruction in Speech of Africa."[18]

Amuka ndiko ni osiepe nyalo luongore ni "ondiek marach." Ng'at ma eka winjo nyingni chieng' mokwongo to bende ok olony gi jalno miluongo kamano, ok nyal ng'eyo ngech nyingno. Nikech ondiek en le marach ma hinyo nego dhano koda dhok gi jamini, kamoro ng'ano nyalo paro ni jalno miluongo kamano en ng'at marach aduwa, ni en ng'a ma timbene richo miwuoro. Ng'a ma paro ni mano e tiend nyingno ni mabor ahinya gi adiera ngech nyingno. Wich matiyo ok bi yie gi parono, wijno biro temo fwenyo adiera mar ngech nyingno nikech ong'eyo ni osiepe ma pakore ok luongore kamano. E pakruok, ng'ato inyalo luong ni ondiek marach ka en jamuandu kata ka oloyo mbesene e yore mang'eny kaka e tuke kata somo. Samoro bende, ng'ato ma nyiri ohero ma jachode inyalo luong ni ondiek marach. Ng'ato be ipako ni sibuor ka ji oluore nikech oger kata otek ka sibuor. Jalno ma ong'eyo goyo mawi, ma meno mbesene te idendo ni sibuor. Le moro ma Joluo ohero pakorego en liech. Ng'ato inyalo pako ni liech ka luwore gi timbene madongo kata tiyone matek. Seche moko bende iluonge kamano nikech delne maduong' (ma ogangore). Achiel kuom josiasa ma ne ong'ere e piny Luo koda Kenya ngima e higni mag piero aboro, Odongo Omamo, ne Joluo dendo ni Kaliech. Odongo Omamo ne en wuoi marabet, to kendo moloyo ne ogero ot maduong' ma ne iwuoro.

Apuoyo kata ogila en le ma ithoro winj e sigend Luo. En le mathin ma dende ok ogangore. Kendo en le ma ok kwiny ma nego dhano kaka le ma moko kaka sibuor kata ondiek. To kaka othinno to kendo ok okwiny, rieke to ng'eny ma iwuoro. Omiyo osiepe thoro luongore ni apuoyo kata ogila nyarondo. Amuka e oboke ma ondiko nyiso malong'o gin ma omiyo jal ma ne iluongo ni Ochuti ne idendo ni Ochuti Ogila. Ochuti, Amuka wacho, ne en ng'a ma ok rabora to dende bende ne tin. Kata kamano ne ong'eyo goyo mawi tweta. Ne onyalo meno ji ma ohewe gi duong' del mana kaka e sigend Luo ogila nyarondo ne loyo le ma dongo kaka liech e yore mang'eny nikech riekone. Ochuti bende ne ong'eyo lungo wach, dhoge ne mit omiyo nyiri mang'eny ne ohere. To gi ma ne miyo jo moko wuoro ne en ni Ochuti ne otho ka en ja dhako achiel kende. Ma ne omedo ji luonge ni ogila nyarondo. Ka iwacho adiera, ji ne paro ni Ochuti wat ka ne en jadoho to ma ling' ling, en mana ni rieko, ujanja, gi bedo motang' machalo koda mar ogila ema ne otiyogo ba ogalo ji ni en jadhako achiel. Bedone jalemo mar Adwen ema ne ochune ni ogal ji mondo gipar ni en jalemo motegno ma luwo puonj misa mar ng'ato bedo gi dhako achiel. Ochuti bende ne ipako ni apuoyo tin to goyo rude. Ma ne en nikech ne onyuolo wuoi ma dende dongo to chuiny. Kendo wuodeni ne obedo jathieth mong'ere ma ne nigi huma maber. Wuodeni, ma Amuka ondiko ni ne iluongo ni Samuel Oraw, ne inyalo pim gi rude nikech duong' dende kendo nikech ng'eruokne kaka jathieth mogen.

who is a lecturer at Moi University in Eldoret, did commendable work. We would like to use some of the praise names he uses in his article, written in English and titled "The Play of Deconstruction in Speech of Africa."[18]

Amuka writes that friends can call each other *Ondiek marach* (dangerous hyena). Any person who hears such a name for the first time and who is not familiar with the person called by that name is unlikely to know the meaning of such a name. Since a hyena is a dangerous animal that often kills human beings and livestock, one might think that the person called *Ondiek marach* is a very dangerous and bad person. But whoever might think that is far away from the correct meaning of that name. Any person who carefully thinks about it would not accept such a view, and would try hard to find a proper meaning because friends would not call each other in such a manner. In praising a friend, *Ondiek marach* could be used to refer to a person who has excelled in various undertakings beyond one's contemporaries; such a person could be wealthier, better in sports or education. Sometimes, a lady-killer, or a great seducer of women, would be called *Ondiek marach.* A person may also be referred to as *Sibuor* (lion) when people fear the person because he is as fierce and strong as a lion. A great wrestler who skillfully entangles and fells his age-mates would be called lion. Another animal that the Luo often use in praising is the elephant. Some person would be praised as *Liech* (elephant) if the person is known for great achievements such as hard work. Sometimes a person may be called elephant if the person is huge. One of the well-known politicians in Luoland and Kenya as a whole in the eighties, Odongo Omamo, was fondly called *Kaliech* (literally "like elephant"). Odongo Omamo was not only a huge man, but he had also built a marvelously big house.

Apuoyo or *Ogila* (hare) is another animal often used in Luo folk tales. It is a small animal. And also, unlike a lion or a hyena, it is not fierce and does not kill human beings. However, despite its small size and the fact that it is not fierce, it is a very witty animal. For that reason many friends often use *Apuoyo* or *Ogila Nyarondo* (witty hare) as a praise name in reference to each other. In the aforementioned article, Amuka properly explains why a man named Ochuti was fondly called Ochuti Ogila. Ochuti, Amuka explains, was neither tall nor huge. But he was a great wrestler. He could entangle and fell a huge opponent just as *Nyarondo,* in the Luo tales, could outwit many huge animals such as the elephant in many ways. Ochuti was also humorous, a sweet talker and therefore a darling of many girls. However, he surprised many people when he died a monogamous man. This even made people praise him more as *Ogila Nyarondo.* In reality, many people thought that perhaps he was secretly a polygynous man and that he only used wit, just as a hare, to make people think that he was monogamous. As a member of the Seventh Day Adventist church, he had to be monogamous in order to make people believe that he was a religious devotee. Ochuti was also fondly referred to as *Apuoyo tin to goyo rude* ("Hare, the small animal, that gives birth to twins") because he had a huge strong son. His son Samuel Oraw became a famous doctor. Oraw could be compared to twins because of his huge size and fame as a great doctor.

Kata kamano, Amuka wachoni ji ma ne ok ohero Ochuti ne ok dende ni apuoyo tin to goyo rude, ne giluonge ni nyawang' achiel nikech ne en gi dhako achiel kende. Doho bedo achiel mag timbe Joluo, thoth jodongo kata jomuandu thoro bedo jodoho. Ng'eny oganda Luo machon ne gin jodoho, ne gi kawo jadoho ka ng'a ma nitiere e kang' ma malo moloyo jadhako achiel mana kaka bedo giwange ariyo ber moloyo bedo gi wang' achiel. Ka gimoro dipo ka otucho wang' jawang' achiel to ng'ano dong' e mudho. Kata kamano e ndalo ma tinde, nying' mar "nyawang' achiel" ok ne ka nying mar ayany. Ma en nikech Joluo ti oke e kor piny to thothgi dhi ka thoro luwo timbe mag jorachare, to kit jorachare ok oyie gi weche mag doho. Omiyo tinde ngech nying' mar nyawang' achiel nyalo bedo nying' mapore nono.

Joluo luongo wuodgi ma sani pek e siasa mar Kenya, Migosi Raila Amolo Odinga, ni Aguambo. E dholuo aguambo en ng'a ma rieke gi parone chalo mana ka mar ogila. Aguambo en ng'a ma riekene ng'eny sinawuoya maloyo nyaka tekre dhano; sa ma iparo ni isejuke cha eka koro otony nyamonge nono. E siasa ma Kenya, seche moko osega bedo ma oganda Kenya paroni sirikal kata jok moko kuro osetieko Raila. To seche makamago ema Raila wuokga gi riekni matut miwuoro. Kaka e higa 2002, bang' romo gi Daniel arap Moi mane en jatend Kenya kendo duol mar siasa mar KANU (Kenya African National Union), ne giwinjore ni Raila oketh duol ne mar NDP (National Development Party) mondo joge duto te odonj e KANU. Raila ne otimo kamano. Bang'e ka ne Raila dwaro chung' e yiero mar telo ni Kenya e higano, Moi ne obaro kode yoo. Moi ne oyiero Uhuru Kenyatta ni ema dhi chung' gi otiko mar KANU. Ngeche ne ni Raila koro ne ok nyal chung' gi otiko mar KANU. Ji mang'eny ne owuoro kendo ochogo gin ma ne Moi otimo ni Raila. Ne gineno ka Raila osediwo nikech seche ma ne odong' eka go ombulu ne chuok to bende duonde ma moko ne oseyiero jog gi ma ne dhi chung' gi otikogi. Raila kaka nyarondo ne otuch gi tim ma Jokenya pod wuoro nyaka sani. Ne obaro profesa mar siasa ndas.[19] Piyo nono Raila ne otimo tim ma ne ji ok par ni nyalo timore. Ne owuok e KANU gi ji mathoth moloyo ji ma ne odonjo kodo, KANU ne odong' tambla kendo ka odhier nono. Ayeto piyo piyo, Raila ne otiyo kaliech mar neno ni chama moko duto te obedo e kanyachiel e kwedo KANU. E seche ma yiero ne ochopo, KANU ne olo mabor kendo maduong' moloyo ne en ni ng'at ma ne Raila osiro ema ne oyier kaka jatelo manyien mar Kenya. E seche mane Moi otamo Raila chung' gi otiko mar KANU ne oparo ni osetieko Raila; ne oparo ni oseyudo yo ma ne KANU pod biro bedogo e loch. Ne okiya ni kara ne opiago mana pala mane dhi ng'ole koda duonde; ne okiya ni kara ne otugo mana tugo ma ne Aguambo olonygo. Joluo wacho ni "nyiero machien mit maloyo nyiero mokwongo."[20]

However, Amuka explains that those who did not like Ochuti never called him by the praise name *Apuoyo tin to goyo rude,* but instead called him *Nyawang' achiel* ("one-eyed") because he had only one wife. Polygyny is one of the traditional practices of the Luo, and most elders or rich men tended to be polygynous. In the past, most Luo men were polygynous and such men were perceived to have a higher social status than a monogamous man, just like having two eyes is better than having one. A person with one eye would become blind if something were to poke out and destroy the eye. However, these days being referred to as "one-eyed" is no longer considered an insult. This is due to the fact that many Luos are dispersed all over the world and most of them tend to follow the practices of white people, whose traditions do not allow the practice of polygyny. Consequently, the name "one-eyed" hardly makes sense these days.

The Luo call their son who is currently great in Kenyan politics, Honorable Raila Amolo Odinga, "*Agwambo.*" In Luo language, *agwambo* (mysterious) refers to a person whose wit is comparable to that of a hare. *Agwambo* is a person with enormous intelligence and wit beyond human strength; such a person easily find his way out of situations that appear insurmountable to most people. In Kenyan politics, Raila has been in tight situations when people thought that the government or some people in the government had cornered him and would politically finish him. But he often got out of such situations with so much ease that people were left wondering. For instance, in 2002 Daniel arap Moi, then president of Kenya and chairman of the political party KANU (Kenya African National Union), agreed with Raila that he would dissolve his political party NDP (National Development Party) and have its members join KANU. Raila did that. Later that year Moi differed with Raila when Raila wanted to contest the presidency of Kenya representing the KANU party. Instead Moi appointed Uhuru Kenyatta to be the one to run for the presidency representing the KANU party. That therefore meant that Raila could not contest the presidency as KANU's representative. Many people were surprised and disapproved of the way Moi treated Raila. It seemed to people that Raila was stranded—he had been tricked out of the presidential race because there was little time left until the elections and other political parties had already nominated their presidential candidates. Raila, like a witty hare, suddenly came up with a plan at which many Kenyans are still wondering today. He thoroughly defeated the professor of politics.[19] Within no time, Raila did what no one could expect. He walked out of KANU with more people than when he came in. KANU was left desperate and destitute. Swiftly, Raila worked like an elephant to ensure that the other political parties were united in opposing KANU. When election time came, KANU was defeated by a large margin and the candidate Raila supported won the presidential election and became the new president of Kenya. When Moi prevented Raila from contesting the presidential race on KANU's behalf, he believed that he had politically finished Raila and had found a way by which KANU would continue to rule. He did not know that he was sharpening the knife that was to cut him and his political party; he

Nyinge ma moko mag pakruok ma Joluo hinyo tiyo kodo gin: jakual wuoth ka paka; fulu ma oro ngenge; kodh yamo; jaidh yath ma malo to weyo ma piny; oyieyo matugo ka paka nitiere; ruath; jananga; chot pim; rech ki siane guok; afuong'o jang'uono, gi ma moko.

WACH MOGIK

Julia Stewart ondiko ni Leonard R. N. Ashley e buge ma iluongo ni *What's in a Name?* wacho ni nying' moro amora ma ng'ato oyiero ng'ano onego ne ni nyingno chiek to kendo ok otek luongo kata ndiko.[21] Ka luwore gi chike Joluo mag chako nyinge mbaka ma Ashley goyono chalo ka ma obayo yoo. Bedone ng'at ma opon e piny Amerka, Ashley loso ka luwore gi kido ma kuno. Kido ma neno nying' mana ka gin ma itiyogo mar pogo dhano, gin ma ka oluong to ng'ato yie. E kidoni, nyinge moko gikawo ni beyo ma loyo moko. Nyinge mayot luongo kendo ma winjore ma mit ka weche man e thum ema beyo moloyo nyinge ma boyo kendo tek luongo. Ngeche en ni nyinge e kidoni chalo kaka maua. Ka luwore gi adiera ni e ndalo ma sani Joluo oke e kor piny ma omiyo giromo gi ji ma nigi chike gi timbe mopogore, Joluo moko tinde luwo timbe ma ok opimore gi mag Joluo. Ng'enygi, moloyo to rowere, thoro luwo timbe jorachare. Ma ema omiyo chike ma Joluo luwo e chako nyithindgi nyinge kanyachiel gi ngech kit nyinge ma ni okang' mar adek gi okang' mar ang'wen dhi ka lal, to ma ok en huma maber nikech onge gimoro marach gi chike Joluo mag chako nyinge kata mana kit nyingegi. Kaka waseneno e obokeni nyinge ma Jaluo chakore nigi gi ma omiyo gin kaka gi bedono. Jaluo chako nyithindo nyinge ka luwore gi wang' chieng', gi seche mag otieno, kaka onyuolgi, ka ma onyuolgi, kaka jogweng' odich e puothegi, kaka piny chalo, gi weche ma kamago (okang' mokwongo). Kendo ka luworegi kanyachiel mar dak Joluo, gimiyore nyinge mag wedegi ma ne osenindo kata mar gweng' ka ma anyuola opon (okang' mar ariyo gi mar adek). Okang' mar ang'wen oting'o nyinge pakruok kata nyinge nyadhi. Ber nyinge ma nitiere e okang' mar ang'wen en ni gimiyo ng'ato paro. Gi machal kendo oriwo nyinge ma nitiere e okangegi duto en ni nyingegi gin ranyis mar ng'ano miluongo kodgi. Nying' ok en nying' anyinga to kata mana dhano ok en dhano adhana, nitiere tudruok e kind nying' gi dhano (jalno ma iluongo gi nyingno). Omiyo ka inyalo penj ni e kind kaka Joluo miyore nying' gi kaka jorachare chako mekgi, ma ne maber ma loyo moro? Dwoko penjono ok tek. Ma ema omiyo onge wach moro maduong' ma onego mi kido gi chike Joluo mag chako nyinge lal. Joluo gi joratenge duto te onego mak matek weche mag Paul Mbuya ni jopiny onego ket chikegi gi timbegi mabeyo ka mise mokwongo; eka giger buche gi timbe welo e wi mise ma giseradho. Kendo omedo ni piny ma kama ema bedo gi huma maber e nyim pinje moko.

did not know that he was playing a game that *Agwambo* knew best to play. The Luo have a saying that "the last laughter is sweeter than the first."[20]

Some other praise names that the Luo often use are: one who walks stealthily like a cat; the haplochromis fish that sends tilapia; the windy rain; one who climbs the upper branch of a tree before the lower; the mouse that plays in the presence of a cat; the bull; the man of clothes; the old woman's lover; a dog cannot be set on a fish; a waist petticoat worn by women without pants is generous, and many others.

CONCLUSION

Julia Stewart tells us that, in his book *What's in a Name?,* Leonard R. N. Ashley states that whatever name one chooses, it should be short and neither difficult to pronounce nor to write.[21] According to the Luo custom of naming, the position taken by Ashley seems incorrect. Being a person who grew up in America, Ashley's position could be reflecting the American tradition. In that tradition, some names are perceived as better than others. The names that are easy to pronounce and are as sweet as the words in music are considered better than those that are long and difficult to pronounce. This means that according to that tradition, names are like flowers. The fact that these days the Luo are scattered all over the world and they meet with people from various customs and traditions means that some of them embrace certain practices that are inconsistent with those of the Luo traditions. Most of them, especially the youth, tend to follow the practices of white people. This is the reason why the Luo customs for naming children as well as the meaning of names in the third and fourth levels tend to be disappearing, and this is not a good development, since there is nothing wrong with the Luo customs of naming or the names themselves. As we have seen in this article, Luo names have meanings and reasons why they are the way they are. The Luo name their children depending on the position of the sun, time of the night, how they are born, where they are born, the kind of agricultural activities in which the community is engaged, the weather/situation in the land, etc. (the first level). In accordance with the living together of the Luo, they name children after dead relatives or give names linked to the places where one's kindred grew up (the second and third levels). The fourth level consists of praise names or names for virtue boasting. The beauty of the names in the fourth level is that they provoke people to think hard. However, what is common to all the names across the levels is that names signify persons who are called by them. A name is not just a mere name or a person just a mere person; there is a connection between a name and the person called by the name. Therefore, if it were to be asked which is a better custom of naming between that of the Luo and white people, answering that question would not be difficult. For that reason, there is no good justification for abandoning the Luo names and the custom of naming. The Luo and all black people should take seriously what Paul Mbuya said: an indigenous people should make their good customs and traditions a foundation

Onge piny manyalo dongo maber ka giwito timbegi to mag welo ema gimako matek. Oganda Luo ka okikore gi joratenge duto onego her timbegi koda chikegi. Wach mifwambo ni timbe gi chike jorachare long'o moloyo mek joratenge en wach ma joratenge onego gol e pachgi, ma ket luore gi ngech Joluo ma wachoni "Alot michayo ema tieko kuon kata dere."

NOTES

1. Ji moko thoro ndiko "Mbuya" ni "Mboya," omiyo ji ma ogoyo buk mar *Luo: Kitgi gi Timbegi* ondiko nying jandiko ni "Paul Mboya." E obokeni, an atiyo gi "Mbuya." Ma ema aparo ni en ranyis malong'o mar luongo nyingno.

2. Nyocha machiegni ne onyisa ni bug Paul Mbuya oselok e dho jorachare gi Mikayi Jane Achieng' e higa mar 2002.

3. Paul Mbuya, *Luo: Kitgi gi Timbegi* (Kisumu: Anyange Press Ltd., 1938) 7.

4. Oginga Odinga ne omako wachni matek turi ma kane otero nyithinde mondo otis, padri ne otamore tisogi nikech Odinga ne oramo ni nyaka migi mana nyinge Joluo. Bang' yuaruok e kinde mang'eny gi angili, nyithinde adek ne otis gi nyinge Luo ni Ng'ong'a Molo Oburu, Raila Amolo Odinga, gi Ngire Omuodo Agola. Oginga Odinga, *Not Yet Uhuru: An Autobiography* (London: Heinemann, 1967) 54-55.

5. Odinga, 40-42, 47-48.

6. Kaka wana nyis bang'e, nyingegi pogore gi nyinge ma oleki kata mag juok.

7. Ochola/Achola inyalo ndik bende ni Ocholla/Acholla.

8. Ojwang'/Ajwang' inyalo ndik bende ni Ojuang'/Ajuang'.

9. Omolo/Amolo inyalo ndik bende ni Omollo/Amollo.

10. Mbuya, 110-111.

11. Onego waler wachni malong'o. Nyinge ma nitiere e okang' mar adek samoro nyalo bedo nyinge wede ma nyicha eka onindo ma podni e pach ji. Kendo moloyo en ni nyingegi ok gin nyinge juok.

12. Ne akwongo winjo ni nyinge nitieraga miluongo ni *surnames* kinde ma ne achako puonjruok mar secondari e higa 1973 e sikul miluongo ni Nairobi School (ka pod ne ka oloki nying' sikundno ne iluonge ni Prince of Wales School). E puonjruokna motelo e skul mar primari, nyinga ma ne ong'ere ne en Ochieng'. Ma en nying' ma ne ochaka ka luwore gi okang' mokwongo. Ka ne adonjo e skul mar secondari, japuonj ma ne otelo kanyo ne oramo ni *surname* ema ne nyaka luonga kodo, ni mano ne e chik. E pache *surname* ne en nying' wuon ng'ato, omiyo ne okawo nying' wuora "Odhiambo" kaka *surname* mara. Chakoregi kanyo nyinga ne obedo Odhiambo ka luwore gi chike koda timbe jorachare. Ka luwore gi weche ma

on which to build foreign organizations and practices. He added that it is such a community that earns a good reputation among other communities.

There is no community that can progress if it abandons its good practices and instead holds firmly to foreign ones. The Luo as well as all black people should love their practices and customs. The spreading of erroneous information that practices and customs of white people are better than those of black should not be entertained by black people; this seems to conform with the Luo proverb that "it is the despised vegetable that finishes *kuon* or empties granaries."§§

NOTES

1. Since some people often write "Mbuya" as "Mboya," the publishers of *Luo:Kitgi gi Timbegi* wrote the author's name as "Paul Mboya." In this article I use "Mbuya." This is how I think the name should be written and pronounced.

2. Recently I was informed that the book by Paul Mbuya has been translated into English by Jane Achieng' and published in 2002.

3. Paul Mbuya, *Luo: Kitgi gi Timbegi* (Kisumu: Anyange Press, 1938), 7.

4. Oginga Odinga took this matter so seriously that when he took his children for baptism he insisted that the children must be baptized in Luo names, but the priest refused. After a long tussle with the Anglican Church, his three children were baptized in Luo names as Ng'ong'a Molo Oburu, Raila Amolo Odinga, and Ngire Omuodo Agola. Oginga Odinga, *Not Yet Uhuru: An Autobiography* (London: Heinemann, 1967), 54–55.

5. Ibid., 40–42, 47–48.

6. As we explain later, these names are different from the names from dreams or ancestral names.

7. Ochola/Achola, but can also be written as Ocholla/Acholla.

8. Ojwang'/Ajwang' can also be written as Ojuang'/Ajuang'.

9. Omolo/Amolo can also be written as Omollo/Amollo.

10. Mbuya, 110–11.

11. We should make this point clearer. The names at the third level may at times be of those relatives who died recently and are still fresh in the people's memory. But more, they are not ancestral names in the sense that they are not acquired the way those in the second category are.

12. I heard for the first time about surnames in 1973 when I joined secondary school at Nairobi School, then called Prince of Wales School. In primary school, I was known by the name Ochieng'. This is the name I was given in accordance with the first-level naming. But when I joined secondary school, the school's head teacher insisted that I must be called by my surname for that was the rule. In his thinking, one's surname is the father's name, and so he took my father's name "Odhiambo" as my surname. From that time my name became Odhiambo according to the tradition and practices of white people. According to the three levels of Luo naming that we have explained, this was not proper. At the beginning, I had a very hard time

wasewacho kuom okange adek mag Joluo e chako nyinge, ma ne ok kare. Kinde ma ne e ka ochak luonga ni Odhiambo, wachno ne orocha ngano—ne ok onyal donjo e pacha. Pile ka ne pod ka wachako somo, sa ma ne japuonj luongo nyinge jo puonjore mondo eka ong'e ji ma nitiere gi ji ma onge, ne japuonj ka oluongo nying' mar Odhiambo to ne kawa seche eka aduok ni "an tiere." Ma ne en nikech e tok pacha nyingno ne ok mara dawe.

13. Ma luwore gi kido margi mag *surnames*.

14. E oganda Luo, ngech min kata wuon ng'ato ok en mana jogo ma ne onyuole. Wuod kata nyar Luo nigi wuone koda mege mang'eny. Owete wuon nyathi bende gin wuone nyathino to nyimine min gin mine ne bende. Thoth ji ma jorachare luongo ni nera Joluo luongo ni wuora, to moko ma giluongo ni waya Joluo luongo ni min. Pogo wede nyalhodia kaka jorachare timo ni moko gin mathenge kata ma ok adiera ok en kit Luo da. Kuom Joluo wach moro ni wat bedo mathenge onge. Kwere, daye, wuoro, mine, owete, nyimine, nyikwayo, gi wede ma moko ok pog ni moko gin mathenge. Ng'ato bedo kwaro, wuoro, min, nera, waya, nyamin, omin,wuod, nyar kata nyakwaro, tinda. Ma en ranyisi mar kanyachiel motegno koda hera madimba e oganda Luo.

15. Kinde ma ne an rawera, chieng' moro ka ne eka ahango dhi e buch anyuola e dala mar Nairobi, achiel kuom anyuola ma ne nitiere e bura ne opakore ni en "sandak." E seche mokwongo wachno ne omako dhoga. Kindego "sandak" ne en nying' wuoch, to ok ne anyal neno gima omiyo ng'ato dipakore gi nying' wuoch—wuoche en gima ji ruako e tiendegi to nyonogo lowo piny! Bang'e ka ne asemiyo wiya tich matin, eka ne amako tiend nying' pakruok mar omerano. Sandak ne gin wuoch mag mon (gi nyithindo bende). Kindego ne tek yudo ng'ama dhako kata nyako ma ne ongegi wuoch mag sandak. Mon ne ohero wuochgo nikech ne ilosogi e range mang'eny mopogore kendo nengogi ne ok rach. E pakore ni "sandak" anyuolano ne nyisore ni en ng'ama mon koda nyiri ohero.

16. Jean-Francois Lyotard, *The Differend: Phrases in Dispute* (Minneapolis: University of Minnesota Press, 1988) 151-161.

17. Mnaye en tugo ma dwaro paro. Mnaye ka otamo jogo ma ogoni mnayeno fwenyo to jogo nyaka mi ng'a ma ogoyo mnaye gimoro amora ma jalno dwaro eka onyisgi ngech mnaye. Gin ma imiyeno en mana wach, ok ni nyaka gimiye gimoro madiera dawe—en mana ka tugo.

18. Peter Amuka, "The Play of Deconstruction in Speech of Africa," in Ivan Karp and D. A. Masolo (eds.), *African Philosophy as Cultural Inquiry* (Bloomington: Indiana University Press, 2000) 89-104.

19. Ma e kaka Daniel arap Moi ne japakore.

20. E dier kinde ma ne andiko obokeni mokwongo gi sani ma koro amedo weche moko machuop manyien, Jokenya ne ogoyo ombulu mar yiero jogo machung' ni dhoudi mopogore e od bura maduong' kanyachiel gi yiero jatend sirikal. Ombulu ne ogo tarik 27, dwe mar 12 e higa 2007. E goyo ombulu mar yiero jatend sirikal, jogo madongo ma ne ochung' ne gin jatelo mar duol mar PNU (Party of National Unity), jatelo mar ODM-K (Orange Democratic Movement-Kenya), gi Raila Odinga

responding to the name Odhiambo. Every day before lessons begun, when the class register was read out in order to know which students were present, it took me some time to respond to the name Odhiambo. This was because, at the back of my mind, that name was not mine.

13. This is in accordance with their tradition of surnames.

14. Among the Luo, the meaning of one's mother or father is not confined to the parent who gave birth to the person. The son or daughter of Luo has many fathers and mothers. The brothers of one's father are one's fathers too, and the sisters to one's mother are one's mothers too. Most of the people referred to as uncles by white people are referred to as fathers by the Luo, and many others that they refer to as aunts are referred to as mothers by the Luo. The Luo tradition does not make such simple distinctions between relatives as white people easily do by referring to some as distant or not real relatives. The Luo do not refer to a relative as a distant relative. None among grandfathers, grandmothers, fathers, mothers, brothers, sisters, grandchildren, and other relatives is referred to as a distant relative. Among the Luo, a person is a grandfather, grandmother, father, mother, an uncle, an aunt, sister, brother, son, daughter, or grandchild, period. This is an indication of togetherness among the Luo.

15. One day, as a young man, when I first went to for a clan meeting in Nairobi, one member in self-praise said that he is "sandak." Initially that name astounded me. In those days, "sandak" was a name of a particular kind of shoes, and I could not see any reason why one would call himself by the name of shoes—shoes are worn by people when stepping on the ground! Soon after I had set my head working I got the meaning of the praise name of my "brother." Sandak were shoes for women and children. It was hard those days to find a woman or girl who did not have this kind of shoes. Women liked sandak because they were made in several colors and were not expensive. Therefore in calling himself sandak, my clansman implied that he is a person loved by women and girls.

16. Jean-Francois Lyotard, *The Differend: Phrases in Dispute* (Minneapolis: University of Minnesota Press, 1988), 151–61.

17. The game of riddles requires thinking. If people cannot get the meaning of a riddle, then they have to give the person who presented the riddle whatever he/she wants so that the person can tell them the answer. Whatever is given is just a verbal gift, not a real gift—it is just a game.

18. Peter Amuka, "The Play of Deconstruction in Speech of Africa," in *African Philosophy as Cultural Inquiry,* ed. Ivan Karp and D. A. Masolo (Bloomington: Indiana University Press, 2000), 89–104.

19. Daniel arap Moi used to brag that he is the professor of politics.

20. Between the time I first wrote this paper and now, when I am adding few new things, the Kenyans held elections for parliamentary representatives and national presidency. The voting took place on December 27, 2007. In the presidential elections, the main contestants were the leader of the PNU (Party of National Unity), the leader of ODM-K (Orange Democratic Movement Kenya), and Raila Odinga who was the leader of ODM (Orange Democratic Movement). Most people believed Raila was the one who would win the race. But what was not known to people is that the

jatend ODM (Orange Democratic Movement). E seche ma ne ji dhi goyo ombulu, thothji ne ong'eyo ni Raila ema ne dhi yombo. Gima ne gikiya ne en ni kara jogo ma ne sirikal oyiero ayeto omiyo ting' mar tayo yierono chalo ka ne nigi pachgi mayore. Ka ne ose go ombulu, jogi ne okwano ombulu eyo ma ne ng'enyji ok oyiego ayeto gilando ni jatend PNU ema oyombo. Jatend PNU ema be ne en jatend sirikal kindeno. Bang' landogi, piny Kenya ne omuoch mach—goch ne ogore, ji ne otho, ji ne ohinyore, ute ne owang', muandu ne oketh. Ma ne ochuno pinyje ma oko mondo obed piny kanyachiel gi jatend sirikal ma ne en jatend PNU koda Raila mondo one kaka wach lweny ma ne nie Kenya dilos. Bang' ndalo mathoth e bura, jatend sirikal ne oyie riwre gi Raila e pogo telo. Bedo gi jotelo ariyo en gima ne pod ka otimore e Kenya chakre 1963 higa ma ne joratenge okawo loch kuom jarachare. Ng'enyji ong'eyo ni ombulu ne okual ni jatend PNU mondo eka ogeng' Raila etelo ni Jokenya. To kata kamano, Raila bedo Aguambo ne ok geng're. Chakore higa 1982, ji mathoth ma tekregi ng'eny e siasa mar Kenya osega temo geng'o Raila e yore mang'eny, to nyalo osega tamogi—rieko Aguambo osega bedo ka tut tweta. Bang' ombulu mane ogo e higa 2007, Jokenya kendo ne ogoyo ombulu moro tarik 4, dwe mar 3 higa 2013. E goyo ombuluno, Raila kendo ne obuogo thoth Jokenya. Kata kane ok oyiere telo ni sirikal, ji ne owuoro kaka ne onyalo tudore gi, kendo kelo bute, Migosi Kalonza Musyoka (jatelo mar duol mar Wiper Democratic Party) gi Migosi Moses Wetangula (jatelo mar duol mar FORD-K). Ji ariyo gi ne gin ji mane ok gimodhore go pi kuom kinde mang'eny. E siasa mar Kenya sani Raila Aguambo en ng'at achiel ma josiasa te oluoro bed gin osiepe kata wasigu.

21. Julia Stewart, *African Names* (New York: Citadel Press, 1993) xiii.

people the government had appointed to oversee the elections had a different plan. After casting the votes, these people counted the votes in a manner that most people did not agree with and declared the leader of PNU the winner. The leader of PNU was also the president then. After that announcement, the country of Kenya burst ablaze—it was a fight, people died, people were injured, houses were burnt, property was destroyed. This forced foreign countries to talk with the president who was also the leader of PNU and Raila to see how to bring to an end the fighting in Kenya. After many days of protracted meeting, the president agreed on power sharing with Raila. Having two leaders is something that had never happened in Kenya since 1963 when black people took over the government from white people. Most people know that the votes were stolen for the leader of PNU to prevent Raila from leading Kenyans. However, Raila, being mysterious, was unpreventable. Since 1982 many powerful politicians in Kenya have tried to prevent Raila in many ways, but they could not succeed—the wit of *Agwambo* has been too deep. Following the general election of 2007, Kenyans had another general election on March 4, 2013. In the latter election, Raila again surprised many Kenyans. Despite the fact that he never won the presidency, people were surprised at how he managed to bring close and work with Honorable Kalonzo Musyoka (the leader of the Wiper Democratic Party) and Honorable Moses Wetangula (the leader of FORD-K Party). For a long time before, the two could not see eye to eye with Raila. In the current Kenyan politics, Raila Agwambo is one person all politicians fear, be they his friends or rivals.

21. Julia Stewart, *African Names* (New York: Citadel Press, 1993), xiii.

*The Luo response, "Here I am," or, "Me," when one's name is called is equivalent to the English response, "Yes," when one's name is called.

†*Jater* or *jalako,* according to the Luo custom, is a surrogate husband who assumes the roles of a deceased husband. This is a sort of leviratic practice, but not strictly so since *jater* can be a brother or paternal cousin to the deceased, or a foreigner or a non-Luo who has been adopted into the community.

§*Chi liel,* in the strict Luo sense, is not a widow because death does not nullify marriage in the Luo culture. The wife of the deceased remains married to the deceased—hence "wife of the grave"—and is not eligible for remarriage. In the Luo customs, remarriage is possible only after divorce.

***Okew* is a son of a sister, but the daughter of a sister is *nyakew*. Okew Onyango is therefore the son to Onyango's sister. In Luo, "sister" refers also to a daughter to a brother of one's father or daughter to a sister of one's mother; "brother" refers also to a son to a brother of one's father or a son to a sister of one's mother; "father" refers also to brothers of one's father; "mother" refers also to any other wife of one's father, a wife to a brother of one's father, or a sister to one's mother; "uncle" is a brother to one's mother; "aunt" is a sister to one's father; "son" refers also to a son of a brother, and, "daughter" refers also to a daughter of a brother. The Luo do not seem to have the concept of cousin, nephew, or niece in the strict sense of the terms.

††"*Jaod*" literally means "one who belongs to the house of," but it refers to a spouse.

§§See the second of the two explanatory notes on p. 51 for an explanation of what *kuon* is.

Kũgeria Mĩario

Atumia, Ciana, Mbũri, Mĩgũnda

Betty Wambui

GĨTONGORIA

Ciũrĩa imwe iciaragwo, na meciria mamwe makoima mĩario-inĩ ya andũ. Kahinda kanini gathiru-rĩ, twaragia na mũirĩtu mũrata wakwa na tũkiaria o ũguo rĩ, akiuga atĩrĩĩrĩ, atĩ gĩkũyũ-inĩ; atumia, ciana, mbũri na mĩgũnda no ta kĩndũ kimwe. Kaũndu gaka oigire nĩ gaikarĩte meciria-inĩ makwa mũno na gagatũma ndĩyũrie atĩrĩrĩ, kuga atĩ atumia na ciana na mbũri na mĩgũnda no ta kĩndũ kimwe nĩ kuga atĩa? Na ningĩ rĩ, ndeto ĩrĩa kohete na karatuhee ni ya ma? Nĩ tugerie gũkoibũria hamwe.

Nĩguo menye ciugo ici mũirĩtu ũcio oigire ciugĩte atĩa rĩ, nĩngeretie gwĩciiria niĩ ũria ciugĩĩte na ningĩ ngaaria na andũ angĩ—ethĩ na aniaru, ni ũndũ wa mũrĩgarĩgo wa cio. Nĩ ndĩmahoyete kĩrĩra nĩguo ngerie kũnyita ũhoro ũrĩa ciugo ici ihithĩte tondũ harĩ niĩ nĩ mata na nditũ. Wa mbere nĩ ndiyũrĩtie niĩ, na ningĩ ngamoria o atĩrĩĩ, kuga atĩ atumia, ciana, mbũri na mĩgũnda nĩ ta kĩndũ kimwe nĩ kuga atĩ indo ici ciothe nĩ cia gĩkundi kimwe? Tũkiuga gĩkundi rĩ, tũroiga atĩ nĩ cia ikundi imwe indo uria ihuanine o na ikundi ici inyitanĩtio nĩ atĩ indo cia ikundi ici itire ngurani kindũ o kindũ kii gika kana atĩa? Kana nĩ kuga atĩ ciothe hamwe nĩ ciganaine? Kana, nĩ kuga atĩ nĩ imwe bũrũri-inĩ—ĩĩ atĩ cionagwo kana ituwagwo ta imwe bũrũri-inĩ? Kana mĩciĩ-inĩ? Kana nĩ ta imwe mĩario-inĩ na meciria-inĩ? Kana cĩĩko-inĩ na mĩtũrire-inĩ?[1]

Angĩkorwo indo ici nĩ cia gĩkundi kimwe rĩ, ũguo nĩ kuga atĩ ciana na atumia moonagwo kana monagwo ta mbũri ona ningĩ ta mĩgũnda? Ta nyamu na ningĩ ta indo itarĩ ũhiũ? Ati nĩ maiganagio na indo ici? Ningĩ rĩ, kuuga atĩ nĩ ta kindũ kimwe nĩ kuuga atĩ atumia na ciana ni maiganitio? Moonagwo, na ningĩ o ringĩ monagwo ũndũ ũmwe?[2] Atĩa ũguo? Mũno atĩa; mũndũ aririkana atĩ ciana nĩ ikũraga, ikaneneha, ikagimara, igatuĩka andũ? Kai ũũ karĩ kuga atĩ atumia matigimaraga magakorwo andũ ĩĩ ati nĩ indũ ti indo? Ningĩ rĩ kindũ na ti indo?

Conversations

Women, Children, Goats, Land

Betty Wambui, *SUNY-Oneonta*
Translated by Evan Mwangi, *Northwestern University*

INTRODUCTION

Some questions are born of, and some ideas emerge from, conversations held with people. Not so long ago, I was talking with a friend of mine, and she remarked that among the Gĩkũyũ people of Central Kenya, women, children, goats, and land are regarded as one and the same thing. This comment has stayed on my mind and has prompted me to ask myself: What does such a claim mean? What is meant when one says that, among the Agĩkũyũ, women and children and goats and land are the same? Furthermore, does this statement literally capture that which is the case? Let us try to unpack and unravel the comment together.

So as to try to understand what my friend said that day, I have personally reflected on her comment as well as consulted with others, both young and old, because of the ambiguity of her words. First, I have asked myself and others: Does saying that women, children, goats, and land are the same mean that all of these things belong to the same category? In making the claim that they belong to one category what do we mean? Do we mean that each of the items on this list belongs to a group of its own, different from the others, even as the groups are similar in their lack of individuality and distinction; or, do we mean that they are all of comparatively equivalent value? Alternatively, do we mean to say that they are perceived as equivalent in society—that is, that they are perceived as and/or treated as the same in this space? Or in the household?[1] Or, do we mean that they are the same thing in conversation and thought? Similar in practice and culture?

If we understand these things to belong to the same category, is this then an assertion that children and women are seen or were in the past seen as the same as goats and land? Furthermore, that these two human categories are viewed as equal to livestock and inanimate objects? In addition, does this mean that women are considered equivalent to children among the Agĩkũyũ? How can that be, especially when we remember that children grow up and

Ciũria ici ciumete ciugo-inĩ icio cia mbere nĩ nyingĩ na no iciare ingĩ ningĩ. Nĩ getha twambiririe gũcicokia mũno gũcokia iria cinjũkire no mũhaka twambĩrĩrie na kuga atĩrĩĩ, atĩ kũicokia gũgũtũria twĩmenyithie ũhoro wa mĩturire ya Agĩkũyũ. Gĩthomo gĩkĩ nĩ gĩgũtumbũrĩria ciugo ici na ona ningĩ gĩtũcokerie ciũria iria tworia.

Tukwambĩrĩria na kwiririkania atĩ Agĩkũyũ o ta andũ arĩa angĩ nĩ mathiĩte magikũraga na makigarũrũkaga o ũrĩa kahinda gathiĩte. Nĩ undũ wa ũguo-rĩ, kũngirĩ kahinda ciugo ici na ciũrĩa iria ciciarĩte no icokio maita maingĩ kuma miena mĩingĩ ta—kuma gĩthomo kia rũthiomi rwa gĩgĩkũyũ, nginya maũhoro ma andũ a tene na mĩĩkĩre na mĩtugo ya Agĩkũyũ. Ningĩ no icokio na gĩthomo kia mĩturire ĩigana ona ya Agĩkũyũ kuma kahinda ga tene rĩrĩa twĩragwo kwagĩire andũ kuma nyũmba ĩmwe—ya *Mũũmbi,* ĩrĩa yakũrire ĩgĩtuĩka bũrũri ũmwe; wĩĩtaga *Gĩkũyũ,* nginya hingo ĩrĩa makorirwo andũ a matũra mangĩ ona marĩ andũ a bũrũri ũmwe gatagatĩ ka mabũrũri maingĩ. No tũmarũmĩrĩre o tũkimathomaaga nginya kahinda ka mĩtukano ya mĩhĩrĩga na ndũriri ĩrĩa ingĩ, tũmakinyĩrire o nginya kahinda ka mũgarũrũko ũrĩa warehire Coomba na mbara ya wiathi na thutha ũyũ nginya kahinda ka wiathi, na ningĩ mahinda ma thutha wa wiathi.

Nĩ twogerere gĩthomo-inĩ gitũ atĩrĩĩrĩ, atĩ o ta ũrĩa tũũĩ rĩ, mahinda mothe na maũndũ mamo nĩ mathiaga mathererete na manyitanite. Kwa ũguo rĩ, harĩa kahinda kamwe kambĩriirie na kangĩ gagathirĩra nĩ haritũ gwatura kana kugayania o ta ũrĩa harĩa andũ amwe mambereirie na magathirĩra hakũragwo haritũ kumenya na kuga. Tuugĩite ũguo rĩ, twirikanitie ũhoro wa mĩtukano ya kahinda, andũ, mĩtũro, meciiria na mĩtugo ona mĩturire rĩ, no tuge atĩ tũgwĩcirĩria ũhoro ũrĩa twambĩrĩrie naguo tuuwe atĩ tũtigũthoma mahinda maya mothe wega kahinda-inĩ karĩa twĩnako; ona tũkimenyaga atĩ meho, na atĩ o kahinda o kahinda na maũndũ mako nĩ makinyanagĩra na makanyitana. Atĩ mahinda na maũndũ ma mbere na mathutha nĩ manyitanaga na magatukana. Nĩ ũndũ wa kahinda rĩ, tũgugithaca mahinda na maũndũ maya mothe meciriainĩ maitũ na tũmagayanie maita merĩ nĩguo tũhote gũthereria wĩra wiitũ wega. Tũkiaria tũgwiita kahinda kamwe kahinda ka mbere—*tene*, na kahinda karĩa kangĩ ga thutha ũcio tugete kahinda gaka kana *rĩu.*[3]

MĨIKARĨRE

Nĩ twambe tũcere kahindainĩ ga tene, kahindainĩ kau ka hau mbere, iceera rĩrĩ riahota gũtũtegera. Nĩ tuone kana ciugo iria twambĩriirie nacio nĩ cigiataukirwo nĩ mũndũ wa hau kabere. Angĩkorwo nĩ cigia ruũkirwo rĩ, nĩ tũgerie kuga ũria andũ a kahinda gaka magia cinyitire tũũi wega atĩ ona tũgĩgeria gũcitaura haitũ rĩ, atĩ cio ii kieene kia hau kabere. Miario-inĩ ĩtũ rĩ, nĩ tũgĩtũmĩre ciugo iria twambĩririe nacio gũcanjarĩkia gikũyũ na ũgikũyũ, tuone na na twĩcirerie kana ndũmĩrĩri ya ciugo icio no ĩtũhingorĩre mũrango wa hau kabere na gũtũmenyithia ũrĩa Agĩkũyũ matũũraga na hihi nĩ ũndũ wa mĩtugo ya kahinda kau rĩ, ũrĩa tuonanaga, tuonaga na twĩciragia o nginya rĩu. Rũgendo rũrũ ruitũ

leave behind their childhood to become adults? Is this assertion a claim that women do not develop to full human maturity? That women are really things, not property or even human beings?[2]

The questions that arise from my friend's comment are many and they may provoke many others. To begin to ponder them, particularly the ones that have occurred to me, it is necessary to familiarize ourselves with Gĩkũyũ culture, because knowledge of this culture will help us answer some of the questions we have raised as well as serve to help us capture the meaning of the statement that got us started.

Let us begin at the outset by noting that the Gĩkũyũ, like any other cultural group, have progressed and changed over time. Given this fact, the comments and the questions raised by our original claim can be approached and answered from a variety of perspectives: study of the Gĩkũyũ language, their history, or the culture of said people. This is a people who, according to mythology, began as a single house—the House of *Mũũmbi,* which then grew into a nation calling itself the Gĩkũyũ, a large community made up of different villages belonging to the same nation, living amongst other nations. We could, if we had time, trace its development through the changes wrought by intermarriages between its clans and with other ethnic communities. We could, as part of this review, follow this community into its experience with the coming of the Europeans to Africa and the changes this brought. We could continue our study through the period when the community was engaged in a struggle for political independence, and even into the early postindependence period and then later into the postcolonial period.

Let us add that, as we know, periods of time and events flow into each other. As such, it is hard to clearly determine where one period starts and another ends, just as it is difficult to state with certainty where one group of people ends and another begins. Considering the dynamic temporal overlap and the intermixture of people, cultures, thoughts, and practices, we can say that, because of the limitations of our time, we cannot discuss in detail all the periods mentioned above, even as we know that those periods are there and that every period has its own distinct practices which at times intersect—that earlier eras influence, shape, and merge with later ones. For the sake of time, we'll heuristically divide all these periods into two major groups. Let's call them *tene* (the past, traditional times) and *rĩu* (the present or now).[3]

CULTURE AND TRADITION

Let us then begin our investigation with a visit to an earlier time. In this process let us use the words we began with to open and expose Gĩkũyũ community and society in that earlier period. Let us see if these words that we began with—ones that equate women, children, goats, and land in conversation—would have made sense to a speaker and listener of that earlier time. If they would have, let us articulate what these earlier conversationalists would have understood by them, conscious as we decode them that they may contain previously encoded meanings and practices that may have left traces that are felt even in our time.

rũgũkorũo rwa gũtuĩrĩria na kũgeria gũcokia ciũria ciitũ ona harĩa rũkugeria gũthima ciugo iria iciciarire hamwe na gũcaria ĩtũmi cia cio mĩtugo-inĩ na mitũrĩre-inĩ ya Agĩkũyũ na ona kũgeria gũcinyita.

Nĩ twambĩrĩrie rũgendo ruitũ o kiambĩrĩria,—gũciara na kũrera. Andiki a mabuku na aheani a ũhoro nimatũheaga ũhoro wa ũrĩa ciana cia nyitagwo ugeni cia ciarwo kahinda-inĩ ka hau mbere. Aingĩ nĩ moigaga atĩ ciana ciothe ciarĩ bata na ona amwe makongerera atĩ ciothe cia nyitagwo o ũndũ omwe. Ona makiugaga ũguo rĩ, kana ithuĩ ene tũkiuga ũguo rĩ, no mũhaka tũĩtĩkĩre atĩ nĩ ma nĩ kwarĩ ngũrani ũria ciana cianyitaguo ũgeni wa mbere. Nĩ tũririkane ati ngemi cia kũmenyithania atĩ mwana nĩ aciarwo nĩ ciatiganite—ithatũ cia kairĩtu, ithano cia kahĩĩ. Ona ũguo rĩ, twĩraguo atĩ ngemi ici ciarĩ o cia kũmenyithania ũhoro na atĩ kũnyiha kana kuongerereka gũacio gũtiari gĩtũmi kana bata ũngĩ.

Ningĩ rĩ, mũndũ ũkwaria ũũ nĩ atũririkanagia atĩ thutha wa gũciarwo ciana ciothe ni ciaroragwo o ũndũ ũmwe irĩ nini, atĩ twana turi tunini tuothe twaikaraga na nyina nyũmba-inĩ yake na ningĩ tuothe twetagwo twana. O na tumenyete ũũ rĩ kana ona tũgetikania na mũndũ ta ũcio rĩ, no wega kũrĩa atĩ rĩĩ, nĩ rĩ ningĩ twana twa garũrũkaga—kana tũkagarũrũo na tũgakorũo atĩ tũmwe nĩ twatũo kana twatuĩka andũ na tũmwe indo ũguo mũrata wakwa ahuteririe? Nĩ twambe tũrũmĩrĩre ũreri wa ciana na gũkũra gwacio nĩ getha tuone kana nĩ kũrĩ handũ, hĩndĩ kana ũndũ warehaaga mũgarũrũko ta ũyũ kana ona ngũrani ĩrĩa ingĩtũma ciugo ta iria twambĩrĩrie nacio ciario.

O ta ũguo twoiga haha igũrũ rĩ, twĩragwo atĩ kahĩnda-inĩ ga tene ciana ciothe ciambagiria mitũrĩre o ũndũ ũmwe nyũmba-inĩ cia *nyina*. Nĩwe wamaroraga na kũmatungata. O nyũmba-inĩ iyo ya nyina ciana nĩ ciambagĩria githomo giacio. Nĩ amonagia maũndũ na mawĩra marĩa we, mbarĩ, ndĩra na itũũra cionaga ũrĩ wa bata na ona akamonia wendi wa bũrũri.

Thutha wa kahinda o nyũmba-inĩ ĩo ya nyina twana nĩ twa gayanagio. Mũgayũ ũyũ warĩ wa mĩkomere nyũmba-inĩ ya nyina nĩguo tũirĩtu tokome *kĩrĩrĩ* hakuhii na nyina na tũhĩĩ *kwerũ* na mbũri. Mũgayũ ũyũ nyũmba-inĩ o ĩyo ya nyina o na ciana ikĩreragwo hamwe nĩ nyina warĩ mũtigithũthokanio wa kerĩ mitũrĩre-inĩ[4]. Ningĩ rĩ, kuma kahinda gaka rĩ, ii kau tũirĩtu na tũhĩĩ twatigithanagio mĩkomere-inĩ, twana nĩ twambagĩrĩria gũkũra tũkũranĩtio.

Nĩ ũndũ wa meciria ma mawĩra marĩa ciana ici cionagwo atĩ cikana ruta hau kabere rĩ, na bata na gĩtĩo kĩrĩa andũ a tene maahete miaka rĩ, mbari na ĩkundi rĩ, ciana nĩ ciakoragio inyiitithĩtio andũ arĩa akũrũ[5], mũno aria a *nyũmba* yao, a gĩkundi kiao, itũũra riao na bũrũri wao. Ĩkundi iria cia tũmagirwo ũreri-inĩ wa andũ na bũrũri mũno ciarĩ *mbari* na *riika*.

Our journey will be exploratory and explanatory in nature; it will try to weigh and explicate the meanings of these words within the context of the practices and traditions of the Gĩkũyũ even as it tries to figure out that which prompts them and how we are to read them.

Let us begin our journey at the very beginning—birth and nurture. Authors and narrators tell us of how children were in this past period welcomed into Gĩkũyũ community at birth. Many people are of the opinion that all children were highly valued and others go as far as to insist that they received equal treatment. In spite of such claims, whether another's or ours, we must accept that there was distinction in their first reception. There was, we note, disparity in the ululations uttered in celebration of infant arrival—three ululations for a girl and five for a boy. Be that as it may, we are told that this distinction was of no special significance or value besides its obvious informational one.

Furthermore, one denying any implication of inequality in treatment may in corroboration direct us to what they insist was the equal treatment and nurture of infants after birth. Consequently, in support of their claim they may say that all infants stayed with their mother in her hut, and they were all known as *twana* (babies), regardless of their sex. Still, whether one accepts their claims or not, it is also appropriate to ask at this point when children changed or were changed so that children of one gender came to be seen as or became persons while the other came to be seen as or became property or things, as my friend suggested. To answer this question, let us carefully observe the upbringing and socialization of Gĩkũyũ children, so as to see if there is anything in its process that would bring about the kind of change or gender differentiation that the statement we are considering points to.

As we remarked above, we are told that in traditional times, children started their life-journey on an equal footing in the hut of their *nyina* (mother). It was she who looked after them and nurtured them. In her house, a mother would start her children's education. Under her care they began to learn those things that she, their clan, blood-relatives, neighborhood, and village regarded as important for the welfare of the community.

After early childhood, girls and boys were separated from one another—the girls to sleep in *kĩrĩrĩ* (the girls' room) near the mother's bedroom and the boys in *kwerũ* (the boys' room) near where the goats slept. Although they continued to live together in the same house, this division in sleeping arrangements is significant. It is the second distinction in treatment that children experienced.[4] Also, from this period on, there was differentiation in the way the children were brought up and socialized.

Given the group's anticipation of children's future roles and jobs, and the honor that society placed on age, family, and social groups; children were apprenticed to older people[5] among their kin in their homesteads, villages, and the nation. The units that were utilized the most in this process of growth and fostering were the *mbarĩ* (clans) and the *riika* (age-set).

Ĩkundi ici nĩ cionagwo ci cia bata nĩ ũndũ nĩ ciateithagia ciana kwĩĩruta maũndũ maingĩ o na ningĩ ciga cihe mweke wa gũcidana na gwĩkũrania nĩ getha atongoria na arũmĩrĩri meyonanie na ona nĩ ũndũ wa ciako ciao—mũndũ o mũndũ, memenyithie. O ĩkundi-inĩ ici noho andũ magĩyaga na magathondeka ũrata. Ndũgũ ya ũrata yarĩ ĩngĩ ya tĩĩtwo mũno. Nĩ ũndũ wa ũtũmeri ũyũ wa ĩkundi ici—mũno kĩu kia riika rĩ—ĩkundi nĩ cionaguo cii cia bata mũno na ikaheyo gĩtĩo o ta gĩtĩo kĩrĩa kiaheyagũo mbari.

ĨCUNJĨ CIA HAU KABERE

Nĩ twarĩrĩrie ũhoro wa riika hanini na ningĩ tũgwete makinya marĩa andũ ona me ĩkundi-inĩ moyaga magikũra na kũrerũo. Nĩ twambe tũmenye atĩ riika nĩ riateithagia kumenyithia mũndũ o mũndũ, mbari, mũciĩ itũũra na bũrũri mahinda ma imeera na magetha ma andũ na na indo. Riika nĩ ria gitũmagĩraguo gũthima na kũratha, rigatumĩrwo kumenyithia andũ matukũ na maũndũ marĩa magĩrĩire. Nĩ ũndũ wa ũguo rĩ, ciana nĩ cia nyitithanagio na mariika macio nĩguo gukamenyekana harĩa cikinyiite ũkũrũ-inĩ.

Mahĩtũkĩire mariika rĩ, andũ nĩ moyaga makinya maigana ona magikũra. Mwana mũka nĩ akũraga na agatuĩka *kairĩtu*. Akũrakũra agatuĩkaga *kĩrĩgũ*—ũyũ nĩ *mũirĩtu* uria ũtaruate[6], agacoka agakurwo mũirĩtu—tondũ nĩ muruu. Thutha wa kahinda gaka na ahika nĩ etagwo *mũtumia*. Mũndũ mũka wĩ twana etagwo *kang'ei* o nginya rĩrĩa kana gake ka mbere karua. Kana ka mbere karua kang'ei nĩ etagwo *nyakinyua* tondũ kuma kahinda gaka nĩ etĩkĩrĩtio kũnyua njohi.[7]

Mwana mũndũrũme o nake nĩ arumagĩrĩra mũtaratara ũrĩa watumagirwo kũmũrera nĩ getha o ta mwana mũka aimĩre na akũre. E mũnyinyi mũndũ mũrũme nĩ etagwo mwana no a kũra kũra we etagwo *kahĩĩ*. Kahĩĩ gakũraga gagetwo *kĩhĩĩ*. Kĩhĩĩ kia rua gĩĩtagwo mwanake. Anake nio mathiaga ita. Me miaka ya kũrua na gũthĩ mbara metagwo *njamba*.[8] Macoka kuma mbara na mahikania metagwo *athuri*. Nĩ athuri maikaraga kiama-inĩ magacira ũhoro wa mĩciĩ, itũũra na bũrũri.

Athuri othe a *kiama* matiahianiĩne. Nĩ matigithanĩtio nĩ indo iria marĩ—atumia, ciana, mbũri, ng'ombe, mĩgũnda—na ona thenge iria maahete kiama.[9] Ningĩ nĩ matigithanitio nĩ kahinda karĩa matungatite kiama, itũũra na bũrũri. Kuongerera rĩ, ũũgĩ ũrĩa monagwo menaguo, ũcamba ũrĩa mũnanĩtie mbara-

These groups were seen as important because they helped children learn and develop skills and mastery in many fields. They also gave children an opportunity to compete with one another and, in the course of this, forge independent identities. They provided children a chance to demonstrate their abilities so that the leaders amongst them could distinguish themselves, and the followers become apparent from the interactions they engaged in on the platforms offered. In these groups too, members made friendships in a community where such relationships were highly valued. Because of these important functions that these groups—and particularly the age-set—played in fostering children, age groups were as much respected as blood lineage.

SOCIAL DIVISIONS OF THE PAST

Let us further discuss the age-sets as we review the steps that children took in and out of age-sets as they grew up. We begin by noting that age-sets helped individuals, homesteads, clans, villages, and the nation track and plan seasons and the activities of planting, growth, and harvest. In this role, then, the age-set was used to measure and estimate time and operate a calendar of events. Children on their part were grouped into various age-sets, so that their stage of development would be determined.

Within age-sets, people took various steps as they grew up. A female* baby (*mwana*) would grow into a *kairĩtu* (girl). After some years, she grew into a *kĩrĩgũ*—an older adolescent girl who is not yet circumcised.[6] After circumcision, a female became a *mũiritu*. After circumcision and marriage, a female became a *mũtumia* (a married woman). A woman with children was called *kang'ei,* that is, until her first child was circumcised. After her first child was circumcised, a *kang'ei* graduated and become a *nyakĩnyua* (one who drinks) because from this time on she had license to drink alcoholic beverages.[7]

The male child followed a pattern similar to that of the female. As an infant, a male was called *mwana* (baby). After a while, he would grow and be called *kahĩĩ* (small boy), then with some more time and further growth, a *kĩhĩĩ* (big boy). After circumcision, a male would become a *mwanake* (young man). Young men were the ones that went to war. During this period of their growth, they were called *njamba* (warriors).[8] After this stage and on marrying, they would be called *athuri* (elders). It is elders who sat in *kiama* (council of elders), passing judgment on matters relating to homesteads, villages, and the nation.

There were different ranks among the elders in the *kiama.* Members were distinguished one from another by their property—wives, children, goats, cows, farms—and also by the number of he-goats they had offered as dues to the council of elders.[9] They were also differentiated and ranked by their period of service to the council, to the village, and to the nation. In addition to one's wisdom, one's courage as a young warrior, the leadership positions one had earned within one's age-set, the skills with which one led one's homestead, and one's wealth all came into play in determining status.

inĩ, ũtogoria ũrĩa riika riao ria maahete na ũtungatĩri ũrĩa matungatĩte naguo mĩciĩ yao na ũtonga wao o nacio nĩ cia matithithokanĩtie. Kwongerera rĩ, kiama-inĩ no kwoimaga *mũthamaki* kana *mũramati*. Ũyũ ari mũthuri ũrĩa warĩ gĩtĩo kĩrĩa kiingĩ mũno gĩkundi-inĩ kĩu na itũũra-inĩ.

KŨIMBŨRIA ICUNJĨ NA MAKINYA MA GŨKŨRA

Tondũ nĩ twarikia kwaria ũhoro wa makinya marĩa ciana ciarũmagĩrĩra igĩkũra rĩ, rĩu no twĩyũrie ũũ, makinya marĩa ciana cioyaga nĩ marĩ gĩtĩo kĩmwe? Maũndũ mao na mĩikarĩre yao nĩ yarĩ coho ũmwe? Agĩkũyũ aingĩ magĩcokia kiũria gĩkĩ moigaga atĩ ciana na makinya macio marĩ gĩtĩo kĩmwe. O naguo rĩ, nĩ kũrĩ arĩa moigaga atĩ kuga ũguo ti kwaria ma. Nĩ tũgerie gũtuithia cira ũria wĩ haha.

Arĩa moigaga atĩ ciana ciothe ciarĩ gĩtĩo kimwe moigaga atĩ nĩguo mũndũ ahote gũcokia kioria gĩkĩ na aige kana ciana na makinya macio nĩ ciaiganaine rĩ, no nginya tũririkane bata wa makinya marĩa tũrarĩrĩria gĩkũyũ-inĩ. Andũ ta aya magĩtwĩraga atĩ mũndũ ũkũrora makinya maya atarĩ na itherũ no one atĩ makinya maria ciana cioyaga cioyaga ci ciothe cirathĩte ũgima, ũhiki, gũciara, ũreri na ũtugateri wa matũra na bũrũri. Andũ arĩa monaga mbica ĩno irĩ ya ma na itũmi ici irĩ cio ciarĩ rĩciria kana thugunda iria yaicũhagia mĩtugo, mitũrere na ũreri wa ciana cia gĩkũyũ matũririkanagia atĩ ona akorwo arũme na aka nĩ marutaga mawĩra matiganite, mawĩra maya mothe marĩ ma bata bũrũri-inĩ. Makĩria rĩ, bata ũcio nĩ wa menyetwo na ukaheyo gĩtĩo.[10]

Amwe a mwena ũyũ wa ngarari ĩria ũhoro witũ ũciarire nĩ mathiaga na mbere na makoiga atĩrĩĩrĩ, atĩ mũndũ ũtegwĩtĩkĩra kĩhooto gĩkĩ no ũrĩa ũrarora mĩtũrĩre ya ũgĩkũyũ o igũrũ. Mũndũ ũrĩa ũramakararia woni-inĩ ũyũ—ĩĩ mũndũ wa mwena ũria ũngĩ ngarari-inĩ, no aige atĩ twana twa ĩhĩĩ na ona ningĩ anake na athuri nĩ maarĩ gĩtĩo kia mwanya marorithanio na tũirĩtu na atumia. Mũno mũndũ ũyũ no aige ũũ aririkana atĩ makinya ma ũtumia kaingĩ makinyagĩrio nĩ ũndũ wa ũtũmeri wa mĩrĩ yao nĩ arũme—kwendio, kũhika, gũciara na kũrera ciana na ona kwĩnyihia he arũme; harĩa athuri makinyagĩra na makagĩya ĩtĩo nĩ ũndũ wa cĩĩko ciao itũũra-inĩ na mbara-inĩ, nĩ ũndũ wa ũria ma umũkanagia ciugo ciao, ũũgĩ ũria monanagia kiama-inĩ na marĩhi maria maneanaga kiama-inĩ, nĩ ũndũ wa wathani wao igũrũ wa ciana na atumia mĩciĩ-inĩ.

Besides the ranks that emerged in the council, there was also in every group a *mũthamaki* or *mũramati* (a leader). This was the man held in the highest esteem by all the elders in the group.

INVESTIGATING THE STAGES OF GROWTH AND EMERGING DIVISIONS AND GROUPS

Now that we have talked about the steps that children took as they grew to adulthood, I think it appropriate to now ask: Were these steps equally valued? Were their experiences and roles equally respected? While many Agĩkũyũ may respond affirmatively, there are equally many others who would answer negatively. To resolve the question, let us interrogate this matter further. Those who hold that all children were treated equally argue that a serious response to this question must take into account stages of human development as woven into Gĩkũyũ culture. Such consideration, they insist, reveals them to have been engaged by all with a similar aim or purpose—the ambition of successfully achieving adulthood, marriage, bearing and nurturing children, and service to the village and the nation. Those making this kind of a claim argue that even if men and women performed different duties, their tasks and participation were equally accepted as crucial in society. Furthermore, they remind us that the importance of each task was clearly understood and well recognized.[10]

Some supporters of this position would go farther and argue that failure to see the veracity of their position is a consequence of looking only superficially at Gĩkũyũ culture. In response to such a claim, a challenger may argue that boys, and even young men and male elders, received preferential treatment when compared to their female counterparts. Such a challenger may cite the fact that the graduation of women to improved status was determined by the use of women's bodies, as women were exchanged from father to husband in marriage, in marriage itself, childbirth, parenting, subordination and service to husbands. This is in contrast to a man's change in social status, which was determined by personal deeds and contributions in one's village, personal bravery at the battlefield, wisdom displayed at council of elders' deliberations, payment of one's required dues therein, as well as one's success in presiding over wives and children at home.

While agreeing with this critique, advocates for the argument of equality point out that it is imperative that we remember that marriage and childbearing were as important to young men and male elders as they were to their female counterparts. A male's graduation to eldership and eventually the determination of consequent status required the measure of children and wives, of family and its organization, which was why, just as with women, these were used to determine one's worth and to grant respect and honor to those who met these general social criteria. Furthermore, proponents of this view hold that even if measures of value for women and men were different, the evaluations were related and similar. In addition, they say that the division of labor along gender lines was pragmatically necessary for

O na magĩtĩkagĩra ciugo ici rĩ, andũ a mwena ũrĩa ũngĩ miario-inĩ ĩno nĩ moigaga atĩ no mũhaka tũririkane atĩ o na kũrĩ anake na athuri, kũhikania na kũgĩa ciana kwarĩ bata na atĩ ni ũndũ ũyũ makoria twĩtĩkire ati mĩĩrĩ yatũmagiruo o ta ũndũ ũmwe. Magakĩririkanania atĩ o ta ũria kwarĩ kũrĩ aka, mũndũ mũrũme atuwagwo mũthuri nĩ kũhikania na thutha kana iguru wũ ũguo atumia arĩa mũndũ arĩ nao. Igũrũ wa atumia aya rĩ, ciana iria mũndũ agĩayaga ni ciaroraguo. Kuongerera ũguo rĩ, ũtogoria wa mũciĩ wake nĩguo watũmaga mũthuri amenyekane atĩ nĩ njaba itũũra-inĩ na aheyo kana ongereruo itĩo. Andũ aya makiugaga atĩ ona angĩkorwo athuri na atumia matiathimagwo na githimi kimwe rĩ, ithimi ciao nĩ cia konianie ona ika hanana. Ningĩ rĩ, nĩ mogagĩrĩra atĩ no mũhaka mawĩra ma mũciĩ, ma mbari, ma itũũra na ma bũrũri makũranio ona mothe me ma bata nĩ guo matura na mabũrũri makure. Kuongerera haha rĩ, andũ a mwena ũyũ nĩ moigaga atĩ tũgithiĩ na mbere tũĩjeririe ũhũro ũyũ tũrorete tũrikĩririe wega nĩguo tũmenye ũrĩa athuri na atumia mathimagwo ri, no tuone atĩ ithimi ici ciao ciarĩ o ta ũndũ ũmwe. Makoiga atĩrĩrĩ, atĩ ota ũrĩa mũtumia ũtari ciana atarĩ gĩtĩo rĩ, no guo mũthuri ũtarĩ ciana atarĩ gitĩo. Ona amwe nĩ maugaga atĩ mũthuri nĩ atuwagĩrwo itua rĩnene gũkĩra mũtumia agĩagire mwana.

Andũ ta aya moigaga atĩ mũthuri agĩamenyekanire ndagiciarithia nĩ onaguo ta atarĩ bata o na hanini. Twĩraguo nĩo atĩ mũthuri ta ũcio nĩ amenaguo ginya akorio ĩyurage na aremwo agateithio nĩ arũme arĩa angĩ.[11] Nĩ ũndu wa ũguo rĩ, mũtumia agiyamenyire atĩ mũthuri wake ndagĩhota guciarithia nĩ acaragia mũndũ wa gũciara nake, (mũno mũndũ wa riika ria mũthuri wake kana muru wa nyina na mũthuri wake), nĩ guo ahithie ũhoro ũcio tondũ kũngiamenyekanire atĩ mũthuri mũna ndaciarithagia mũciĩ wake nĩ wagaga atumia angĩ tondũ ndagionire airĩtu agihikia. Na, agiagire atumia a kũhikia, mũtumia wake nake o take nĩ agaga andũ a kũmũteithia mawĩra-inĩ ma mũciĩ wao.

Andũ a mwena ũrĩa ũngĩ wa ngarari ĩno nĩ makararagia woni ũyũ na macokia—kana no macokie na moige atĩrĩĩrĩ, atĩ ti ma atĩ athuri na atumia nĩ marĩ bata ũmwe. No moige atĩ ngũrani iria yari ho, ngũrani ithererete nginya kahinda gaka gaitũ nĩ yonaguo na no yonagwo hau kabere nĩ mũndũ ũngĩ ũire kahinda ga kũrora ũrĩa erĩ maruragwo na makonwo. Nĩ twambĩrĩrie na kũririkana atĩ kuma thutha wa kahinda karĩa kaganagwo ka Wangũ wa Makeri rĩi, ũgĩkũyũ-inĩ atumia matiahikanagia, nĩ kũhikio ma hikagio. Igũrũ wũ ũguo nĩ turirikane atĩ o matigia hikĩire mũthuri gukĩra ũmwe ũria mahikĩire atakuĩte, kana atamatete. Arũme rĩ, o nĩ mahikagia atumia kuma ũmwe o nginya arĩa mũndũ agiahotire. Ũngĩ ĩciririaa ũhoro ũyu rĩ, ngwĩciiria hihi mũndũ no ĩtĩkire atĩ nĩ ta atumia na athuri matiaganinie ũgĩkũyũ-inĩ.

HITHO YA CIUGO—GŨCĨRUMBŨYIA

Nĩ tucoke twĩciirie ũhoro wa ciugo iria arũme na aka metagwo na ũria cionanagia ũtiganu ũyũ twageta. Tugire atĩ mahika "airĩtu" metagwo "atumia." Kiugo gĩkĩ gĩa kerĩ kiumete kuma kingĩ—"tumia." "Tumia" ("gũtumia")

the development of the homestead, clan, and village, as all tasks are important and valuable. Besides, this group argues, if we carefully consider the assessment of men and women in society, we would see that the standards of value were similar for both genders in the sense that just as a woman without children was considered worthless, so was a man without children. Indeed, some of the proponents of this position argue that a man without children would be treated more harshly than a woman in a similar situation.

They observe further that if a man was suspected to be impotent, he would be derided and considered completely useless. We are told that such a man was advised to kill himself and, if he was unable to do so, he was assisted by other men in the taking of his life.[11] For this reason, if a woman realized that her husband was impotent, she would look for an alternative sex partner (especially a man of her husband's age-set or her husband's brother) in an attempt to conceal this fact about her husband's conjugal incapacity, not only because of the danger such knowledge posed to him but also because such a failure would impact her own quality of life, since an impotent man would not be able to attract other women to their home, women who, if he successfully made them his wives, would help the first wife with their domestic chores.

This argument could be countered with the claim that it is not true that men and women are equally important in society. These opponents may insist that there are now, even as there were in the past, some major and important differences between the sexes, that there were distinctions signifying inequality that existed in the past that have been sustained and can be traced and tracked to current time, distinctions that would have been apparent in the past to anybody looking at the different ways men and women were treated and perceived in Gĩkũyũ culture. Let's start by recalling that since that legendary period in which we are told that Wangũ wa Makeri, a woman, reigned, Gĩkũyũ society has not been matrilineal (women did not marry but rather were married, as it is they who joined the husband's family upon marriage). In addition to this, they could not be married to more than one man if their husband was still alive or if they had not been divorced. Men, on the other hand, could marry as many women as they could afford. In observing this fact, it seems apparent, this side argues, that men and women were not valued or treated as equals in Gĩkũyũland.

WORDS AND HIDDEN MEANINGS—INTERROGATION AND EXPOSURE

Let us also consider the words used to designate men and women in Gĩkũyũ and how these words emphasize this difference. Earlier, we indicated that upon marriage, "*airĩtu*" ("girls") were called "*atumia*" ("women"). This latter word comes from another—"*tumia*." "*Tumia*" ("*gũtumia*") brings to mind another word—"*kira*"—*gũkira*. These words—"*kira*"/"*gũkira,*" "*tumia*"/"*gũtumia*"—bring to mind silence or even further, not speaking one's mind, even when

nakio nĩ kiugo kĩnyitanĩte na kĩngĩ, "kira"—gũkira. Ciugo ici—kira—gukira, tumia—gũtumia; irehaga meciria ma kwaga kwaria ona ningĩ kwaga kuga ũrĩa mũndũ arieciria, mũno mũndũ atũrĩĩtio kana atahetwo rũtha rwa kwaria. Ningĩ nĩ ciugo irehaga meciria ma mũndũ ukumenya nĩ atĩa ee kuga na nĩ atĩa atekuga, mũndũ ũkũmenya handũ hake miario-inĩ na ona ningĩ ũrĩa ekwaria. Nĩ ciugo (tumia na ũtumia) ningĩ ikũnie ũhoro wa gũkindĩrĩria na kũhorera. Na kwoguo atumia (kuma mũtumia), ni kiugo kiumete gũtumia na nĩ ta kiugo gĩkĩ kiugaga atĩ atumia nĩ aria magĩrĩirwo gũkiraga na kwĩnyihia. Wĩrĩgĩro ũyũ ũtumia-inĩ nĩ wũonagio airĩtu, ahiki na atumia na ona rĩu nĩ umenyagithio airĩtu, ahiki na atumia. Othe nĩ meragwo kaingĩ atĩ wega ũmwe wa Aka nĩ kwĩnyihia—ũrĩa ũngĩ nĩ kũrora na kwĩrutanĩria wĩra—inĩ wa mũciĩ wao na wa mũthuri wao.[12]

Ningĩ nĩ turore kiugo kĩrĩa kĩnyitanĩte na gĩkĩ (ĩĩ na kiugo mũtumia)—mũthuri. O ta ũrĩa tũgire rĩ, anake moima mbara—*njamba cia ita*—na mahikania metagwo "athuri." Kiugo "mũthuri" gĩkonaine na kiugo kingĩ, "gũthura." Gũthura nĩ gũcagũra, na gũcagũra kũrehaga meciria-inĩ wĩtĩkio atĩ mũndũ ũrĩa ũracagũra kana agathura nĩ oii wega na ũru. Ũtumĩri wa kiugo gĩkĩ nĩ wonanagia atĩ mũndũ ũrĩa ũcagũraga kana agathura nĩ akũraguo ahetwo uhoti na agakorũo na ũgi wa kũhota kũrĩkĩrĩria wĩra ũcio ciugo ici inyitetie. Ũthuri rĩ ũgĩkoragwo ũhoro wa kwaramia na ningĩ wa kũramatia harĩa ũtumia ũgĩkoragwo ũhoro wa kũnyihia na gwathwo.

Ũthuri na ũtumia, warehaguo nĩ ũhiki. Thutha wa gũthaũra ciugo ici, ciako na mĩtugo iria ciahiohagia rĩ, gwiciria atĩ no tuge atĩ nĩ kũrĩ ũrĩa ciothe ciarĩ cia kunyihia mũtumia na kunenehia mũthuri rũthiomi-inĩ na ona bũrũri-inĩ. Ona twĩtikĩrĩte ũguo rĩ, nĩ tuongerere atĩ ũhiki, to guo wekagа. Nĩ tuge atĩ ũtungatĩri wa ũhiki na maũndũ marĩa maokonie ta mũciĩ na ũreri wa ciana matiohaga mũtumia e ika kana kũhe mũthuri itĩ na itĩo e ika. Maũndũ maguo ma makinyagiria na makahaicĩria atumia na athuri marĩ erĩ. Kaingĩ rĩ, erĩ no mũhaka magiahĩtũkĩire bara ino ũhiki worotete, bara ĩria bũrũri wa corete na ũhiki nĩ guo magiye itĩo cia arĩa ahiku; itĩo ciĩririrwo mũno bũrũri-inĩ na itũũra-inĩ; nĩ guo riika-inĩ, mbari-inĩ na mũciĩ-inĩ magiye mũgambo. Nĩ tũthiĩ na mbere na miario itũ. Tũtikorugama haha tondũ wĩra witũ ti mũthiru na twĩna maũndũ mangĩ magũthima na gũthathaura tũtacoketie kiũrĩa kĩrĩa tũwambĩrĩrie nakio nĩguo naĩthue tuge nĩ twa rĩkia thabarĩ itũ.

RIIKA NA MAŨNDŨ MARĨKONIE

O harĩa kabere ni tũkũgwetete bata na gĩtĩo kĩrĩa kiahetwo riika. Ngwĩciria ni kahinda kega ga gũcokerera gĩkundi gĩkĩ na kwĩririkania ũrĩa mwako ũyũ warutaga wĩra mĩturire–inĩ. O ta ũrĩa tũkugĩite rĩ, riika nĩ ria teithagia bũrũri na itũũra kũmenya ũrĩa mahinda marahĩtoka na ningĩ mawĩra marĩa andũ magĩrĩiruo gũkorũo makĩruta. Ningĩ rĩ, nĩ ũndũ wa ũrĩa andũ makũragio thĩinĩ wa riika rĩ, riika na andũ arĩa marĩkoniĩ—ĩĩ riika-inĩ ria mũndũ, nĩ marĩ gĩtĩo gitahunanaga na kĩrĩa kiaheaguo andũ arĩa angĩ. Anake aya arĩa mũndũ athũndikagwo nao nĩ monagwo o ta mahana arũ a nyina na mũndũ (ta mũrũ

offended and especially when not given permission to speak. They bring to mind one who knows what to say and what not to say—someone who knows "their place." They are words (*tumia*/*gũtumia*), then, that connote composure and calm. And so *atumia* (plural of *mũtumia*), as it is a noun derived from the verb *gũtumia,* suggests that women are those who are expected to maintain silence, submit, and humble themselves. This expectation of women is made clear to girls, newly wed brides and all females even today. They are told often that an important feminine virtue is humility; another is care and commitment to their homes, devotion and service to their domestic duties and to their husbands.[12]

Let us now consider the antonym of *mũtumia* (woman)—*mũthuri* (man). As we said above, after young men came back from war as *njamba* (warriors) and got married, they were called "*athuri*" (plural for *mũthuri*). The word "*mũthuri*" comes from the word "*gũthura.*" *Gũthura* is to select; the word brings to mind the idea that a person who makes choices is able to tell what is good and what is bad. The use of this word thus suggests that the choice- or decision-maker exercises agency. It appears then that the status of men as husbands is one that increases the extent of one's power, while that of women as wives promotes humility and subordination.

The status of being a man or woman was brought about by marriage. After unpacking these words and the habits and customs or culture they promoted, I think it is fair to argue that they worked to diminish the status of the female and promote that of the male in language and society. Still, even if we admit this claim, let us also admit that marriage did not only do this. Let us also say that marriage and those other things that concerned it, such as parenting, did not serve only to limit and curb women nor did it privilege men alone. Rather, both gained status in its performance. Generally, both men and women were expected to journey down the path it signified, down this road that society had drawn, if they wanted to enjoy the privileges that were reserved for married people—privileges that were highly coveted in this community—so that they could have their voices respectfully heard at any level of society. Let us continue our conversation rather than stop here, as our task is not yet complete. We have many things to consider and evaluate, before we can say that we have answered the questions that prompted our discussion and fully traveled our own route in this discussion.

AGE-SETS AND RELATED MATTERS

Earlier on, we mentioned the honor and respect that was granted the age-set. I think it fitting to revisit this structure so as to remind ourselves of its function within Gĩkũyũ culture. As we said before, the age-set helped the village and the nation to estimate time, and to plan and make judgments in the execution of social activities. Also, because of the way people were brought up within the age-set, fellow members in the group were treated with special honor. These young men with whom one was tightly bound were treated like one's own brothers and their friendship was first-class. These people, with whom one had been circumsized,

wa nyina na mũndũ) na ũrata wao ũgakorwo wa gĩtĩ kia mbere. Andũ ta aya rĩ, ĩĩ arĩa mũndũ aruate nao, metanaga "*wakini*."[13] Ũrata wao nĩ weyonanagia na ciako nyingĩ. Gĩko kimwe ũrata ũyũ weyonanagia naguo rĩ, nĩ atĩ athuri; magiacereiruo nĩ mũrata ta ũyũ rĩ—wakini—nĩ mamũheyaga mũtumia ũmwe wao aga koma nake angĩkorwo nĩ ekũrara. Niĩ ngĩigua ũhoro ta ũyũ ndĩyũragia atĩ rĩĩ, kũngia hotekire atĩa ũũ? Kai atumia matonaguo ta marĩ meciria mao? Ĩĩ angĩkorwo ndarenda gũkoma na mũthuri ũcio aheo? Kai wendi wao ũtarĩ bata? Ũtahetwo gĩtĩo? Ningĩ rĩ, ngeyũria atĩrĩrĩ, kai mũtumia arĩ kindũ atĩ no aheo mũndũ o ũria wecirerio? Atĩ atia, atĩ mũtumia agakorwo nĩ agũcagũrĩrwo wa kũmũhikia na ningĩ wa kũmũhikia akamũcagũrĩra wagũkoma nake?[14] Githe ti mĩtugo ta ĩno na maũndũ ta maya matũmaga andũ marie ta mũrata wakwa makiugaga atĩ atumia no ta indu? Na gĩthe tũtuone haha ũria ciugo ciake cirauga?

Kũrĩ ciũria ta ici arĩa maheanaga ũhoro nĩ maririkanagia mũndu atĩ ona tũkinegena nĩ ũndu wa ũrĩa tũrona ta atumia maagagiruo gĩtĩo, makahinyĩrio na makanyarirwo rĩ, nĩ wega kwaga gũtwa cira naihenya ũhoro-inĩ wa aka. Nĩ wega, matwĩraga, tũgĩciira tũririkane mĩtugo ya kahinda gaka na mĩeke ĩrĩa ya kumbatĩte, ta mwanya ũrĩa nao o aka matigĩrũo ũhoro-inĩ wa wendo wa mwĩrĩ. Andũ ta aya nĩ magĩtũririkanagia atĩ mĩrorere ya mwĩrĩ na miri ndiahanaga ũrĩa ĩhuana kahinda-inĩ gaka ka rĩu. Kahinda-inĩ kau ga tene gatahana rĩu rĩ, nĩ twĩraguo atĩ anake na airĩtu nĩ metikagĩrio kũmenyana kĩmwĩrĩ—gũthakania na gũthangania, bata matikoye ikinya rĩria riarĩ ria mũico tondũ riri nĩ riaigiruo kĩrĩrĩ kia ũhiki. Ningĩ ri, hihi nĩ ũndũ kaingĩ ũhiki ndwarehaguo nĩ wendo rĩ, andũ amwe nĩ moigaga atĩ aka nĩ marekagĩrwo na magetĩkĩrio magĩĩ ũrata wa mwĩrĩ na andũ angĩ tiga athuri ao ona marĩ ahiku, bata; mbere, matiga conore athuri ao—hihi thoni ya kuonania ũrata ũyũ mũno kana njono ya gũotũmĩra ũrata ũyũ gũcinora athuri ao kana gũthũkia mĩcĩĩ yao. Kerĩ, ati mũndũ ũcio mũka agia ũrata wa mwĩrĩ nake ndagakorwo e wa riika ĩnini gũkĩra mũtumia ũcio na mũthuri wake—ndagakorwo ta mwana wao, na haha riika nĩ rĩatumagĩrwo ta gĩthimi. Nĩ ũndu ũyũ rĩ, mũthuri agiakorire itimũ ria mũndũ wa riika riake nja wa nyũmba ya mũtumia wake rĩ, nake ndagianegenire; ndagiarehiire thina, kana ona onanie marakara makuga atĩ mũtumia ũcio wake nĩ araagana. Nĩ tũgũthiĩ na mbere tũgĩcaragia mĩeke na mĩanya ta ĩno ĩrĩa atumia matigĩirwo kahinda-inĩ gaka ga tene thutha-inĩ.

KŨRIGICANIA MIARIO—AKA NA MAŨNDŨ MAO

Hamwe na maũndũ maya rĩ, no tuge atĩ nĩguo gĩthimi gitũ gĩkorwo kĩigananu rĩ, no mũhaka ningĩ tuongerere na tũrehe mbere maundũ mangĩ ma o ũgĩkũyũ. Maũndũ maya nĩ megũtongithia miario itũ tondũ nĩ mekuongera ũmenyi witu wa gĩgĩkũyũ na ona ningĩ matũhee mbica ya ma ya ũria atumia monagwo kahinda-ĩnĩ gaka ga tene nĩguo tũhote gũtuĩria wega ciugo iria twambĩririe nacio, na ona ningi tũamũre cira ũria irehire tũtarĩ hitho kana wagi. Andũ megwĩtĩkania na ithuĩ bata wa wĩra ũyũ-rĩ, no mambĩrĩrie na kuga atĩrĩrĩ, atĩ ona angĩkorwo nĩguo atĩ kuma thutha wa kahinda ka "Wangũ wa Makeri" athuri

addressed one another as "*wakinĩ*."[13] This friendship and bonding manifested itself in different ways. One of these ways is observed in the fact that when a *wakinĩ* came to visit, the host would allow the visitor to sleep with one of his wives if he (the *wakinĩ*) planned to spend the night at the homestead. When I hear this, I ask myself: How could this happen? Were women seen as lacking in intelligence, agency? What if a woman did not want to share her body with this man to whom she had been handed over? Were women's desires and choices not important? Were these not recognized and respected? Further, I ask myself: Is this practice an indication that women were considered inanimate objects that could be given out to any person? Is this not odd, that husbands would be chosen for women and then husbands could choose others with whom their wives "slept" with?[14] Isn't this the kind of thing that leads to conclusions such as the one drawn by my friend that, in Gĩkũyũland, women are seen as mere objects, as things? And is it not now clear what she means?

In response to questions like those above, individuals well versed in Gĩkũyũ culture tell us that, when complaining about how women were disrespected, oppressed, and victimized, we must not be too hasty in our judgment. They insist that, when thinking about this issue, we should remember the culture of this period and the opportunities that accompanied it, especially those gaps preserved for women in relation to conceptions of the body and intimacy. Individuals holding such an opinion also remind us that perceptions of the body and intimate relations have evolved in the period between these more traditional times and now. For example, we are told that in traditional times in contrast to our own, young people were allowed to investigate their bodies and sexual responses, to engage in foreplay as long as one did not have sex, as this was reserved for marriage. Also, maybe because marriage was often not a love match, some people say that married women had a right to engage in a love affair on the side as long as the relationship met some established criteria. First, the relationship ought not shame her husband—for example, by being too openly conducted or being used to mock him or destroy their home. Secondly, the partner one took ought not be young enough to be one's child, and in this the age-set was used as a measure. Given this social attitude, it was well understood that if a man found a spear of an age-mate planted outside his wife's hut, he was not to make a fuss or accuse the wife of loose behavior. We will continue to seek gaps and spaces such as these in our discussion.

COMPLICATING THE DISCUSSION—WOMEN AND THEIR EXPERIENCES

In addition to the discussion above, we may say that if our evaluation is to be fair, we must bring to the fore other elements of Gĩkũyũ culture. Such a presentation will enrich our understanding of this society, particularly that of women, and so allow us to more accurately comprehend the perception of women that characterized this era. This may in turn allow us to unravel the words we started with and consequently allow us to more comprehensively

nĩ mamberĩrie kũhikagia atumia aingĩ rĩ harĩa mbereinĩ nĩ atumia mahikagia athuri aige rĩ, ũhoro ũyũ tũrarĩrĩria ndũthiragĩra haha, nĩ kurĩ ũngĩ wa kwario. Arĩa magiuga twongerere ũhoro rĩ, no mauge atĩ ona maahikio marĩ aingĩ rĩ, atumia gĩgĩkũyũ-ini nĩ marĩ gĩtĩo kiao. Ta, nĩ tũgwete atĩ mũthuri enjagwo no mũtumia wake wa mbere tu, ũyũ nĩ ũrĩa na rũtĩo wetagwo "*mũtumia ũrĩa mũkũrũ*" kũrĩ andũ arĩa akũrũ, na kũrĩ ciana cia mũciĩ wao kana nyũmba yao "*maitũ mũkũrũ.*"

Nĩ tũcũthĩririe na tũrore harĩa gĩtĩo kĩu twagweta kĩrĩ. Makienjana rĩ, matũmĩrite gĩko gĩkĩ rĩ, mũthuri na mũtumia wake nĩ ta meranaga atĩ erĩ nĩ maiganine—mũtwe kwĩ mũtwe. Nĩguo twĩtĩkie atĩ gĩĩko gĩkĩ kĩarĩ kĩritũ rĩ, reke ngwete atĩ ona mũcemanio-inĩ wa athuri—*Gĩcigĩ-inĩ,* no mũtumia ũcio wa rũgamagĩrĩra mũthuri wake hĩndĩ ĩrĩa mũthuri ũcio atarĩ ho nĩ ũndũ hihi thabarĩ, ndwari kana maũndu mangĩ nĩ mamũhingĩrĩria. Ningĩ rĩ, no mũtumia ũyũ wa mbere wacagũraga atumia arĩa mekũmũrumĩrĩra mũciĩ-inĩ ũcio wao. Uũ nĩ kuga atĩ rĩĩ, atĩ ona mũthuri angĩonire mũirĩtu na amwende handũ agienda kũmũhikia, no mũhaka agĩyaririe na mũtumia ũcio mũkũrũ, marĩrĩrie wendi ũcio wake nĩguo ahote kũhikia mũtumia ũyũ ũngĩ.[15] Angĩkorwo ũhoro ũyũ nĩ wa ma rĩ, niĩ haha no mũhaka nyambe ndũgame kahinda nĩguo njuge atĩrĩ, atĩ haha heena mweke, ihoro, gĩcheng'ũ na ona hamwe ningĩ harĩ na mũhĩnga, mũtego, mũtaro mĩtugo-inĩ na mĩtaratara-inĩ ĩno tũrathoma. Yerĩ nĩ tukũhumbũria.

Mũtaro[16],—ni tũririkane atĩrĩ, atĩ kaingĩ, athuri macagũragĩrwo mũtumia wa mbere nĩ maithe mao—na hihi (ngwĩciria kaingĩ) maanyina nĩ mũragio woni wao. Haha mĩtugo-inĩ ĩno ya kahinda gaka nĩ tuone atĩ ningĩ mahikania, thutha wa makorwo athuri, arũme matigia cagũrire aka o arĩa mekwenda. Mweke[17],—no mũhaka mũthuri agiaiguanire na mũtumia ũcio mũkurũ na thutha wa ũyũ, angĩ moka, atumia othe maiguane agĩcagũrĩra mũtumia ũngĩ. Kũhana ũguo rĩ, no tũgwete atĩ nĩ taari athuri mohetwo ona angĩkorwo mũndu aigua ũhoro wa mĩtugo na mĩturire ya Agĩkũyũ ĩĩ hunyĩrĩrio no aiige atĩ athuri nĩ meyathaga na atumia magathwo na makohwo. Ĩĩ kai aka na arume maigananio?

Ithuĩ tũtatwiite cira rĩ, nĩ tuongere gĩthimi-inĩ gĩtũ meciiria ma Agĩkũyũ ũndũ-inĩ wa kũnyita mwana, mũirĩtu, kana mũtumia na hinya; na gũkoma nao. Cĩĩko ici nĩ ciĩtigĩrĩtwo mũno o na ningĩ cikamenwo makĩria hihi nĩ ũndũ wa ũria cionagwo ci cia gũthombotha andũ na mĩturire yao. Kwa ũguo rĩ, mũndũ agiendire kwĩĩhĩta ni getha onanie ma na ũritũ wa ũria araiga rĩ, nĩ ehĩtaaga oigĩti atĩrĩĩ—"ingĩka ũndu mũna niganakoma na mwana," kana, akĩongerera mwĩhĩto hinya rĩ, akaiga eka kana aga gwĩka ũndu mũna akana koma na nyina (ĩĩ acoke kũrĩa aimete); kana, o na ningĩ gũkĩria—mũndũ akaiga acoke kĩhĩĩ, aruithithio. Mĩĩhĩto ĩno nĩ ĩgũtũhe handũ hangĩ ha gwĩcirĩria ũria atumia na ona ciana cionagwo.

answer and resolve the debate they triggered. Those who would agree with us on the value of this activity may at this point begin by saying that, while it is the case that, after the era of Wangũ wa Makeri, men started taking more than one wife while before it was women who used to marry more than one man, that is not all there is to the matter. Those making this case may argue that even when married in a polygamous setup, Gĩkũyũ women were respected. For instance, let us mention the fact that after marriage a man's head was shaved only by his first wife, known by the honorific title of "*mũtumia ũrĩa mũkũrũ*" (the senior wife) by other adults and in the homestead among the children as "*maitũ mũkũrũ*" (our senior mother).

Let us seek to determine where the respect that we just mentioned lies, in this view. When shaving each other, husband and wife in this symbolic act seemed to say to one another that they were equals. To demonstrate the significance of this act, let me add that, during council meetings, only this wife could represent her husband if he was away on a journey, had taken ill, or, due to any other unforeseen circumstance, was absent. In addition, it is this woman who chose the other women with whom she would share her husband. This is to say that even if the man identified a female that he wanted to propose to, it was understood that he needed to consult with and gain the consent of this senior wife.[15] If this claim is true, I must pause right here and note that there is, here, in this claim, an interesting opening, a gap and breach, even as there is also an obstacle, a trap and obstruction, in the culture and tradition we have talked about. We will discuss both.

The obstruction first[16]—let's remember that men had their first wives chosen for them by their fathers (I imagine that their mothers' views were sought in the choice). Here in the mores of the period, let us note that, a man could not choose the wife that he wanted to marry freely. The opening now[17]—it was expected that a man would come to some agreement with his first wife and eventually with those that followed her on any new marriage partner. This being the case, I think that we can say that men were restricted in really significant ways even though at first sight it may appear as though they were at great liberty and exercised free choice while women were constrained and subject to them. Have the scales just been rebalanced?

Before we reach a verdict on our discussion, let us also factor in how rape and sexual harassment were taken among the Agĩkũyũ. These acts were greatly feared and despised because of their potential to disrupt the lives and traditions of the community. Consequently, if a person wanted to swear and thus demonstrate the truthfulness and seriousness of one's words, one would say: "If I ever do such and such a thing, may I have sex with my own child"; or, to further add weight to an oath, one might say that if one ever did or did not do such and such a thing, may he sleep with his own mother; or, even more seriously, if he failed to keep his word in some regard, become a *kĩhĩĩ* again, that is, may he be uncircumcised. These oaths give us another opportunity to see how women, and children as well, were viewed in this culture.

Nĩ twambe tũge atĩrĩ, atĩ mĩĩhĩtwa ĩno ndiathakagwo nayo. Yehĩtagwo rĩrĩa mũndũ endaaga kuonania atĩ ũria aroiga nĩguo, atĩ ndarathaka na ningĩ ndarahenania. Tondũ ndĩari ya gũthakwo nayo rĩ, andũ makiĩhita makĩgwetaga indo ira gũtari ngaja atĩ cionagwo ci cia bata na maũndũ marĩa monekaga ta matagĩ ĩkĩka. Kwa ũguo rĩ, arũme makĩĩhita na mwana. Ona atarĩ hinya rĩu rĩ, mwana nĩ iciaro ria ũmũthe rĩrĩa rĩkanakorwo mũndũ wa bũruri na itũra rũcio. Ningĩ rĩ, mwana nowe njĩra ĩrĩa mũndũ aciaraga aciari ake nake we mwene akagĩa kĩrĩgĩrĩro atĩ nĩ agaciarwo na ningĩ nĩ ũndũ wa gũciara na kũrera mwana akagĩa wagũkanamũrora kahinda-inĩ karĩa we atagakorwo ena hinya wake we mwene.[18]

O ta ũria mũndũ mũgima atagicoka ihu ria nyina rĩ, kũria atĩ mũndũ akorũo nĩ ta atarĩ arua nĩ kũria ũhoro wa kĩndũ gĩtagĩriruo gwĩkĩka. Andũ nĩ makĩĩhĩtaga na maanyina, ĩĩ mũndũ ũcio wamũkuire na mwĩrĩ wake nĩguo mũndũ aciarwo, na agĩcoka akĩmũtungatĩra arĩ mwana. Ningĩ, ni mĩĩhĩtaga mũndũ akagweta gũcokera irua riake tondũ ta ũrĩa tũgire harĩa kabere rĩ, irua kũrĩ andũ othe rĩarĩ rĩa bata mũno.[19] Gũkĩgweta maũndũ maya nĩ kũrĩa gũcoka na thutha na ningĩ kuga mũndũ acokio wanaine na nĩ ũndũ wa ũguo aimwo itĩo na itĩ cia ũgima. Ningĩ rĩ, nĩ kũririkanania[20] atĩ mũndũ nĩ ciako na mũndũ ũngiĩka maundũ maya magwetetwo mĩĩhĩtwa-inĩ ĩno rĩ, no ta nyamũ kana, irimũ, ti mũndũ.

Nĩ tũkiuge atĩ mĩĩhĩtwa ĩno nĩ ũndũ wa ũria yonagwo itarĩ ya itherũ rĩ, na ningĩ yonangwo ĩĩ mĩritũ o nayo no yonanie indo iria cionagwo ci cia bata andũ-inĩ aya na atĩ ningĩ twamĩrũmĩrĩra tũmehumbũrie no tũkore atĩ ihithete ũria andũ aya monaga umũndũ. Kũrĩ ũũ rĩ, mũndũ nĩ ũria ugaga na ageka, mũndũ wĩĩ kĩrĩko, mũndũ oĩ atĩ aikaraga na andũ na atĩ nĩ kũrĩ ciĩko imwe itekagwo nĩ andũ—ta kwĩriga nginya mũndũ akaagĩra ciana, atumia nawe we mwenyewe gĩtĩo.

MĨEKE NA ITHERI—MĨHAKA NA MĨARAMANO

Nguona haha ta hari handũ hega ha gũthuthuria mieke ĩrĩa yari ho mĩtugo-inĩ na mĩtũrĩre-inĩ ya Agikũyu ũhoro-inĩ wa andũ aka na ningĩ hari hega ha kuarĩrĩria ũrĩa mĩeke ĩno yatũmagĩragwo nĩ arĩa mĩthondekagĩra njĩra cia mwanya magatiga iria maakĩirwo kana metĩkĩrĩtio bũruri-inĩ. Nĩ tũkiarie ũhoro wa aka aya a mwanya.[21] Aka aya nĩ mathithokanĩtio na arĩa angĩ na makonwo marĩ atiganu nĩ ũndũ wa ciĩako ciao ta wooni (atumia ooni), wĩra marutaga wa bata bũruri-inĩ (ta atumia aruithia na ago), kĩyo marĩ (atumia ehoti) kana ũrume na ũcamba (njamba). Aka aya no tuge marĩ a mĩthemba ĩrĩ—atumia ahiku na nginge angĩ arĩa matahikaga. O erĩ marĩ itĩo ciao maheyaguo nĩ ũndũ wa ciĩako, uhoti na utoria wao. Gĩtĩo kĩrĩa mahetwo nĩ gĩatomaga maingĩrio Gĩcigĩ-inĩ. No ona guo rĩ na mũno magĩagĩkorũo marĩ ahiku rĩ, maikaraga thutha wa athuri a o hanini mahinda-inĩ ma miario na magoti.[22]

Let us start this part of our discussion by emphasizing the fact that these oaths were never uttered in vain. They were said only when one wanted to convince others that what one was saying was true and not a joke or a lie. Because they were not a game or prank, by and in these oaths people put at stake those things and people thought to be of the greatest value then went farther and invoked activities that were culturally taboo. And so men swore by a child. A child, however powerless today, has the potential to become a thriving a member of society tomorrow. Also, a child in its birth, naming, and nurturing offers one an opportunity to present one's parents with a chance of rebirth and, in the process of parenting, one gains the hope of being reborn as well as the security of loving care in their old age.[18]

Just as an adult cannot literally return to her mother's womb, so too is it impossible to become uncircumcised. One would swear by one's mother, that is, the person who carried one in her body so that one would be born and the person by whom one was raised. One would swear by mentioning the idea of repeating circumcision because, as we have said, circumcision was very important to these people.[19] To invoke either of these "returns" is to ask for regression. It is to ask that one return to their childhood and forego all the gains and privileges of adulthood. In these oaths also is a reminder[20] that to be human is to act a certain way, that one who acts in any of the ways mentioned is just like an animal or an ogre—a beast or some other unnatural thing, not a human being.

Let us also then say that because of the seriousness with which these oaths were viewed and the emphasis placed on the things and people they referenced, they also serve to reveal how this community viewed personhood. According to this community's view, a human person is one who keeps their word, one who recognizes that they are social beings who live in community with other beings, one who recognizes that there are certain actions that such beings do not engage in, such as forgetting oneself to the point where one loses respect and care for children, women, and even for oneself.

GAPS AND SPACES—LIMITS AND OPPORTUNITIES

I find this is an apt moment to examine the opportunities available to women in Gĩkũyũ tradition and culture, a chance to discuss how such junctures were utilized by those women who chose to chart different, sometimes unusual, even unique life paths; in contrast to those dictated by society and history. Let us discuss these extraordinary women who dared to chart a unique way of being and the strategies they employed.[21] Such women were seen as special and different from other women because of the uniqueness their special abilities exemplified, for example, that of prophecy (women seers), or competence in special skills that allowed them to perform important duties within the community (such as female circumcisers and medicine women), or hard work (self-reliant women), or courage and heroism (warrior women). These special unique women were of two categories—married and unmarried.

Tũtarĩkĩtie kwaria ũhoro wa aka aya a mwanya rĩ, nĩ twarie ũhoro wa ĩkundi ingĩ igĩrĩ cia aka a mwanya tondũ ona cio no cia bata ũhoro-inĩ ũyũ tũrarĩrĩria. Mbere nĩ twambe tũgwete ũhoro wa atumia thata. Atumia thata kaingĩ marĩ aka ahiku no o ene matigiahotire gũciara. O ta ũria tũkũhũtĩirie mbere-inĩ na tũkagweta rĩ, ũhoro wa gũciara na kũgĩa ciana nĩ wa tĩĩtwo mũno gĩkũyũ-inĩ. O rĩngĩ rĩ, ciana cio nĩ cionagwo ci cia bata makĩria. Wa mbere, nocio ciarĩ cia kũrinda na gũtirĩra bũrũri kahinda ka mbere. Ningĩ kerĩ rĩ, tũtathiete haraya ũguo mono rĩ, nĩ tũririkane ũria tugire, atĩ mũndũ warĩ mwana nĩ ari kĩrĩgĩrĩro gĩake tondũ mwana-inĩ wake—rĩ nĩ ari mũndũ wa gũkanamũrora we akũra. Ningĩ rĩ, gũciara mwana kwarĩ kũgĩa mũndũ wa kũnengera indo iria mũndũ atũraga acaragia; na mũndũ wa kumuciara, nĩguo rĩĩtwa rĩake rĩtikanae kũriganĩra. Kwa ũguo mũndũ aciara mwana nĩ onaguo ekite maũndũ maigana ona mega. Wa mbere, nĩ ũndũ wa kumaciara rĩ, agakorwo nĩ akinyĩria aciari ake wĩrĩgĩrĩro wao. Kerĩ, we akehandĩra kĩrĩgĩrĩro gĩake gĩa gukana ciaruo mwana-inĩ ũcio. Nĩ ũndũ wa ĩtũmi ici cia tĩĩtwo muno na ningĩ nĩ ũndũ wa bata urĩa wa hetwo ciana rĩ, atumia·thata nĩ metekĩrĩtio mahikanie o ene nĩguo magĩĩ ciana ciao o ene. Kaũndũ gaka ga kuga atĩ no mahikanie, kaũndũ karĩ ho, nĩ gegũtwĩtĩkĩria twarĩrĩrie ũhoro wa indo gĩkũyũ-inĩ, mũno nĩ ũndu wa arĩa moigaga atĩ gĩgĩkũyũ-inĩ atumia matiarie indo ciao na ningĩ makĩria gatwĩtĩkĩrie tũcokerie arĩa maigananagia atumia na indo.

Nĩguo mũtumia—thata, kana ũngĩ—ahikie ũngĩ rĩ, no mũhaka agĩagũrire ũcio arahikia na indo ciake we mwene. Tũngĩ ĩcirĩria ũhoro ũcio rĩ, no tuge atĩ rĩ, atĩ nĩ ta tũrona atĩ gĩkũyũ-inĩ nĩ ta atumia metekĩrĩtio kũgĩa indo ciao. Ndarorania meciria macio na mĩtugo ĩngi ya Gĩgĩkũyũ rĩ, nguona ta ita hĩtĩtie. Nĩ tũrore na tũroranie mĩtugo ĩngĩ—ona kana ũrĩa ĩririkanaguo. Andũ arĩa makaanaga woni ũyũ makoiga atĩ atumia matiari indo ciao na atĩ indo cia mĩciĩ yothe ciarĩ cia arume—athuri ene mĩciĩ na anake ao rĩ, no mũhaka macokie ũhoro ũria ũturanĩrwo na ũkanyitĩrĩrwo nĩ ciugo na mĩtugo ĩno ya atumia thata na ona ningĩ marĩrie mĩtaratara ya mĩciĩ ya kahinda gaka ga tene. Nĩ tugwete mĩtugo ĩmwe ĩrĩa yarĩ kuo nĩguo twĩcirerie kana hihi no tũcokerie andũ ta aya makanaga ũgĩi wa indo hari aka na tũgĩremwo kũmacokeria rĩ, tũitĩkanĩrie nao.

All these categories of women commanded respect because of their actions and character, their capabilities and enterprise. The honor accorded them granted them opportunity to participate in special committees and earned them room in the ultimate political office—the council of elders. Still, and especially if they were married, they would sit behind their husbands in council of elders' meetings as they exercised these special rights.[22]

Before we finalize our discussion of exceptional women in Gĩkũyũ culture, let's talk about two other groups of exceptional women, as they are also relevant to our discussion. Let us first start with a discussion of barren women.† These were often married women who could not themselves bear children. As we already mentioned earlier, childbearing and rearing were valuable, honored activities among the Gĩkũyũ. Children were considered to be of the utmost importance. In the first place, it is children that would form the nation's defense force, they who would maintain and sustain the community in the future. But, secondly, before appealing to this more abstract and distant role, let us look closer to home and remember that more intimate value attached to children that we mentioned earlier, that of future care. One with a child had hope and expectation of a loving source of care in their old age. Also, with the birth of a child, one gained a steward who would inherit that which one had spent one's life accumulating and an opportunity to keep one's name in living memory. Hence, in the birth of one's child, one achieved several good things: first, one fulfilled one's own parents' hopes of continuing life and, secondly, one established the possibility of one's own rebirth. Given these reasons and the important role of children in this community, barren women were allowed to marry other women so that they could get their own children. This point—that women could and did get married to other women—allows us to discuss property and ownership in Gĩkũyũland especially as a way of addressing those who insist that women in this culture did not and could not possess property, and even more urgently, those who equate women to property in this community.

For a woman, barren or otherwise, to marry another woman, she would have to pay bride-wealth with her own property. When we consider this fact, it seems to me as if it by itself clearly indicates that women could and did own property legitimately. When we contextualize this claim, situate it within the background of other practices, and compare it to these, it seems to accurately represent that which was the case. Let us consider those other practices that I am referring to, or at least how they are remembered, as those who deny that women could and did own property, those who assert that all family property was owned by male members of society—husbands, fathers, and sons—must respond to the challenge posed by these practices and procedures surrounding the phenomenon of childless women in traditional times. Consequently, let us mention some of these practices so that we can give a rejoinder to those who reject the idea of females owning property and, if we are unable to provide a compelling rebuttal, accept our opponents' argument on this issue.

Mbere, nĩ tugwete atĩ angĩkorwo andũ aka matiari indo ciao rĩ, atumia aya thata matigarĩ gĩa kũgũrana na mũtugo ũyũ wa aka kũgũrana na ũtaũri waguo ũngĩri ta ngano cia gĩcenji kana urimũ, no, ti ngano. Nĩ twĩraguo atĩ nĩ kwarĩ aka mahikanĩtie na ona tũkona maciaro mao. Ningĩ rĩ, nĩ tũririkanagio atĩ watho warĩ atĩ mũka wa mũndũ agĩahikanirie nĩwe (mũka ũyũ mũgũranĩ) wathaga mũtumia ũcio ahikiya ti mũndũ ũngĩ ona angĩkorwo ũcio ũngĩ nĩ mũthuri wake we mwene.[23] Na, nĩ tũririkane atĩ athanaga tondũ indo iria ciagũranite ciarĩ ciake, na, ndagĩarĩ ciake agĩkorũo gũtiamenyekanete na gũgakoruo atĩ aka no makorwo na ciao.

Kerĩ, nĩ tũririkane gĩkundi kĩu kĩngĩ tũgwetire harĩa igũrũ, kĩrĩa kia Aka Ehoti. Aka aya kaingĩ marĩ atumia merutanĩirie makagĩa indo ciao ciakũigana na nĩ ũndũ wa ũguo magatĩo. Nĩ tuongerere ũhoro ũyũ na tũgĩthima cira tũgwete atĩrĩĩ, atĩ andũ angĩ nĩ metĩkanagĩa na niĩ haha na makauga atĩ mũciĩ-inĩ, o mũtumia nĩ arĩ ikumbĩ rĩrĩa aigaga irio iria wee arimaga na irio ici itingĩarutirwo tiga aheane rũtha. Ningĩ rĩ, nyũmba cia atumia cigĩakwo nĩ ciathondekagirwo *kwerũ,* harĩa mũtumia aigaga mbũri ciake. Ningĩ, ona angĩkorwo ng'ombe ciarĩ cia mũthuri wa mũciĩ, na nĩcio we (mũthuri) atũmagĩra kũigũrĩra[24] kana kũgũrĩra anake ake atumia rĩ; ona agĩkoruo mĩgũnda mĩngĩ yarĩ ya arũme rĩ, ona aka nĩ marĩ indo ciao ta maciaro ma mĩgũnda iyo ya athuri na ya mĩgũnda yao o ene ona angĩkorwo ti mĩgũnda mĩngĩ yarĩ ya atumia; na mbũri ciao[25]. Atumia nĩ matũmagĩra indo ici ciao kũruta mawĩra mao kana ona kũhigia mabataro mao, ta, mbũri cia aka nĩcio nao matũmagĩra kana mongagĩrĩra wĩra-inĩ wa ciana ciao—ta marua kana mahiki. Mũndũ agĩnyitithania maũndũ maya mothe gwĩciria no etĩkĩre atĩ atumia o nao nĩ marĩ indo o na angĩkorwo itiari nyingĩ ta cia athuri.

Tiga atumia thata na aka ehoti rĩ, gĩkundi gĩkĩ nĩ kĩarĩ aka agĩ. Ta, nĩ kwarĩ aka arĩa matoimire mĩciĩ ya maithe mao. Aka aya nĩ magaga kuma mũciĩ nĩũndũ wa ĩtũmi nyingĩ itiganĩte—ta mĩrimũ ĩmwe, wĩra marutagĩra mũciĩ wao kana ona magakorwo o matiendaga gũkanahika. Airĩtu arĩa matendaga gũkanahika o nao nĩ metĩkĩrĩtio kwĩgũra nĩguo ithe ndakanamedie.[26] Airĩtu ta aya nĩ mathĩnjagĩra ithe nake ithe agetĩkĩra mbũri iyo maaruta na akamĩrĩa na athuri a kiama. Kuma kahinda karĩa ithe etĩkagĩra mbũri ya mũirĩtu wake ya kwĩigura nake nĩ ambagĩrĩria gũtua mũirĩtu ũcio ta mwanake wa mũciĩ wake o nginya egayaga, akamũgaĩra indo ciake o ta ũria aragaĩra anake ake. Mũirĩtu ũyũ nĩ agĩtuĩkaga wa nyũmba thĩni o ta anake na athuri a mũcĩĩ ũcio wao tondũ ti wa nja ta airetu arĩa angĩ a mũcĩĩ ũcio, aria makana thĩĩ mahika; kana ta atumia arĩa nĩ undu wa kũhika mahikĩĩte magoka nyũmba-inĩ yao, ĩĩ "andũ a nja aria mokire kuma kũnge."

Our first and most obvious rebuttal is that if women did not and could not own property of their own, these barren women would not, in a community where the marriage contract required an exchange of property, have the means to marry another women and hence this practice or even its claim, would be like a fairy tale or a form of nonsense without any basis in reality. But, as we know, the practice is real. We are matter-of-factly told about woman-to-woman marriages and we have seen living testament of the practice in their offspring. We are also reminded that traditional law demanded that if one's wife got married to another woman, the latter was under the authority of the dowry-paying wife, not the husband of the homestead or any other person.[23] Let us also remember that the authority such a woman exercised in this relationship was hers because she was the one who had paid bride-wealth and she could not have paid such if it was not known and understood that she (and women in general) could own property and was authorized to make the kind of exchanges this practice entailed.

Second, let's also remember that other exceptional group that we mentioned earlier—that of self-reliant women. Economically independent women had worked hard to accumulate personal wealth, and for this reason were highly respected. In discussing them, let us also note a related fact, that many would agree with me that in every household, each woman had her own personal granary which she used to store her agricultural produce. Such produce could not be used without her permission. Also, during the construction of a woman's hut, room was always made for a "*kwerũ*"—a kraal in which her goats would spend the night. Let us note that even if the cattle and most of the tilled land belonged to men—husbands who used their cattle to "buy" wives for themselves[24] or for their sons—it was accepted that women owned the produce of the land and their goats.[25] They used these resources to finance their own activities and to meet or at least contribute to the fulfillment of their personal obligations such as, for example, the circumcision and weddings of their children. If one takes the time to put together all this information and considers its significance, I think one will agree that women had a right to property, one that they exercised, even if men in general held more wealth.

Besides barren and self-reliant women, the category of exceptional women had other members that are of interest to us. For example, it included females who for various reasons never left their parents' homes, ones who never married. The reasons why a female may have remained unmarried are varied and include certain illnesses, duties and responsibilities that they were committed to in their parents' homestead, or even an inclination against marriage. Those females who could have participated in marriage but were averse to it were allowed to pay bride-wealth for themselves and purchase themselves from their father so that their father lost the right to accept bride-wealth for them from a suitor.[26] A female would slaughter a goat for her father, which he would share with his age-mates and other elders. Upon accepting this payment of a goat, a father would start treating his daughter "just like a son," which meant that she gained a right to inherit his property just like her brothers. She became part of the inner circle of that household

Ũhoro ũyũ twaria wa aka a mwanya na mĩtugo ĩria yamarigicĩirie nguona ta ũkũhigũra njĩra njeru cia gwĩcirĩria ũhoro wa aka Gĩkũyũ-inĩ. Nĩ tũcirũmĩrĩre. Wa mbere nĩ atĩ tũgĩĩtĩkia njĩra ĩrĩa miario ĩno itũ yonania ciari ho na atĩ nĩ cia cagũraguo na cigatũmĩrwo nĩ aka rĩ, no twambĩrĩrie na kuga atĩ nĩ kwarĩ mĩeke ya aka gwĩthondekera na gũtũra mĩtũro ya mwanya. Atĩ ona angĩkorwo nĩ kwarĩ mũtaratara wa ũtũro ũria wabangĩtwo rĩ, to mũhaka aka magĩarũmerire makinya marĩa mabangitwo na makabagĩruo nĩ bũrũri ũhoro-inĩ wa ũtũro wao, atĩ atumia nĩ na nĩ magĩecagũrire makinya mangĩ. Mwahuha wa makinya maya mangĩ ona me maritũ nĩmo atumia aregĩ moyaga, magĩthũndĩkera ũtũro nginya magatuika ta mĩeke ĩyo na makamĩrũgamira na nĩkio nĩ ũndũ wa kũmooya magĩonwo ta rũũri rwa ĩthuurĩra na rũthooria kana rũkaana. Mĩeke ĩno na ũtũro ũyũ atumia aya "aregi" moyaga ndwarĩ mũhũthũ—o ta ũria o na kahinda gaka ka rĩĩu ũtarĩ mũhũthũ no yarĩ ho.

Wa kerĩ nĩ atĩ mĩeke ĩno nĩ ya rũgamaga ta kiũrĩa gĩa kũria ũrĩa agĩkũyũ mabangitĩ mĩtugo, mĩtaratara na mĩtũrire yao. Ikarũgama kũũria kana ũria kũhuana nĩguo kwagĩrire na o na kana andũ amwe—mũno kana ta aka arĩa kaingĩ matarĩ hinya mũingĩ maũndũ-inĩ ma itũra, bũrũri, wathani na mbara nĩ mahinyerĩirio. Igũru wa ũguo mĩeke ĩno nĩ ya ririkanagĩa bũrũri atĩ andũ matihinaine na o na atĩ kwaga ũhianano tĩ kwaga ũũndu. Ikaririkania arĩa mĩtikagĩra kũigua atĩ nĩ wĩra wa bũrũri ũnyitanĩte na mũndũ we mwene gũcaria na gũthondeka handũ ha kũiganĩra. Ningĩ rĩ, atĩ andũ na mĩtũrĩre yao matibangao biũ, atĩ o na magĩbangwo atĩa no mabangũraga na makabagũrũra. Atĩ andũ no marũũgaga na makaarura kana makahĩtuka mĩhaka ĩrĩa maigĩirwo. Maũndũ maya mothe ni maũndũ tũtagĩrirwo kũriganirwo.

GŨTŨMA NA GŨCHOKANĨRĨRIA

Tũkinyĩte haha no tocokere kiũrĩa gitũ na twĩyurie kana tũkirora mĩtugo ĩno twarĩrĩria na o na ng'ano cia ndũrĩrĩ ĩrĩa twagweta ndũmĩrĩri ĩrĩa twambĩrĩrie nayo nĩ ya taũkĩka na kana nĩ ĩronekana ta ĩtũheire ũhoro wa ma na ona kana ithue nĩtũretĩkania nayo.

Mbere, thutha wa gĩthomo gitũ rĩ, nĩ tũrie kana ciugo ici iroiga atĩ indo ciaigananagio (kana ciaigananĩtio) ni ati mwene ni mũrũme.[27] Ningĩ rĩ, nĩ twĩyũrie kana ĩra iga atĩ indo ici ciothe nĩ cia mũthuri na no acitũmĩre o ũrĩa agienda. Tiga kuorota wa gũcitũmera rĩ, nĩ kũrĩ arĩa magĩuga atĩ bata wa ciugo ici twambiririe nacio, nĩ ma wacio. Ati gũciĩgua na gũcitaũka ni kũruka ũria igwatete mũtaratara wa ndĩra na bũrũri ũgĩkũyũ-inĩ tondũ nĩ mũthuri warĩ (hihi ona rĩu ũrĩ) rũtha rwa mbere gũtũmĩra na kũrũgamĩrĩra indo ici ciothe. Andũ ta acio rĩ, nĩ mataukĩte ciugo ici wega?

in that interesting way that men were—not "persons of the outside" as she, unlike her sisters, would not eventually be married outside of it; nor like her mother or mothers—the wives—"who had come" in from elsewhere, that is, married into the home.

I think that our discussion of exceptional women, their lives, and the cultural procedures and processes that accommodated them offers us an opportunity to think about women in a fresh way in Gĩkũyũ society. In the first place, if we accept the existence of the routes we have revealed, if we see these as actually present and as actually used by women in that time, then we can claim that there were opportunities for women to choose, shape, and experience their lives in unique and interesting ways. We can go farther and claim that while there were prescribed life choices that women were encouraged to take and live, one did not necessarily have to adopt those, as one could construct other options. This latter alternative was the one that the rebel embodied and took. The rebel's choice of customizing one's life, of utilizing the potential opportunities these spaces and gaps represented was not easy, just as it is not easy today; nevertheless, it was there, the choice real.

Secondly, the gaps unveiled by our discussion put into question the popular conception of women in Gĩkũyũ culture, tradition, and procedure. They also stand to ask if it is just that some members of society—mainly women, who often do not have much power in the affairs of the village and the nation, in peace or war—are oppressed. In addition, these gaps stand as reminders that people are not the same even as they remind us that lack of similarity is not lack of humanity. They remind those willing to be reminded that society and each individual have a task to seek and create spaces of accommodation for all members. They are reminders that we can never police and order human beings efficiently enough. That however carefully we try to discipline human beings, they will always explode and exceed the limits and boundaries we attempt to enforce and will always reorder the order at play. These, I think, are considerations we ought not forget.

WEAVING LOOSE ENDS

Having arrived at this point in our discussion, I think that we are ready to return to the claim that prompted our discussion, ready to ask ourselves, especially in view of our study of Gĩkũyũ culture and tradition—if we understand it and to what extent we are in agreement with it.

First, let us consider if upon the reflection we have engaged in, the claim means that all things are made equal—or were made so—by the fact of male ownership.[27] Also, let us ask if the claim made by that original statement is that all the things mentioned—land, children, goats, and women—belong to men and that, as such, a man could and can use or treat them as he pleases. Besides pointing to the one who has jurisdiction, there are those who may say that the value of the words we started with is their truthfulness. That to comprehend these words is to understand how in the operation of this

Ithuwe haha nĩ tũgũcokeria woni ta ũyũ. Nĩ tũge atĩ rĩĩ, atĩ kũigua ciugo ici cikuga ũũ na kũnyitia mbica ta ĩno, ĩĩ ya kũhinyĩrĩria na kwĩnyihia tu, nĩ kwaga kuona, kana hihi kwaga gwĩtĩkĩra maũndũ marĩa mangĩ gĩthomo gitũ kiaumbũra. Makĩria rĩ, nĩ kwaga kuona mĩeke ĩno twarĩkĩrĩrĩa nayo, na ningĩ bata na itĩo cia mwanya iria indo ici tũrathima—mũno mũtumia na ciana ciahetuo. No tuge atĩ wamũri uria ũtagwĩtĩkĩra kuona mwena ũũ wa ũhoro wũrorete mĩtugo na mitũrĩre ya Agĩkũyũ o igũrũ ũmehunyĩrĩirie handũ ha kumĩcũthĩrĩria thĩinĩ, rungu na miena yothe ũrĩa tũgeretie gwĩka haha. Mũndũ ũgĩgeria gwĩka ũũ tweka no akore ati ndĩra na mĩtaratara ya Agĩkũyũ ti mĩhũthũ, atĩ ni mĩrigicanu gũkĩra ũria andũ amwe magienda kuonania na ati ũnyogondeku ũyũ nĩguo gĩthimi kia ũriku wa ciugo ĩria twambĩrĩirie nacio na mĩtugo ĩria ituonetie.

Kerĩ, no tũrie o ta ũria tũkũretie harĩa mbere kana indo icio igwetirwo nĩ ciaiganine cio nyene. Tũgĩcokia kiũria gĩkĩ no tuge haha atĩ aca tondũ kĩndũ o kĩndũ kirĩ; na kĩarĩ, bata wakio mwanya. Nĩ ma atĩ mabata macio nĩ manyitanĩte—atĩ mbũri nĩ ya gũraga mũtumia wa ciaraga ciana cia mũteithagia kũrĩma mũgũnda na kũrĩithia mbũri cia mũciĩ-inĩ urĩa warĩ kaingĩ nyumba ya mũthuri[28], no o naguo rĩ, ciothe itiaiganine. Ona tũcoketie ũguo rĩ, atĩ itaiganine rĩ, tũtikage kuona mĩgayanio ĩria yarĩ ho ũgĩkũyũ-inĩ na mabata mayo.

Tũrĩkĩrĩkĩria rĩ, nĩ tũririkanĩte atĩ ikundi na icunje iria ciarĩ kuo—kana ikoraguo kuo, na mĩhaka ĩria (kana iria) ciaigaga na cigaga; ĩigagwo kana yaĩgagwo nĩ ũndũ wa kũgeria kũhanda na kũnyitĩrĩra hinya na ũhoti mĩciiinĩ, matũũra-inĩ na bũrũri-inĩ. Ati wĩra ũyũ wa kũhanda hinya na ũhoti, gwathana na gũkanania, ni mũritũ na mahinda-inĩ mothe ni kũrĩ ũria kurĩ amwe aria maikaraga nja wa icunje iria hinya na ũhoti ibangagaga na magakararia mibango yacio. Andũ ta aya—"aregi"—nĩ matũcirithagia na mitugo ĩria yumagĩra kana ĩkeyũũmba ĩmathiororokĩre nĩ ya bata miaro-inĩ itũ. O na mĩturĩre yao no—kana o ene nũ matwĩtĩkĩrie tũone ũria tũgĩĩcirĩria ũhoro wa ciugo ta ĩria ciamberĩrie thabarĩ itũ. Ningĩ rĩ, no matwonererie njĩra cia kũhũnga, kuumbũra na kuumbũrũria, kũguthugunda na kũguthugunduthia ciugo ta ici na mĩtugo ĩria ciorotete. Magatũteithia kũhee ciugo ta ici, meciria, mĩtugo na mĩhaka ĩria yumagĩra ho kĩene ona tũkĩmĩkararagia na kũmĩatũra, tũkĩmiururugaga na kũmĩrũrũrũbia, tũkĩmĩrutanagia na kũmethengia o tũkĩgeragia na tũkĩhaaraga mũirigo na mũgiriito uria ciugo ta ici na mĩtugo iciaraga ciambatagia na kũgwatia andũ, bũrũri na mĩtũrĩre.

community, at every level, man stood, and perhaps still stands, as the one with first right to the use and disposal of the things mentioned. Are such persons correct in their reading of the statement?

To this kind of a reading, we respond that on one hand to hear these words in this manner, as only pointing to and reinforcing subordination, submission, and oppression, is to fail to see or maybe, even more, is to fail to accept those other aspects of the Agĩkũyũ that our discussion has revealed and unpacked. It is to fail to see the gaps we discussed above and the distinct value, status, and respect that each of the things we mentioned, especially women and children, enjoyed. Such a view is one that observes Gĩkũyũ culture and traditions only superficially rather than taking the time to engage in a sympathetic in-depth analysis from all sides. A person who tries to do that, as we have, would find the practices and procedures of the Agĩkũyũ are more complicated than some would pretend and that this complexity is the deepest measure of the statement with which we began.

Secondly, we could ask, as we originally did, if the things we mentioned are themselves equal, that is, share equal status. In responding to this question, we can say "not so" as each of these things had, separately, distinct and differing values and functions. It is true that these values and functions were related—that goats were exchanged for women, who gave birth to children, who helped women till the land and graze the goats and other animals that belonged to the home, which was in many cases a man's property[28]—but still, all these things were not equal. Even that being the case, let us not fail to take into account and to emphasize the distinctions that characterized Gĩkũyũ society even as we reflect on their role and function.

As we draw to an end let us keep in mind that the groups and divisions present in this society, the boundaries and limits they signify or signified, played or continue to play an important role in the construction and maintenance of power in the home, the village, and the nation. Let us remember that this work of gaining and maintaining power, of subjection and domination, is difficult and that there are always those who remain outside groups and categories created by a system, those who do not easily yield to it and who resist its work. Such individuals—rebels, and the culture of rebellion that emerges from their resistance—issue challenge and have in part been the focus of our conversation. As we have seen, they and their lives can also help us think about the words we started out with. They can serve to help us contextualize these words and then to move beyond this exercise to interpret and reinterpret them, to invent or reinvent these words, ourselves, and our world, to investigate culture and sentiments to discover that which gives birth to words such as these even as we find ways of challenging and critiquing them, of taking over established boundaries, of finding ways to test and track for traces of the tensions and possibilities that such words feel for and point to as these are felt and found in culture, tradition, and history, promoted in sentiments, myths, songs, proverbs, and conversations.

KŨRĨKĨRĨRIA—CIUGO CIA KŨRIGĨRĨRIA NA ŨTAARANI

Ona tugĩte ũũ rĩ, nĩ tũkuĩririkinia atĩ nĩ ma atumia kaingĩ matiarĩ—na ona riu matire hinya wa gwathana bũrũri-inĩ, itũũra-inĩ ona mĩciĩ-inĩ. Atĩ o na magĩagĩire—na ona rĩu magĩgia—ngumo, igweta na gĩtĩo, kaingĩ no mũhaka menyihie kana magienyihirie mbere ya Athuri ao kana Maithe mao, arũ a nyina na ithe wa mũndũ kana kana ona mbere ya kiama—mbere ya arũme na mĩtaratara ya arũme. Atĩ, bata wa ciana warĩ (kaingĩ ũkoragwo) wĩra ũria cionaguo iroteirwo na kũrathiruo kahinda-inĩ ka mbere, mũno nĩ ta ciakoraguo andũ ciakora. Atĩ mbũri na ona nyamũ ingĩ na mĩgũnda ciarĩ (na ona rĩu kaingĩ) bata nĩ ũndũ wa wĩra wa kũgitĩra hota ya andũ—mũno acio a mbarĩ ĩyo yetagwo ya muthurĩ mũna. Atĩ ciothe—atumia, ciana, mbũri na mĩgũnda nĩ cia thimaga ũtonga, ũgima, itĩ, na itĩo cia athuri na hihi nĩ haha cionaguo kana cionagwo ta ciarĩ (ta ire) o ta kĩndũ kĩmwe ona igĩturokagia, igĩtigithanagia na kwĩhoya kuma mĩtuire ta ĩno; ona (mũno ta atumia ũguo twathoma) ikĩgenyukaga, ikiĩthugundaga na kwethugunda werũ.

NOTES

1. Nĩ tũririkane atĩ gũtuwo kana ona kwonwo ti gũkũrwo. Keri, ni tuone ati haha ni ndagayania rũare rwa mũciĩ na rwa bũrũri.

2. Nĩ tũkwarĩrĩria ũhoro ũyũ thutha-inĩ no haha ni tũgwete ngũrani iria ndĩrageria kũhutithia. Atĩ kĩndũ—"indu"—kiria tũra aririria haha nĩ kindũ kiagu ũruka, ũmũndũ, ũ-mũndũ na ũũmbe tũroranitie na "indo." Tũkĩgweta indo tũraorota indũ inyitanĩte na mũndũ na kwoguo nĩ ũndũ wa gitũũranario ikagia bata ũria kĩndu kĩagaga gĩtari ngwatanĩro-inĩ ĩno. Ona ũguo rĩ, thuthainĩ nĩ tũkuona atĩ nĩ kũrĩ ũria atumia monagwo ta indũ igarũragwo nĩ ũndũ wa andũ ariaene—maaithe, kana aria mamagiaga—athuri, kana makagarurwo nĩ handũ hau megũragira bũrũri-inĩ.

3. Nĩ twĩtĩkĩre kwaga kwaria ũhoro wa ngano cia mĩtũrĩre na mĩtũrere na kana ici nĩ irũmagĩrĩra mũtaratara mũna na igathĩ na mbere na kana ikaga na ona kana ĩcĩ ĩthereraga mũhari-inĩ kana ca.

4. Tũngĩtara ngemi iria ciana cia gwatagũo nacio ũgeni.

5. Na Kwa ũguo bata wa Cũcũ na Guka wa mũndũ kũrĩ ũreri na ũrori wake.

6. Ririkana atĩ kũrĩ Agĩkũyũ kũrua kwarĩ kwa bata mũnene mũno. Andũ othe no mũhaka magia ruire na gũtire ũngĩ etirwo mũndũ mũgima kana etwo mũgima ataruiite.

CONCLUDING CAVEAT

Having said all of this, let us remember that it is the case that women were often, in the past, as is often still the case, powerless within the nation, village, and home. Even if women gained honor, influence, and status, they still had/have to humble themselves before men—their husbands, their fathers, their brothers, or even the council of elders; before men and patriarchal institutions. Let us remember that the importance of children was to a great extent (and often still is) their anticipated future value and that they were (and are) seen as full human beings only upon gaining the age of majority—adulthood. That the value of goats and farms, of land and animals was (and still is to a large extent) their utility as a form of material insurance and security against, for example, hunger in the community—one often signified as "man" or a certain man's family. That all of them—women, children, goats, and land—were/are used to measure the wealth, maturity, honor, and status of men; and maybe in this were seen—and perhaps still are seen—as "one thing," as similarly linked to "man" even as they attempted/attempt to evade and escape, divorce and separate themselves from such characterization, even as they (as we have particularly seen with women) continue to rebel, invent, and reinvent themselves.

NOTES

1. First, note that the fact that they are perceived as and/or treated the same does not necessarily make them the same. Second, I have distinguished the homestead from society.

2. We shall deepen our discussion on this claim and specifically as it relates to property later on. However, at this point, let us note the distinction suggested here between a thing—which implies a lack of character, humanness, form—and property. This is an interesting distinction because property in some way implies a human connection, and in some subtle manner, elevates the status of a "thing." As we shall discover later on, there seems to be a way in which a woman is indeed often a "thing" in this sense, that is, by some kind of ownership claimed by her father or husband or when she "purchases" herself.

3. Let us also sidestep the question of whether history, culture, and development are linear or otherwise.

4. Second if we count the ululations made at birth.

5. Hence the important role of grandparents in children's upbringing.

6. Remember, that among the Agĩkũyũ circumcision was very important. No person would be called an adult or be seen to have matured without undergoing this rite of passage.

7. Ririkana ati Nyakinyua arĩ mũtumia utarĩ twana tũnini.

8. Njamba cia ita kana mbara.

9. O ringĩ "indo" ti "indo na andũ."

10. No haha hagoka kiũria kingĩ, mawĩra maya ni monaguo maiganine? Muno, ni marĩ gĩtĩo kĩmwe?

11. Haha heena ũhoro tũgiarĩrĩria tũũgĩre na kahinda, ũhoro wa ũria ũrume and ũtumia wakagwo na gũthingĩrĩrio.

12. Ona atĩ nĩ kiugo kĩra arĩrĩria mĩtugo, miario na mũikarire ya Aka.

13. Ĩĩ mũndũ wa hakuhe mũno, wa ruiete na kahiũ kamwe na ũrĩa ũngĩ.

14. Ni tũririkane ati kaingĩ gĩkũyũ-inĩ airĩtu macaragĩrio na magacagũrĩrwo athuri nĩ maithe, matithĩtio ni maanyina. Mũndũ akienda kũhikia mũiretu nĩ ithe orogia na no ithe aheaga rũracio—indo cia kũracia.

15. Ĩĩ rĩria mũtaratara ũria wagĩrire ũkũrũmĩrĩrwo.

16. Hee mũthuri.

17. Hee mũtumia.

18. Ciana cia tuwagwo aciari a mũndũ na arĩ na ariũ a nyina.

19. Ririkana ati kũrĩ Agĩkũyũ anake and airĩtu eri ni maruaga.

20. Kũririkania ũria ũrarĩrio, na tũmũhetũkire rĩ, kũririkania itũra na andũ othe aria mekũrĩte kuma ciĩko cia kĩnyamũ na mandũ maria andũ matagirirwo gwika.

21. Ririkana atĩ ti aka othe matũmagĩra njĩra ici.

22. No ona makĩingagĩragio gĩcigĩ-inĩ rĩ, nĩ tũririkane ati maikaraga nja hanini wa gĩthiorore gia athuri—ĩĩ nja wa gatagati ka hinya wa itũũra na bũruri. Kuhinyĩrĩria, gũcokithia na gũcokerera ciako cia kwĩnyihia mbere ya ũrũme.

23. Oni ũria mĩtugo ya kũnyitĩrĩra hinya na ũhoti, kũhaicia na kũnyihia, ũnene na ũnini itũũraga na igacokerera o na mieke-inĩ ta ĩno.

24. Ririkana ati mũtumia wa mbere mwanake agũragĩrwo nĩ aciari ake—nyina na ithe, no acio angĩ nĩ we wegoragĩra. O naguo rĩ, ni tũririkane uria twarĩrĩrie hau kabere—ũrĩa mũtumia ũria mũkũrũ na aria angĩ mũciĩ-inĩ maragĩrĩria ũhoro ũyũ. Ningĩ rĩ, reke hinyererie kiugo gĩkĩ gĩtũmagirwo na atumia haha,—"kũgũrwo," tari indo.

7. Still, remember that the *nyakĩnyua* could only indulge in alcohol if she did not have a young child still dependant on her.

8. Young men of battle or war.

9. Again, note, their "property," not "property and human relations."

10. But here another question arises: Were these tasks perceived as equal? In particular, did they attract the same level of prestige?

11. There is more that we could talk about here if we had the time. We could enter a discussion of how masculinity and femininity were constructed and maintained.

12. See how the word speaks to the behavior, speech, and lives of women.

13. This is a very close person, one with whom one has shared the same knife during circumcision.

14. Let us remember that in Gĩkũyũ tradition, more often than not, it was one's parents—fathers assisted by mothers—who sought and chose husbands for their daughters. Indeed, if a man wanted to marry a girl, it is from her father that he would request her hand and to whom he would pay *rũracio* (bride wealth).

15. In an ideal situation, according to the social rules.

16. For the man.

17. For the woman.

18. Children were named after family members starting with the parents' parents and then going on to one's siblings.

19. Remember, in the Gĩkũyũ culture, both men and women were circumsized.

20. A reminder to all who are being addressed and, through them, to all who have rejected as beastly those acts that are undesirable for human persons.

21. Let me emphasize the fact that not all women chose to activate these possibilities.

22. And so note that even when they were included in these proceedings, they sat in the periphery of the male circle—outside the center of power in the village and community during discussion and court sessions, thus continuing and reproducing the performance of submission to masculinity.

23. Look at how practices of holding power, of constructing hierarchies of power and domination, of domination and subordination, persist and subsist—how they are maintained and reproduced even in the very possibility of their erasure that these gaps present.

24. Remember that a man's first wife was acquired for him by his parents—his father and mother—but that he paid bride-price for the others mainly by himself. Be that as it may, let us also remember our earlier discussion regarding the involvement of his first wife and then those others that one may have married in a man's decision to marry another woman. Also, let me highlight the Gĩkũyũ word that is used in marriage—"*kũgũrwo,*" which translates as "to buy," as if relating to property.

25. Atumia ehoti nĩ ma cokagĩrĩria indo ici makaitũmĩra kũgia hinya na mũgambo bũrũri-inĩ.

26. Nĩ tũririkane ati mũiiretu agiahikire nĩ ithe woriagio rũtha rwake na atĩ indo cia mũiiretu cia ruraciũ cia neagwo ithe. Ningĩ rĩ, nĩ twona ati mũirĩtu—ti mwanake, agiendire kwaga kũhika egoraga kuma kũrĩ ithe. Igũrũ wa ũguo ri, ni tũririkane ati mũirĩtu agiagĩire ihu atahikite mwanake "mwene" ihu atuĩro na arĩhiũ nĩ athuri rĩ, nĩ ithe aneaga indo iria matuaga.

27. Cũthĩrĩria na wone ũria ũyũ arĩ—na hĩhĩ nginya rĩu arĩ—mũndũ ũria warĩ hinya ũria muingĩ bũrũri-inĩ.

28. Na kwa ũguo karũĩmbo ta karia kabundithagio twana na mũno anake makirua *Wakaratha* kanyitithanagia hakuhi indo ici ciothe.

25. It was in part these items that independent women accumulated, manipulated, and deployed to secure power and voice in society.

26. Let's remember that if a girl was to be married, it was the father that would be asked the permission by the suitor and it was the father of the girl who received the bride-wealth. Also, we have seen that if the girl did not want to get married, she would have to "buy" herself from her father. Her male counterpart did not have to meet this condition. On top of this, if a girl became pregnant before wedlock, the man responsible paid the penalty to her father and it was male elders who would determine the fine.

27. Pay attention to the fact that this was the most powerful status in this community and perhaps still is.

28. And so songs such as "*Wakaratha,*" in which all of these things are connected, would be taught to boys as they participated in circumcision rites and prepared for "manhood."

*While aware of the baggage the terms *female* and *male* carry in Western literature, I find it best to use these terms as the rest—that is, English synonyms—are loaded in Gĩkũyũ language as will be shown by the following presentation of the stages of growth in this community.

†Note that I use the term *barren* deliberately. With it I point to the fact that they could not for whatever reason give birth to children. This does not mean that they were "childless" as the subsequent discussion demonstrates.

Okwu na Uche

Emmanuel Chukwudi Eze

(*Maazi Eze, onye nke o-na ewute anyi na o lago muo, anaghi etinye akaranta n'edemede ya.*)

I. MMALITE

Amamihe

Onweghi onye bu omada omachara.

O ruru otu mgbe . . .

Mbe a gaa kpakota amamihe dum tinye ya n'akpa. O choro ka oburu sooso ya maara ihe. O gaghi adi onye ozoo maara ihe n'ihi na mbe ji amamihe dum.

O wee na-acho ebe o ga edobe akpa amamihe ya. O si, "e-hee, a matalam ebe m ga e dobe ya, ka onye abula ghara i metu ya aka. A gam e dobe ya n'elu nkwu; o dighi onye aka ya ga-erute n'ebe ahu."

O were akpa amamihe ya ahu konye n'olu ya jikere iri elu nkwu. O choo ka o ria, o naghi enwe ike. O gbalia n'ebea, mba. O gbalia n'ebe ozoo, o dighi uzu.

Ka o no na-gba ukwu nkwu okirikiri, na-acho otu o ga-esi ria-elu, otu nnunu e fefee, hu Mbe, juo ya si, "e-woo, enyi m Mbe, gini ka i na-eme?"

Mbe a zaa ya si, "o bu akpaa m'nya n'olu m, a choro m i dobe ya n'elu nkwu a, ma a naghi m e nwe ike ria nkwu a"

Nnunu wee chia ya ochi, "He-he-he-he-he-he-e-e-e-e-e-e!"

O juo Nnunu si, "kedu ihe mere i ji na-achi m ochi?"

Nnunu a zaa ya si, "Enyi m, Mbe, i maara na-inyaara akpa ahu n'ihu gi. O buru na i nyafee ya n'azu gi, i ga-enwe ike ria elu nke oma."

Word and Mind

Emmanuel Chukwudi Eze (deceased), *DePaul University*
Translators: Mary Gloria Njoku, *Godfrey Okoye University*; Father Joachim Oforchukwu, *St. Charles Borromeo Seminary*; Christian Ukaegbu, *Northwestern University*; Uchechi Ukaegbu, *Cornell University*

(*Mr. Eze, who, sadly, passed away, did not like to use diacritical marks in his writing.*)

I. INTRODUCTION

Knowledge

No one knows everything.

Once upon a time . . .

Tortoise gathered all knowledge for himself. He wanted to be the only possessor of knowledge. He did not want any rivalry because he had the key to knowledge.

He looked for a place to keep his bag of knowledge. He said, "Yes, now I know where to keep it so that nobody else will ever touch it. I will keep it at the top of the palm tree, where nobody's hands can reach it."

He hung the bag of knowledge around his neck, and got ready to climb the palm tree. Although he tried to climb, he could not. If he tried this way, no success. If he tried another way, it was not possible.

As he circled the trunk of the tree looking for a way to climb, a bird flew by, saw Tortoise and asked him, "My friend Tortoise, what are you doing?"

Tortoise answered, "It is this bag around my neck; I want to keep it at the top of the palm tree, but I can't climb it."

Bird just laughed at him: "He-he-he-he-he-he-e-e-e-e-e-e!"

Tortoise asked the bird, "Why are you laughing at me?"

Bird said, "My friend Tortoise, you are unable to climb the tree with the bag because you carried the bag in front. But if you had put the bag on your back, you would be able to climb the tree."

Ka o nuru nkea, Mbe a nyafee akpa amamihe ahu n'azu ya, nwee ike ria elu nkwu ahu. Oge o rutere n'elu, o juo onwe ya si, "Nkea, o putara na m ewekotachaghi amamihe dum?"

Nnukwu iwe e wee ya, n'ihi na obughi sooso ya ji amamihe niile. Nnunu ahu jikwa ufodu. O site n'elu tupu akpa amamihe ahu. Akpa ahu daa n'ala, tiwasia. Amamihe ndi ahu wee fesaa.

Ya mere ka onye obula jikwara nwee ike i mata ihe.[1]

II. FILOSOFI N'ASUSU IGBO?

Uru gini ka odi idee filosofi n'asusu Igbo? Ajuju a di ime. Enwere uzo di iche iche iji zaa ya. Mana tupu anyi ebido zawa, odi mkpa imata: Obu onye na-aju? Onye ka ana-aju? Obugini mere a na-ajuluu?

Ewekaria ndi Igbo n'onwe ha, maobu ndi na-agu akwukwo n'ala Igbo, odighi otutu ndi mmadu ozoo ga-ekweta, taa, na odi uru ikuzi, maobu imuta, filosofi asusu Igbo. Na ngosi, ewekaria ndi okauche na-aghota asusu Igbo, kedu onye okauche ozoo ga-ekwere na odi mkpa ka akuziere ya filosofi n'olu Igbo? Nezie, ijegodu n'ala Igbo, na Naijiria, enweghi otutu umu akwukwo mahadum [univasiti] na amu filosofi n'asusu Igbo. Na mahadum niile di ugbua na Naigiria, obu sooso n'asusu ndi oyibo ka a na-akuzi filosofi. Ya mere m ji kwu na odi mkpa ijuta: Onye bu onye choro igu filosofi n'asusu Igbo? Kedu udi ndi mmadu choro imee nchomcho gbasara filosofi n'olu Igbo? Maka gini—na n'ebee—ka ndia ji nweta obi ochicho di etu a?

Obaghi uru ichoba aziza ajuju ndia—maobu aziza ndi ajuju ozoo yiri ha—n'ebe tere aka. Site n'igba mbo ikowa isi okwu m nke m ji wee n'ede akwukwo nke i na-agu, anyi nwere ike ighota ihe mere na ufodu ndi mmadu, taa, choro imee nchomcho na filosofi n'asusu Igbo. Mana tupu m ebido kowaa onwe m n'uzo di omimi, biko, otosiri ka anyi mee nkewa—ya bugodu na nkewa a bu sooso n'oke nke ihe gbasara konsept—n'etiti *imu filosofi n'asusu Igbo* na *imu filosofi ndi Igbo*. Ihe ndi a bu udi okwu abuo nke ihe ha tuputara abughi ofu. O bu eziokwu na ntuputa okwu abuo ahu yiebere onwe ha. Ma obukwa eziokwu na, I nene ihe ha n'ekwu na nso, ha anaghi egosi ofu ife. N'itinye n'uzo ozoo: n'otu aka, okwu abuo ahu agaghi anabata nkewa n'uzo di kpakapii; mana odi mkpa ijide n'uche na ha na-ekwu di iche. Na ngosi, onye okaechiche obula bukwa ony na-aghotakwa asusu Igbo mara na ya nwere ike imuta filosofi n'asusu Igbo; mana obughi filosofi obula onye a meputara n'asusu Igbo ka anyi nwe ike ikwu na filosofi a ga-aburiri filosofi gbasara echiche maobu omenala ndi Igbo.

Nkewa m choro imee gbasa imuta filosofi n'asusu Igbo na imeputa filosofi nke ndi Igbo dikwa mpka n'uzo ozoo. *Onye Igbo* nwere ike burukwara onye okauche, mana obughi filosofi obula onye okauche onye Igbo tuputara ka enwe ike ikwu n'obu filosofi *ndi Igbo*. Ihe m na-aju bu nkea: filosofi obu filosofi Igbo sooso maka na o bu onye igbo dere ya? O bu ihe tosisi etosi iji kwu na sooso filosofi gbasara omenala ndi ka anyi ga akpo

When Tortoise heard this, he put the bag of knowledge on his back, which freed him to climb the tree with ease. He asked himself when he reached the top of the tree, "Does this mean that I did not possess all knowledge?"

It annoyed Tortoise to realize he did not possess all knowledge. This meant that Bird had some knowledge too. He became very annoyed, and threw the bag of knowledge from the tree, which tossed the knowledge into the wind and it scattered all over the world.

This is why people today are able to have knowledge.[1]

II. PHILOSOPHY IN IGBO LANGUAGE?

Why is it useful to write philosophy in the Igbo language? This is a deep question. There are different ways to answer this question. But before we answer this question, it is important to know: Who is asking this question? To whom is it being asked? Why is this question being asked?

Apart from the Igbo themselves, or those who study in Igboland, not many other people today will agree that it is useful to teach or learn philosophy in the Igbo language. For example, besides the philosophers who understand the language, which other thinkers would attempt to learn philosophy in Igbo? In fact, in Igboland in Nigeria, there are not many university students who learn philosophy in the Igbo language. Philosophy is taught in English in all the universities in Nigeria. This is why I say it is important to ask: Who would like to learn philosophy in the Igbo language? Who would like to do research in the Igbo language? Why and from where did some people develop the idea to seek this knowledge?

It is not necessary to look for the answers to these questions or similar ones elsewhere. I intend to explain why people want to learn philosophy in the Igbo language. But before I go on to do that, it is proper to explain the difference between the concepts of *the study of philosophy in the Igbo language* and *Igbo philosophy*. These are two different terms which mean different things, although it is true that they are similar. But when you look at them closely, you will understand that they differ. To put it another way, these two terms are not easily distinguishable; this is why it is important to bear in mind that they say two different things. For example, any philosopher that understands the Igbo language knows that he or she may learn philosophy in the Igbo language, but what he or she discovers may not necessarily be philosophy about the Igbo culture.

The difference I am trying to point out concerning philosophy in the Igbo language is also important in another respect. *Any Igbo* can be a thinker, but not every philosophy created by an Igbo thinker can be said to be a part of the philosophy of the *Igbo people*. My question then is: Does the fact that an Igbo wrote philosophy make it "Igbo philosophy"? It is appropriate to ask whether it is only philosophy that deals with our culture that should be

filosofi Igbo? N'uche m, enwere ike ikwu na filosofi gbasara omenala maobu odinala ndi ofu obodo (nke ndi Igbo maobu nke obodo ozoo) bu filosofi nke obodo a. Enwekwara m ike ikwu na filosofi onye Igbo obula meturu ga aburiri filosofi nke onye a tuputara. Ya bugodu na onye okauche a anyi na-ekwu maka ya n'eme sooso ntapia omenala maobu odinala ndi Igbo, okwesiri ka anyi ghota na odi uzo di iche iche onye nwe ike itapia omenala maobu odinala. Ebe obu na onye okauche abughi sooso onye onuokwu nke omenala maobu odinala, odi mkpa ikwuputa n'uzo were anya na filosofi bu uzo ofu onye maobu otu ndi mmadu ji eme nchomcho. Onye na-eme nchomcho na-eme ya maka na onye a na-acho igbazi amamihe nke ya. O bugodu eziokwu na imee nchomcho banyiere omenala maobu odinala nke obodo na-enye amamihe, obukwa eziokwu na oru nchomcho na oru onye onuokwu nke omenala maobu odinala abughi ofu ihe.

N'elu ya kwa, ebe obu na obughi onye obula na-asu Igbo bu Igbo, anyi ga ekweta na obughi onye obula na ede filosofi n'asusu Igbo bu onye Igbo. Ya mere na filosofi edere n'asusu Igbo nwere ike i bu gbasara isi okwu nke ndi na-agbasaghi—maobu na-agbasaghi n'uzo obula di omimi—obodo na uwa nke ndi Igbo. N'otu aka ozoo, onye nwere ike idee maka omenala na odinala Igbo n'asusu na-abughi asusu nke ndi Igbo nwekwara ike ideputa amamihe di mkpa gbasara obodo maobu uwa ndi Igbo.

N'itinye ya n'uzo di mkpemkpe, onye edemede n'abughi onye Igbo nwere ike idee akwukwo filosofi gbasara omenala na odinala Igbo. Ihe anyi ga-aju onwe anyi bu: kedu uru obara ndee akwukwo di otu a n'asusu Igbo? N'ihe na-eso ebe a, aga m agba mbo nye gi aziza nke m. Etu m si enene ihe bu isi okwu, odi mkpa imee nkewa gbasara oru onye na-akaputa uche, dika *okaechiche*, na *echiche* onye a na-atuputa. Na ngosi, obughi uchiche filosofi obula onye okauche onyi Igbo tuputara ka anyi ga-asi na uche a bu echiche nke "ndi Igbo." Nezie, obaghi uru I noro ebe a kowaba na olu ofu onye Igbo abughi olu ndi Igbo mmadu niile.

Mana achoro m ikwu na enwere ihe di oke mkpa—n'ezie, odi otutu ihe mkpa, ihe nwere nnukwu uru o bara—na onye okauche onye Igbo, maobu onye okauche obula n'aghota asusu Igbo, na-edee makwa na-aguu filosofi—filosofi n'udi obula—n'olu Igbo. Ya mere, n'aziza m nke mbu, o na enye m obi uto igosi na isi okwu akwukwo nke a iji n'aka, azago ofu n'ime ajuju nke ndi mkpa anyi juru. N'enweghi nsogbu obula, aga m abara isi okwu a: *igee onwe onwe anyi nti*. Na ndemde nke a m na-ede, ihe m choroo igosi bu na odi mkpa ka ndi okauche ndi n'aghota asusu Igbo—n'ezie, onye okauche obula—na-akpasi onwe ha nkata gbasara echiche nke ha, na na-eme nkpakori uche a sita na omenala nchomcho na ndemde nke ndi obodo na asusu di iche iche. Udi mkpakori nkata di otu a diri filosofi n'onwe ya nnukwu mkpa. Oburu na ndi okauche ndi Igbo choro igee onwe ha nti, ma ha choro igee onwe ha nti gbasara onodu filosofi n'asusu Igbo, maobu gbasara nkuzi filosofi n'olu Igbo n'uloakwukwo ndi di na Naijiria maobu na mba ndi ozoo, odi mkpa iji asusu Igbo na-akpa nkata ndi a.

called Igbo philosophy. I think we can say that it is philosophy about the culture or tradition of a people (whether the Igbo or any other people) that should be regarded as the philosophy of this people. I would also say that philosophy done by any Igbo person must be the philosophy of that person. Even if the thinker we are talking about only interprets Igbo culture or tradition, it is important to understand that there are different ways to interpret culture or tradition. Since a thinker is not merely a spokesperson for culture and tradition, it is important to state clearly that philosophy is one of the ways a person or multiple people can conduct research. One does research because one is trying to improve one's knowledge. Although it is true that doing research into the culture and tradition of a people gives knowledge, it is also true that the work of a researcher and the work of a spokesperson for culture and tradition are not the same.

On top of that, since not everybody who speaks the Igbo language is Igbo, we can also agree that one does not have to be Igbo to write philosophy in Igbo. This is why philosophy that is written in Igbo may not have any connection with Igbo worldviews. On the other hand, one can also write about Igbo culture and tradition and knowledge important to the Igbo world in a language other than Igbo.

To be more precise, a writer who is not of Igbo origin can write philosophy about Igbo culture and tradition. The question we have to ask is: what is the benefit of writing this type of essay in Igbo language? I will attempt here to give my own view. It seems to me that it is important to distinguish between the role of a *philosopher* ["person who produces ideas"] and the *idea* he or she produces. We have to know that not everything a philosopher says should be taken as a reflection of Igbo thoughts. It is not necessary to say that one Igbo voice represents the voice of all Igbo people.

However, I would like to note one important thing, which is very important indeed—namely, that it is highly beneficial for an Igbo philosopher or a thinker who writes and understands the Igbo language to write philosophy of any type in Igbo. This is why, in answer to my question, it makes me happy to say that the purpose of this essay you are reading is to answer multiple important questions. Without difficulty, I propose the theme: *listening to ourselves*. In this paper, I want to expose here the need for thinkers who speak Igbo (indeed, all thinkers) to have a dialogue among themselves about their own ideas, and to have conversations about their thoughts on the cultural research and writing from other places where other languages are spoken. This type of exchange is very beneficial for philosophy as a whole. If Igbo thinkers want to listen to themselves, and if they want to preserve philosophy in Igbo or teach philosophy in Igbo in the Nigerian educational institutions, it is important to use Igbo for such conversations.

III. OKWU NA UCHE

III.a. Uche bu Aku

N'oke nke a, aga m aju ajuju ato di mkpa gbasara uzo di iche iche filosofi nwere ike igee onwe ya nti n'olu ndi Igbo. Ajuju nke mbu: Kedu udi ihe jikora filosofi na asusu—asusu obula? Kedu etu njiko a si di n'asusu nke ndi Igbo? Nke abuo: Kedu etu o si di na, site n'asusu obula, onye mmadu nwere ike ighota uche onye nke ozoo? Gini bu echiche? Gini bu nghota? Onwere otu ihe—maobu otutu ihe—jikoro echiche na asusu? Obu gini bu ihe njiko a? Nke ato: kedu ihe jikoro nghota na asusu? N'ampkemkpe, kedu ife jikoro okwu na uche?

O buru na imee filosofi nwere ike inyere omenala aka n'uzo oru igee onwe ya nti, oga aburiri ezie na igee onwe anyi nti bu kwa igee filosofi n'onwe ya nti. Ya mere na idee filosofi n'olu Igbo ga-edubariri anyi n'iju ajuju gbasara uzo filosofi n'onwe ya si wee nwe ike imee ihe nkowa ya n'asusu Igbo. Oru mchomcho gbasara eziokwu ndi a, na eziokwu ndi ozoo di ka ha, ga-eneyre anyi aka imuta etu otosiri igba mbo ka amamihe na-abawanyie gbasara onodu na njikota okwu na uche n'omenala asusu nke ndi Igbo.

O di otutu ihe anyi nwere ike imuta site na ilebe anya etu filosofi si emepee onwe ya m'obodo ndi Afrika ozoo, dika na Gana. Kwasi Wiredu, onye olu Akan, egosi go uzo enwere ike imee filosofi n'asusu ndi na enwghi omenala ndemde, maobu n'asusu ndi nwere omenala ndemde mana edemede nke ha ebughi nnukwu ibu.[2] Na ndeputa nke ya, nke o kporo *Conceptual Decolonization in African Philosophy* [*Igbaputa filosofi Afrika n'aka usoro Kolonialism*], Wiredu tuputara na odi mkpa igaghachi azu n'asusu na n'omenala ndi Afrika—y.b., omenala Akan, Igbo, Yoruba, weg.—maka iji muta etu filosofi, n'oge taa, nwere ike ikowa uwa na odinala ndi Afrika.[3]

Na udi uzo yiri nke Wiredu, Paulin Jidenu Hountondji, onye Republik Benin, edeputago otutu akwukwo, nke o ji akowara ndi okandemede Afrika ma ndi okandemde nke ndi mba ozoo, na okwesiri ichoputa uzo di ofuu nke nwere ike inyeta aka ka omenala ndi obodo Afrika di iche iche na agam-n'ihu.[4] Etu Hountondji si kwu, ofu uzo iji nweta agam-n'ihu n'ihe gbasara amahihe na filosofi, maobu agam-n'ihu n'ihe gbasara uzo usoro nke sayens obula, bu site n'*imepe* omenala. Omenala, n'echichie nke a, abughi ihe mechiri emechi: omenala bu ihe yere oye. Ya mere, etu Hountondji ji hu ya, o di mkpa ka omenala obula, n'ime Afrika makwa n'ebe ndi mba ozo, gbaa mbo na-emezi onwe ha site na imuta uzo di iche iche, na uzo di ofuu, iji n'ewetara omenala na odinala ha, oga-n'ihu nke kwesili ekwesili.

Sooso omenala nke yere oye—y.b., nke na-acho kwamgbekwamgbe etu oga esi na-emezi onwe ya site n'mmepe—bu omela nke tosiri idi nsopuru. Ugwu a na-enye omenala maobu odinala obughi naani maka na omenala maobu odinala ahu nweburu ugwu n'oge gara aga; omenala na odinala na-enwekwa ugwu taa n'ihi na ha nwere ike idu ndi nwe, na ndi na-asopuru ha, gawa n'iru. Ya mere na n'ime akwukwo nke ya, nke o kporo *Endogenous Knowledge*, Hountondji katoro ndi na-aghotaghi uru omenala na odinala na-

III. WORD AND THOUGHT

III.a. Thought is Wealth

In this section, I will ask three important questions concerning the different ways philosophy can listen to itself in the Igbo language. First, what is the relationship between philosophy and language—any language? How does this relationship exist in the Igbo language? Second, how is it that, in all languages, one understands what another person is thinking? What is thought? What is understanding? Is there something or things that tie thought and language together? What is this relationship? Third, what is the relationship between understanding and language? What, precisely, is the relationship between word and mind?

If philosophy can help culture to listen to itself, then it is a way for us to listen to ourselves and to philosophy. This is why writing philosophy in Igbo will definitely lead us to ask questions about the ways in which philosophy can explain itself in Igbo. Research about these and other related truths will help us learn how to make sure that knowledge about the nature of words and thoughts in the Igbo culture continues to increase.

We would learn a great deal by looking into how philosophy itself developed in other African nations, such as in Ghana. For example, Kwasi Wiredu, one who speaks the Akan language, has demonstrated how to do philosophy in the language of a people without a writing culture or even within cultures that have writing but have few writings.[2] In his work entitled *Conceptual Decolonization in African Philosophy,* Wiredu argued for the need to go back to African language and culture—i.e., cultures such as Akan, Igbo, and Yoruba, etc.—to learn how philosophy today will enable us to explain the African traditions and world.[3]

Similar to Wiredu, Paulin Jidenu Hountondji, from the Republic of Benin, has written several books in which he has emphasized the need for African writers and writers outside Africa to explore new ways of developing African cultures.[4] According to Hountondji, one of the ways to develop knowledge and philosophy, or scientific methods, is to *open* culture. In this way, culture is not a closed system, but an open one. According to Hountondji, it is important for African cultures or any culture, for that matter, to devote themselves to learning new and various ways of advancing their cultures and traditions along the right path.

Only an open culture—i.e., one that always seeks ways to improve itself by being open—is a culture that deserves respect. This respect is accorded to the culture or tradition not only because it had it in the past; this culture or tradition is respected today because it can lead its owners and those who respect them to progress. It is because of this that, in his work titled *Endogenous Knowledge,* Hountondji criticized those who do not recognize the value of culture and tradition in African nations. What Hountondji criticized is the discourse according to which the culture and

aba n'obodo ni Afrika. Ihe Hountondji na-akato bu ntuputa nke na-ekwu na, etu omenala na odinala ndi "Afrika" di, ha enweghi ike imepe onwe ya maka oga n'ihu. O si na ndi nwere udi echiche di otua gbasara Afrika bu ndi choro imechi ndi Afrika anya; o di noo ka ha na-acho igba "Afrika" gbururu site na "mystical halo of values arbitrarily grafted . . . by the ideologies of identity." N'uche nke Hountondji, okwesili ka anyi hapu iche maka obodo di na Afrika, maobu maka ndi Afrika n'onwe ha, n'uzo di otua. Omenala, nke Afrika maobu nke ndi obodo ozoo, enweghi naani otu uzo otosiri idi. Obu n'ihi nkea ka o ji kwuo na o di mkpa ka ndi okauche ndi Afrika nyeta aka n'iji "weaken resolutely the concept of Africa, to rid it of all its ethical, religious, philosophical, political connotations, etc., with which a long anthropological tradition overloaded it and the most visible effect was to close horizon, to prematurely close history."[5]

III.b. "Central Igbo": Ngozi na nsogbu

Ofu ihe anyi nwere ike ighota site n'ekwumekwu nke Wiredu, maobu nke Hountondji, bu na ndi okauche nwe ike inyeta aka na-mmepe na n'agam-n'ihu nke omenala na odinala nke ndi Afrika. Anyi nwere ike inyeta aka na oga n'ihu ndi Afrika site n'immuta udi uzo di ofuu, na udi uzo di di iche iche, etu amamihe ga-esi n'abawanyie.

Obu ezie na Afrika agaghi emepe ofuma n'ihe gbasara filosfi, sayensi, na teknoloji maoburu na ndi Afrika wereanya etinyeghi obi ha n'ime oru ikowa echiche ndi Afrika n'olu na n'asusu nke ndi otutu mmadu bi n'obodo Afrika na-aghota. Mana odikwa mkpa ikwu na obughi sooso n'asusu nke ndi Afrika ka amamihe nwere ike iji bata n'obodo na uwa ndi Afrika. Di ka etu anyi si ghota na akuko gbasa Mbe—akuko nke anyi ji bido edemede nke a—ihe omumu nke na na-edozi obodo na-esi n'uzo atughi anya bata.

Onye Afrika ozoo—n'ezie, onye Igbo—tinyegoro anya n'ihe ndia bu onye oka-edemde Chinua Achebe. Onye choro ighota, n'uju, echiche nke Achebe gbasara isi okwu ndi anyi bu n'uche ebe a, ga-aguriri akwukwo nke Achebe bdia: *Hopes and Impediments* [Ntumanya na Nsogbu], *Morning Yet on Creation Day* [Ututu n'Uboshi Okike], na *Home and Exile* [Ulo na Ezi].[6] Mana ebe m choro ka anyi tinye anya ugbua bu na ekwumekwu Achebe nyere n'olu Igbo, n'Owerri, n'oge emume Odenigbo nke aro 1999.[7] Achebe ji asusu Igbo dee na ndi Igbo aluchabeghi "agha" (p. 42) gbasara nkwado asusu na omenaala ndi Igbo. Agha nke a, n'etu Achebe si kwu, bidoro site n'oge ndi oyibo, ndi mishionari si ala ni ocha, ji bata ala Igbo.

Kedu ihe bu isi agha a? Achebe kwuru: "Ka m gwazie unu ihe bu uche me maka nsogbo a anyi no n'ime ya taa. Obidoro otu nari afor ise gara mgbe ndi C.M.S [Christian Missionary Society] ziputara otu naokorobia ukochukwu a na-akpo T.J. Dennis. Dennis rutere Onitsha n'afo 1894. Dennis amaghi asusu Igbo mgbe o biara Onitsha, mana odi ya mkpa hienne imuta ya. Mana ihe o kwuru ka otu afo gasiri bu na ya enweghi ike ghota otu mpkuru okwu n'ime iriise n'okwukwu e kuru n'igbo." O di mkpa ka-anyi koo akuko a n'uju, etu Achebe si dee ya:

tradition of "Africans" are unable to open themselves to progress. He said that people who think in this way want to close African people's eyes; it seems that they confuse Africa through a "mystical halo of values arbitrarily grafted . . . by the ideologies of identity." According to Hountondji, it is proper to avoid such ideas about Africa and Africans. Culture, in Africa or anywhere else, has no one way of being. This is why Hountondji challenged African thinkers to fashion strategies to "weaken resolutely the concept of Africa, to rid it of all its ethical, religious, philosophical, political connotations, etc., with which a long anthropological tradition overloaded it and had, as its most visible effect, the closure of the horizon, the premature closure of history."[5]

III.b. "Central Igbo": Its Advantages and Problems

One thing we can learn from the works of either Wiredu or Hountondji is that thinkers can contribute to opening and developing the culture and tradition of Africa. We can contribute to this progress of African people by exploring new and various ways to increase knowledge.

It is true that Africa cannot develop well in matters of philosophy, science, and technology if knowledgeable Africans fail to put their souls into the work of explaining African ideas in their own mother tongues, which many people understand. But it is also important to note that it is not only through African languages that knowledge might come to the nations and lives of Africans. From the story of Tortoise with which we began this essay, we learned that knowledge useful for development could come about from unexpected sources.

Another African, an Igbo in fact, who has reflected on this issue, is the writer Chinua Achebe. For one to understand the stance of Achebe on this, it is imperative to know some of his works: *Hopes and Impediments, Morning Yet on Creation Day,* and *Home and Exile.*[6] But I want us to consider his speech in Igbo given in Owerri during the celebration of Odenigbo in 1999.[7] Using Igbo, Achebe observed that the Igbo people are still fighting a war supporting Igbo culture and language (42). According to Achebe, this war began when white people, the missionaries from Europe, came to Igboland.

What is the source of this war? Achebe said: "Let me tell you my thoughts concerning the trouble in which we find ourselves today. This war began 105 years ago, when the Christian Missionary Society sent T. J. Dennis, a priest, to Igbo society. Dennis came to Onitsha in 1894. He had no knowledge of the Igbo language, yet he was interested in learning it. But he said he could not understand some Igbo expressions even after one year from his arrival." It would be proper to narrate this story in its entirety as Achebe wrote it. According to Achebe:

Otu ihe di nnukwu mkpa n'oru igbasa ozioma bu itinye Baibul n'akwukwo ndi ozoo sonye n'asusu ndi a na-ezi ozi. . . . Onye bidoro oru a bu nwoke a na-akpo J.C. Taylor nke ya na [S. A.] Crowther so bia Onitsha n'afo 1857. Taylor bu onye Sierra Leone mana nne ya na nna ya bu ndi Igbo a gbaputara n'ohu. Taylor amaghi Igbo ofuma oge o biara Onitsha mana o bu onye Igbo na mmuo ya. Ihe ozoo nyere ya aka bu na o nwere nwoke onye Sierra Leone ozoo a na-kpo Jonas, nke na-asu Igbo ofuma, so Crowther na Taylor wee bia. Obu Taylor ka a ga-asi toro ntoala uka C.M.S. n'Onitsha. O bu akwukwo olenaole n'Agba Ohuru o tinyere n'Igbo ka Naija Mission ji aka uka mgbe Dennis biara Onitsha n'afo 1894.

Owere Dennis otutu oge iji kwuo na ntapia Taylor tapiara adabaghi, n'ihi na [Taylor] amachaghi oyibo ofuma. Mana nke a bu kwa ihe o kwuru, ihe Dennis na-acho bu ka ya onwe ya buru onye ga-atapia Baibul n'asusu Igbo. . . . [N]'afo 1910, ndi n'ebi Baibul n'obodo oyibo eweputa Agba Ohuru zuru ezu n'olu Onitsha. Anyi ga-echeta na o bu sooso afo isii gara aga ka Dennis zoro ukwu n'ala Igbo ejighi otu mkpuruokwu [Igbo]. . . . Dika onye mgbali obu, Dennis were Agba Ochie, tapia, bie, weputa n'afo 1906.

O buru na akuko Dennis jedebere ebe a, ase ajuju a anyi na-aju taa, aro a anyi zukotara na-atu, agaghijiri adi mkpa. Mana Dennis yiri nwanyi ugwuoba a siri na "o na-ebi oka ede ochiri ukwu abuo wunye n'oku." Maobu udi nwanyi Asaba a siri na nwa ya amaka, o si n ya awubeghi ya ahu. O bu udi ahu ahu Dennis wuru [asusu] Igbo ka Igbo no na-nsogbu ya taa.

Dennis choputara na Igbo na-asu n'olu n'olu, were hu oru ozoo o ga-aru. Mana Igbo amarala kemgbe uwatuwa na mba na-asu n'olu n'olu. Mba a na-ekwu abughi Hausa maobu Yoruba, kama akuku Igbo ndi ozoo. Mba na-asu n'olu ma na ndi ukwara ibe ha amarala ihe obu. Mana Dennis aghotaghi amamihe a. Olu iche iche Igbo na-asu wee bido chuwe Dennis ura. Kedu ihe a ga-eme asusu a bu Igbo ka o wee buru ezigbo ngwaoru a ga-eji gbasa ozioma kraist n'ala Igbo? Ihe o cheputara bu ka ha kpokota mmadu olenaole site na Bonny, n'Onitsha, na Unwanna, na Owerri ka ha nodu n'Egbu Owerri cheputa Igbo ohuru na-abughi nke ony obula iche, ma buru ha niile n'otu, ya bu Central Igbo.

One very important thing in the work of spreading the gospel was to put the Bible and other books in the languages of the people who were being taught. . . . The one who began the work was a man called J. C. Taylor, who came to Onitsha along with [S.A.] Crowther in 1857. Taylor was a Sierra Leonean, but his mother and father were Igbo who had been repatriated from slavery. Taylor did not know Igbo well when he came to Onitsha, but he was an Igbo at heart. Another helpful thing was that there was another Sierra Leonean called Jonas who came along with Crowther and Taylor, and who spoke Igbo well. It was Taylor who, one might say, laid the foundation for the C.M.S. church in Onitsha. There were a few books in the New Testament that he had put into Igbo that the Niger Mission used in the church when Dennis came to Onitsha in 1894.

It took Dennis a long time to say that Taylor's interpretations did not fit well because he did not know English very well. But this was the way he expressed it. What Dennis wanted was that he himself should be the one to translate the Bible into the Igbo language. . . . In the year 1910, those who printed the Bible in the white man's land brought out the complete New Testament in the Onitsha dialect. We should remember that only six years had passed since Dennis had set foot in Igboland without knowing one word of Igbo. . . . But like the ambitious person he was, Dennis took up the Old Testament, translated, printed, and brought it out in the year 1906.

If Dennis's story ended here, the inquiry we make today, the many problems we have had to deal with, would not have been necessary. But Dennis is like the Ugwuoba woman of whom it is said that "she cut cocoyam expertly and then used her feet to put it on the fire," or the type of Asaba woman who, if one says that her child is beautiful, says that she has not had a bath. That is how Dennis treated Igbo, so that Igbo is in such trouble today.

Dennis discovered that Igbo was spoken in various dialects, so he realized that he had more work to do. But the Igbo had known from time immemorial that communities had different dialects. The communities referred to were not Hausa or Yoruba, but in other parts of Igboland. The townspeople spoke in a dialect, but their compatriots knew what it was. But Dennis did not understand this bit of wisdom. The various dialects that the Igbo spoke started to disturb Dennis's sleep. What was to be done to this Igbo language so it would become a real working tool one could use to spread the word of Christ throughout all of Igboland? What he thought of was that he should call together a few people from Bonny, Onitsha, Unwana, and Owerri to meet in Egbu Owerri and think about a new Igbo not belonging to any particular person, but belonging to all of them as a group, which was Central Igbo.

> Etu m si ako akuko a, ikekwe unu ana-eche na o bu sooso Dennis no na C.M.S. na Naija Mission. Ndi ozoo no, ma ndi ocha ma ndi ojii. Onyeisi C.M.S. n'Onitsha bu Achideakon Dobinson, onye norola ala Igbo otutu afo; Ukochukwu Smith na Basden; Miss Warner, onye bidoro Saint Monica, uloakukwo izizi umunwanyi b'ala Igbo; na ndi ozoo ga. Ndi ojii nokwa ya, ma ka anyi hapugodu ha maka na o bughi ha nwe uka. Kedu ihe ndi ocha ndi ozoo chere maka aro dennis na-atu maka Central Igbo? Onye dika Basden bidoro gboo kwuwe na owekwaghi ya anya, nke on-ewe Miss Warner na Smith. Mana nke a enyeghi ennis nsogbu tumadi ebe onyeisi kpatakpata bu bisho Tugwell bi na Lagos kwadoro Dennis. Mana oburugodu na bishop akwadoghi Dennis, Chukwu kwadoro ya, etu uche si gwa ya. Ana m eche na otu ihe kasi ndi ozoo niile o ji di ndi C.M.S mkpa ikwado Central Igbo bu na o ka mfe inwe otu baibul mmadu niile na-agu karia ma inwe at maobu ano. O ga-adikwa onu ala n'ego. O were m anya na o bughi odinihu maobu oganihu asusu Igbo ka ha-ero maka ya.[8]

Isi okwu akuko a gbasara mbido edemde n'asusu Igbo di ohere ituputa "Central Igbo" di ka asusu a na-akpo "Esperanto": odi mma n'echiche mana onweghi onye n'asu ya. Central Igbo, n'etu Achebe si aghota ya, bu *a language in search of people.* Ndi oyibo n'aghotaghi asusu maobu omenala ndi Igbo biara n'ala ndi Igbo wee nuru Central Igbo nukwasi ndi Igbo n'isi.[9]

Ya mere Achebe ji kwuo na obu ndi missionari ndi ocha—n'etiti ha, Dennis—bu ndi doghachiri azu nkuzi na omumu edemede n'olu Igbo. N'ezie, etu Achebe si ako akuko a, nsogbu dakwasiri asusu Igbo site n'aka Dennis kariri nani idoghachi ya azu: obu oya nke mmuo bu ihe dakwuru ndi Igbo. N'uche Achebe:

> Asusu abughi igwe okpuuzu ga-ewere tinye n'oku, weputa kuziwe maobu kugowa etu soro ya. Asusu di nso, di omimi, di egwu. O di ndu. O na-eku ume. O bu ya bu ihe kewaputara mmadu na umu anumanu. Ya kewaputara ndi na ibe ha; mba na agbatobi ha.[10]

Etu akuko a si di, ihe ana-akpo Central Igbo di ka okwu onwu ezugara ndi Igbo. ("Afo 1913 kwesiri ka anyi na-echeta y adika ubochi Achideakon Dennis hara mmiri na-ama asusu Igbo taa."[11])

Odi mkpa ikwuputa na isi okwu akuko a Achebe koro di na ndoro-ndoro. Etu ofu onye okammuta bukwa onye ntapi nke Achebe si dee n'olu oyibo:

> The way I have told this story, maybe you are thinking that Dennis was the only one in the C.M.S. Niger Mission. Others were there, both whites and blacks. The head of C.M.S. in Onitsha was Archdeacon Dobinson, who had been in Igboland for many years; pastors Smith and Basden; Miss Warner, who started Saint Monica, the first school for girls in Igboland; and others. There were blacks there, but let us leave them for now because they did not own the church. What did the other whites think of Dennis's idea about Union Igbo? Someone like Basden began early to say that it was not clear to him, nor was it clear to Miss Warner and Smith. But this did not bother Dennis, especially when the head man himself, Bishop Tugwell who lived in Lagos, supported Dennis wholeheartedly. But even if the bishop had not supported Dennis, God supported him, according to his own thinking. I think that one thing more than all the others that he put forth as important to the C.M.S. support of Central Igbo was that it was easier to have one Bible everyone could read, rather than to have three or four. It would also cost less. It is clear to me that it was not the future or the progress of the Igbo language that they were thinking about.[8]

The point of this story concerning the beginning of writing in Igbo is that it provides an opportunity to see how "Central Igbo" is like the language called "Esperanto"—it is a fine idea, but nobody speaks the language. Central Igbo, according to Achebe, is like a *language in search of people.* White people, who did not understand the Igbo language or culture, came to Igboland, discovered Central Igbo and imposed it upon the people.[9]

That is why Achebe said the white missionaries, especially Dennis, set back the teaching and learning of writing in Igbo. Indeed, according to Achebe, Dennis inflicted a problem on the Igbo language which, worse than taking it backward, can be likened to a spiritual sickness. According to Achebe:

> Language is not a piece of iron that the blacksmith takes and puts into the fire, takes out and knocks into shape or molds as it pleases him. Language is sacred, it is mysterious, it is awesome. It lives and breathes. It is what separates humans from animals. It separates people from their companions; towns from their neighbors.[10]

According to this story, Central Igbo is like an announcement of death sent to the Igbo people. ("The year 1913 should be remembered as the year that Archdeacon Dennis brought down the rain on the Igbo language."[11])

However, it is important to note that Achebe's view is considered controversial. According to Achebe's translator, who writes in the English language:

> Although it would appear that most professionally-trained Igbo linguists see the need for standardization very clearly, their much-revered novelist, Chinua Achebe, has made no bones about his distaste for it. As I struggled toward accurately translating his speech into English, my impression was that he was so stung, and I believe rightly so, by the impertinence of Western missionaries in telling native speakers how they should speak--all the while scorning them as childish and inferior beings--that his vision of what was best for Igbo speakers was obscured.[12]

N'otu aka ahu, ototu ndi okammuta asusu kwere na Standard Igbo bu ezigbo ihe.[13] N'elu nke ndia kwa, ufodu ndi Igbo (Achebe n'onwe ya di n'ime ha) ajugo: Kedu ebe ndi Igbo n'onwe ha no oge a Dennis na ebi akwukwo Baibul n'Igbo? O bu aziza juru afo ikwu sooso na ndi Igbo "no ya, mana o bubeghi ha nwe uka"?[14]

III.c. Amamihe di n'iche n'iche

Achoro m imata ma akuko ndia niile—ya bugodu nke Achebe gbasara asusu Igbo, nke Hountondji gbasara omenala nke ndi Fon maobu ndi di na Republic Benin, maobu nke Wiredu gbasara Akan—nakwa ndoro-ndoro n'eso ha, tosiri ka anyi tinyekwa anya na uche n'uzo kasiri omini. Kedu ihe ndi Igbo, taa, na ndi obodo Afrika ndi ozoo choro gbasara asusu na omenala nke ndi obodo ha? N'iji juo ajujua n'uzo ozo di iche: Kedu uru obara idebe filosofi n'asusu Igbo, na ngosi?

Anyi nwe ike ikwu na azago ajujua: iji filosofi gee asusu Igbo nti bukwa igee filosofi nti n'Igbo. Mana anyi nweka ike ijuu: Kedu uzo kacha mma ka filosofi gee asusu Igbo nti? Kedu uzo kachama mma filosofi nwe ike igee onwe ya nti n'asusu na n'omenala ndi Igbo? Maobu, kedu uzo kacha mma ka onye Igbo gee filosofi nti n'olu Igbo? Enwere uzo tosiri ka filosfi nye aka n'oru ikwalita nkuzi na omumu asusu Igbo? Onwere etu nkuzi na omumu asusu Igbo ga-esi nyee aka n'iweta oganihu nke filosofi? Iza ajuju ndia bu oru ghasara ony Igbo obula guru akwukwo. Mana ebe obu eziokwu na obughi sooso ndi na asu asusu Igbo ka oru a dirir mkpa, ka anyi jugharia negaria isi anjuju mchomcho anyi n'uzo di etu a: Kedu uzo asusu Igbo nwere ike ikowa udi nti otosiri ka filosofi—n'mba obula—gewe asusu na omenala?

Ofu uzo di mkpa iji bido okwu mkpakori a bu itupta, site n'olu na n'asusu Igbo, ihe ndi okauche n'Igbo na-eche gbasara ihe ndi ufodu di mkpa na n'omenala mchemche nke a na-akpo filosofi. Na ngosi: Kedu etu ndi okauche n'omenala Igbo si aghota ihe jikoro uche na asusu—asusu obula? O bu na ndi okauche ndi Igbo kweta na asusu Igbo bu ihe tosiri inye ugwu, obu maka gini ka eji jide okwukwe? Taa, ototu ndi Igbo guru akwukwo mara etu

> Although it would appear that most professionally-trained Igbo linguists see the need for standardization very clearly, their much-revered novelist, Chinua Achebe, has made no bones about his distaste for it. As I struggled toward accurately translating his speech into English, my impression was that he was so stung, and I believe rightly so, by the impertinence of Western missionaries in telling native speakers how they should speak—all the while scorning them as childish and inferior beings—that his vision of what was best for Igbo speakers was obscured.[12]

Similarly, some scholars of language agree that Standard Igbo is a good thing.[13] On top of this, other Igbos (including Achebe) have asked: Where were the Igbo people when Dennis published the Igbo Bible? Is it satisfactory to answer that, although the Igbo people "were in the church, they did not own the church at that time"?[14]

III.c. There Are Different Types of Knowledge

I want to know whether all these stories—whether Achebe's concerning the Igbo language, Hountondji's concerning the traditions of the Fon or of those in Republic of Benin, or Wiredu's concerning the Akan—and the controversies that follow them merit our in-depth examination. What do the Igbo of today and indeed all other Africans want concerning their language and culture? To ask this question in another way: What is the importance of writing philosophy in the Igbo language?

We may say that this question has been answered: to use philosophy to listen to the Igbo language is to listen to philosophy in Igbo. But we can also ask: What is the best way for philosophy to listen to the Igbo language? What is the very best way for philosophy to listen to itself in the language and culture of the Igbo? Or in other words, What is the best way for an Igbo person to listen to philosophy in Igbo language? Is there any way that philosophy could help encourage the teaching and learning of the Igbo language? Is there any way that the teaching and learning of Igbo language could help in the advancement of philosophy? To answer these questions is the task of all Igbo persons who are educated. But since the reality is that not only those who speak the Igbo language have to engage in these tasks, let us go back to our original research question in this way: How might the Igbo language explain the way philosophy—in every nation—can listen to language and culture?

One of the best ways to start this discussion is to point out, through the Igbo language and voice, what Igbo thinkers are thinking concerning some of the important things in the tradition of thought called philosophy. For example: How do thinkers in the Igbo culture understand the relationship between thinking and language—any language? If Igbo thinkers think that the Igbo language should be respected, what is the reason for this faith?

esi ede makwara etu esi asu asusu ndi ozoo: Yoruba, Hausa, French, Inglish, Jaman, weg. O bu gini mere ndi ji hu asusu Igbo n'anya? N'ezie, iju ajuju di otu a (gbasara asusu Igbo) bu iju ajuju gbasa ndi Igbo na onwe ha. Kedu ndi bu ndi Igbo? Ugbua, gini bu onodu uwa nke ha? Gini ka ndi umunna na umunne obodo Igbo—ma ndi bi n'ulo ma ndi bi n'ezie—na-acho? Kedu udi obianihu ndi Igbo taa choro gbasara oga-n'ihu nke umu na umu-umu ha?

"Filosofi" bu sooso ofu n'ime uzo ririnne nke ndi were anya ji akpa nkata. N'ezie, ime nkowauche nke di otua na-ebido dika nkata uche nke onye na-akpasi onwe ya. Na ngosi, oge obula anyi kwu na mmadu nwere "uche abuo," ihe anyi na-ekwu bu na uche onye a na-akpasi onwe ya nakata. Inwe uche abuo bu etu anyi ji akowa itughari okwu n'ime mmuo. Ya mere anyi nwe ike ikwu na onye okaechiche obula mara oru nke ya, nwere ike inwe "obi" maobu mmuo abua, ato, ino, ise, wegabazia, gbasa ofu ajuju. Ya bogudo n'oge anyi ji kwu na onye a (maobu otutu mmadu) nwe "ofu obi," ihe anyi na-ekwu bu na onye maobu ndi mmadu ahu akpachago nkata, wee site n'ime nkata ahu nwee nkweta gbasara uzo aga eso mee ihe nke a maobu ihe nke ozoo.

Ya mere oji karia mma ikwu na onye a maobu onye nke ozoo, ndi otu mmadu a maobu ndi otu mmadu nke ozoo, *ji* ofu obi (ji ofu mmuo, maobu ji ofu uche) gbasara ihe nke a maobu ihe nke ozoo. Onye a maobu ndi ahu a na-ekwu banyere ha *jikotara* obi ya maobu obi ha. Obi onye ma obu obi nke ndi otu mmadu—tupu akpawa nkata—na-adiri n'iche n'iche. N'ezie, "ikpa nkata" di mkpa nani maka na onwe yi onye na-atu anya na onye obula, ebe obula, ji ofu obi. N'elu nke a kwa, ebe obu na mkpakori abughi udi oru na-agwu agwu—obughi ihe a na-emecha kpakapii—odi nkpa ighota na nke a bu maka na mmuo onye obula na-akpaso onwe ya nkata kwamgbekwamgbe.

Onye obula nwere ako-na-uche nwere ike ijikota n'ofu, otutu obi o nwere gbasara ihe nke a maobu ihe nke ozoo. Ofu mmadu, otutu uche. Ndi okaechiche bu ndi ghotara nnukwu mkpa odi ka omenala na odinala obula nwee ike ikpasi onwe ya nkata kwamgbekwangbe. Onye okaechiche, na mba obula, bu onye ghotara na onye bu *ka* onye na-eche: n'ezie, onye bu ihe onye n'eche. A bu m uche m. A bu m ihe m jikotara n'uche. Abu m ihe uche m jikotara *ka* onwe m. Uche m jikotara n'ime onwe m bu ihe anyi na-akpo inwe ofu obi, iji ofu mmuo na-adi, maobu inwe obi maobu anya di n'ala. Onye jiri asusu Igbo si na ya nwere "nkpuru" obi, ihe onye a na-ekwu bu na ya nwere uche: o na ekwu na ya nwere ike nke mmuo nke eji ejiko echiche ndi nke a maobu echiche ndi nke ozoo dika nke onye. Ya mere m ji kwu na uche bu ihe na ejikota echiche di otutu *na* ofu. Uche bu ihe anyi na-akpo ike nke mmuo nke na-eme njikota echiche nke onye. Oge obula any kwu na onye a ṃaobu izugbe otutu ndi mmadu ji ofu obi, ihe anyi na-ekwu bu na onye ahu maobu ndi ahu jikotagoro uche ya maobu uche ha.

Ofu—*nkpuru*—obi enweghi nkewa, ya bugodu na obi a si n'uche na n'amamihie di iche iche metputa onwe. Njikoka. Ya mere na uche si n'otutu echiche tuputa onwe ya, ka-mgbe obu ofu uche, enwezighi nkewa. Ebe obu na nkpuru obi—ofu obi—ekeji ekeji abuzighi *nkpuru* obi, n'otu aka ahu, uche

Today, many well-educated Igbos know how to speak and write in other languages: Yoruba, Hausa, French, English, German, etc. Why do these individuals love the Igbo language? Indeed, to ask these questions (concerning the Igbo language) is to ask questions concerning the Igbo themselves. Who are the Igbo? At present, what is their situation? What do brothers and sisters of the Igbo—both those at home and those abroad—want? What is the future that today's Igbos want for their children and grandchildren?

"Philosophy" is one of many ways that wise people use to dialogue. Indeed, thinking of this kind is like a dialogue that one engages in with one's self. To illustrate: whenever we say that somebody has "two minds," we are saying the person is having a dialogue with him or herself. Having two minds is our explanation of how we mull or think things over in our minds. That is why we can say that all philosophers who know how to do their job can have two, three, four, five, six "souls" or spirits (or more) concerning a question. Even when we say that one person (or many people) can have "one soul," what we are saying is that the person or the people have had a dialogue, and through the dialogue have arrived at how to do one thing or another.

That is why it is better to say that this or that person, this or that people, *use* one soul (one spirit, or one thought) concerning one thing or another. This person or those people are talking about what *unites* their soul or souls. A person's soul or a group's soul—before dialogue—is always different. Indeed, "to dialogue" is necessary because there is no person who expects that every person in every place has the same soul. On top of this, since discussion is not something that comes to an end—it does not just stop abruptly—it is necessary to understand that each person's spirit dialogues with itself all the time.

Anybody who has common sense can bring together in one all his varied souls concerning one issue or another. Therefore, one person, many minds. Philosophers understand the necessity of each culture and tradition dialoguing with itself every so often. A philosopher, in all countries, is someone who understands that people are as they think. Indeed, a person is as he or she thinks. I am my mind. I am what I unite in my mind. I am what my mind unites as me. The unity of my mind within myself is what we call having one soul, using one spirit to continue to be, or having one's soul or eyes on the ground. When a person uses the Igbo language to say he has a "core" soul, what he is saying is that he has a mind: he is saying that he has a spirit which can unify thoughts as if they are his. That is why I said that the mind is what unifies many ideas. The mind is what we call the strength of the spirit to hold together one's ideas. Whenever we say that a person or group of persons have one soul, we are saying that the person or group has become united in thought.

One soul—a *core* soul—has no division, even if this soul is derived from a variety of thoughts or knowledge. Unity is strength. That is why a thought that emanates from many ideas, since it is of one mind, has no division.

onye echiche, ka-mgbe obu nke onye a, enweghi okike. Na ngosi: obu na m kwuo na enwere m ofu ahu, ihe m ga akowa bu na ahum di ofu. Mana ofu ahum a nwere otutu oke: enwere m aka abuo, ukwu abuo, udi mozuru di iche iche, we gaba. Mana o bu ihe ndi a nile di iche iche, n'ofu, ka m na-akp ahu *m*: ha bu nke m.

O bukwa ezie na adighim iche site na ahum. Ebe obu na adighi m iche na ahum, ya mere m nwe ike iji kwu na ahum bu nke m: obughi nke onye ozoo. N'otu aka nke a, adi m otu etu ahum di otu-na-otutu. N'otu aka nke ozoo, ahum di otutu mana na mmuo nwere ike idi n'ofu. N'otu aka nke a, obi m (mmuo m, weg.) di ofu mana na uche m di otu-na-otutu. N'otu aka nke ozoo, uche m (echiche m, weg.) di otutu mana na mmuo m nwere ike idi ofu. Na mkpemkpe, etu anyi nwere ike ikwu na amara m na ahu m di n'otutu oke sooso maka na enwe m ike idi ka m di: ofu na mmuo, anyi nwekwara ike ikwu na mmuo m bu ihe obu maka na abu m onye nwere uche. Adi m ofu dikwara otutu maka na uche bu mmuo.

IV. USORO MKPAKORI OKWU

Etu o di banyere uche na mmuo, ya ka odi banyere olu na asusu, maobu odinala na omenala. Onye nwere otutu echiche nwekwara ike inwe ofu obi. Anyi nwekwaraike ikowa na odinala bu uzo ndi mmadu nwere otutu uche ma ofu obodo ji ejikota uche ha gbasara ihe omenala di iche iche. Dika etu eji asu n'Igbo na onye a "nwe uche abua" maobu "obi ubuo," ana m akowa na anyi nwekwara ike ikwu na otu onye ahu ji uche (maobu obi) ato, ano, ise, weg. Gini me m ji chee nke a? Ka-anyi neneenu ihe anyi na-eche oge anyi kwuru nkpuru okwu, "uche." Anyi ga-eneneekwa ihe anyi ji n'echiche oge anyi kwuru nkpuru okwu, "obi." Site na nnenee ndi nkpuru okwu ndi a, aga m azaa n'uzo di etu a: (a) uche bu (inwe) echiche, etu iche uche bu iru oru icheputa echiche. (b) A ga m ekwu kwa na echiche di n'otutu. O bu oge anyi jikoro otutu echiche n'uzo kwesiri ekwesi, n'uzo n'ewe anya, na n'uzo n'ewata amamihe gbasara ihe uwa, ka anyi nwere ike ikpo njikota echiche di etu a, "uche."

O bu gini mere na mmadu nwere ike inwe otutu uche? Anyi ga-azaa na nke a bu maka na uche, n'onwe ya, gbasara ihe uwa di n'otutu (n.g., ahu m, uwe m, okwute, ukwu osisi, weg.). N'uzo ozoo kwa, anyi nwe ike ikwu na uche n'onwe ya bu ihe uwa na otu aka ahu eji ekwu na obi onye bu ihe di na mmuo dikwa n'uwa. Ya mere na otutu ihe di "n'uwa" bu ihe anyi ji uche na asusu tuputa gbasa ihe mmuo maobu ihe uwa. Sooso okwu nkowa nke a ga-enye anyi ike igosi etu ihe uwa bukwa ihe ntuputa nke mmuo, ji nweta udi ndimadi ha nwere n'onwe ha, maobu udi onodu ha nwere banyere ihe ndi uwa ndi di n'udi ozoo. Uche bu ihe di n'uwa, mana udi o si diri bu ihe enwere ike ikowa sooso site na ntuputa echiche. Mana enweghi uche nwere ike ituputa onwe ya, na mmuo maobu na okwu, karia site na mmekorita.

Since the core soul—one soul—divided is no longer a *core* soul, the mind of someone who thinks, especially when they are his thoughts, cannot be divided. For example, if I say that I have one body, what I am saying is that my body is unified. However, this body has many different parts: I have two hands, two legs, different muscles, and so on. It is all these different things in one that I am calling *my* body: they are all mine.

It is also true that I am not different from my body. Since I am not different from my body, I am able to say that my body is mine: it does not belong to another person. On the one hand, I am one while my body is one and many. On the other hand, my body is many but my spirit is one. On the one hand, my soul (spirit, etc.) is one although my thoughts are one and many. On the other hand, my thoughts (ideas, etc.) are many although my spirit is one. Simply put, since we could say that I know that my body is of many parts simply because I know how I am, one in spirit, we can also say that my spirit is what it is because I am someone with a mind. Multiple, I am also one, because mind is spirit.

IV. LOGIC OF DIALOGUE

As it is concerning mind and spirit, so it is concerning voice and language, or tradition and culture. The person who has many ideas can also have one soul. We can also say that tradition is the way people who have many thoughts but one nation gather their thoughts concerning different aspects of culture. Just as it is said in Igbo that a person has "two minds" or "two souls," I am explaining that we can also say that the same person could have three minds (or souls), four, five, etc. Why do I think this way? Let us examine what we mean by the word *thought*. We should also examine what we mean when we say the word *soul*. Through the examination of these two words, I will answer this way: (1) thought means (having) ideas, just as thinking means developing ideas; (2) I will also add that ideas are varied. It is when we join many ideas in a proper way, in a way that is clear, and in a way that brings about knowledge concerning the world, that we can say these joining of ideas is "thought."

How does it happen that a person could have various thoughts? We will answer this by saying that thought itself concerns various things in the world (e.g., my body, my clothes, stones, a tree, etc.). On the other hand, if we can say that thought itself is of this world, then in the same way it is said that one's soul is in the spirit as well as in the world. That is why the various things "in the world" are what we use thought and language to pick out, whether spiritual or the worldly. This explanation alone can help us to show how worldly things are also spiritual things. Thought is something in the world; however, the way things are can only be explained by ideas. But thought that cannot explain itself, either within the spirit or through words, except through interaction.

Echiche—ya bugodu echiche nke nkowa okwu anyi na-eme ebe a—si na mmekorita puta: mmekorita uche n'ime mmuo (nkata uche na-akpasi onwe ya); mmekorita mmadu na na ibe ya; na mmekorita mmadu na necho. Kedu ihe mere ka uche, site na mmekorita ndi di etu a, nwee ike ijikota onwe ya n'ofu, n'uzo nke anyi nwegaziri ike ikwu na onye na-eche echiche bu (ofu) onye ji uche; na onye a nwere (ofu) obi; maobu na o bu onye nwere (ofu) mmuo? A choro m ituputa na, n'ezie, ihe anyi na-akpo "mmuo" maobu "obi" enweghi nke n'ime ha nwere ike idi, ma asopu na onye a si na onwere mmuo maobu obi nwekwara ike iche uche. N'etu m si hu ya, n'omenala asusu Igbo, onye a si na mmuo ezughi ya oke (maobu onye mmuo ya na aighi "ala"), bu etu anyi na-akowa onye (anyi chere) na onweghi ike iche echiche n'uzo juru afo. Anyi na-ekwu na onye di otu a bu onye na enweghi uche: o bu onye uche iberibe!

"Onye enweghi uche" bu kwa etu e si akowa onye na-enweghi amamihe. Atumatu okwu ndi ozoo di omimi eji akowa onye na-enweghi amamihe bu ndi a: onye na eweghi anya; onye na enweghi isi oma; na onye isi ngbaka. Etu inwe "isi" bu nkpuru okwu ozoo na-egosi inwe echiche, "mmuo" bu nkpuru okwu eji egosi, n'otu aka, otutu echiche, na n'aka ozoo, oru nke di omimi banyere njikota echiche n'ihe anyi kporo "uche." Ya bugodu gbasara umu natakiri ka anyi ana-ekwu, anyi nwe ike ikwu na onye nke a maobu onye nke ozoo nwere ezigbo uche; na uche di ya n'ala; maobu na onwere isi oma. N'uzo di etu a, anyi na-asi kwa na mmadu nwere obi oma, obi ala (umeala); maobu na anya di ya n'ala. Obi na mmuo (ume); maobu isi na anya: ndia bu ntumatu okwu anyi ji akowa ihe omume mmadu na egosi gbasara ako-na-uche onye ya.

Ya mere na obughi ihe ndaputa maobu ihe di na ndoro-ndoro na ana-eji "ala" kowaa ihe gbasara njikoa nke uche onye obula na ihe ozoo ndi di n'uwa, ma nke a bu ihe uwa di necho maobu ihe di na omenala. Na ngosi, "onye anya di n'ala" bu onye mara etu esi egee ezigbo nti banyere ihe ndi uwa nke gbara onye a ugburugburu; "Onye nwere amamihe" bu kwa onye nwere ewemanya gbasara etu ije ihe ndi uwa si di; "Onye obi oma" bu onye a na-ekwu na onwere ezi mmuo; weg. Ihe ndi ngosi nke a niile mere m ga-emechi nkowa m nuzo di etu a: Asusu Igbo gosiri na uche obula nwe onye tuputara ya; a na-ekwu na onye a maobu onye nke ozoo nwere uche maka na, n'ezie, uche ahu bu nke *ya*. (Maobu nke m, nke gi, nke ha, nke anyi.)

Ya mekwara a na-ekwu n'asusu Igbo: Mmadu bu uche ya; Onye na uche ya yi; Onye bu ihe o bu n'uche. Anyi nwekwa ike ituputa na o bu site na amamihe udi ndi nke a ka, na mba ndi ozoo, eji na-ekwu maka uche nke onye a maobu nke onye ozoo n'asusu na ntumatu okwu nke a na-akpo "intellectual property." Ya bugodu n'oge udi asusu ndi a na-abatabeghi ala ndi Igbo, ndi Igbo nwere odinala di mkpa nke ha na-eji akwado ha mara n o bu onye nwere amamihe. N'ala Igbo, taa ma n'oge gboo, ndi omenka, ndi dibia, ndi okammuta, ndi nkuzi, weg., bu ndi a na-akwanyere ugwu n'otutu uzo di n'iche n'ichie.

Ideas—even if they concern explanation of words as we are doing here—come from interaction: interaction of thought within our spirit (dialogue that the mind has with itself), interaction between a person and fellow human beings, and interaction between a person and nature. How does it happen that thought, through all these interactions, could unite itself into one, in such a way that we could say that the person who is thinking is one person with one mind, that this person has one soul, or one spirit? I want to stress that, in fact, what we call "spirit" or "soul" cannot by itself be, unless we say that the person who has the spirit or soul is capable of thinking. The way I see it, in the Igbo culture and language, the person of whom we say his or her soul is not rested (his or her spirit is not grounded) is someone we are saying cannot think in a meaningful way. We say such a person has no thought: his or her thought is foolish!

"A person without thought" is another way of referring to someone who is lacking in knowledge. Other profound ways of explaining that someone is without knowledge are: a person who has no eyes, a person who does not have a good head, a person who is mad. Just as having a "head" is another word signifying possession of ideas, "spirit," on the other hand, is a word used to signify many thoughts and, at the same time, an understanding of the interaction between ideas and what we call "thought." Even if we are talking about children, we could say that this one or that one has good thought, that his or her thought is grounded, or he or she has a good head. In this way, we also say that a person has a good soul, his or her soul is grounded (i.e., humble), and his or her eyes are grounded. The soul and spirit (breath) or the head and eyes: these are different words we use to explain how a person's behavior shows the person's common sense.

That is why it is not by accident or something disputable that we use "ground" to explain unity between the mind of each person and other things in the world, the world of nature and what obtains in culture. For example, "a person whose eyes are on the ground" is a person who knows how to listen carefully concerning the things of the world around him or her. "A person who has knowledge" is a person who has insight into how the world functions. "A person with a good soul" is a person who is regarded as having a good spirit, etc. All these examples will help me to conclude my observations this way: the Igbo language shows that all thoughts come from someone who has developed them. We say that this or that person has thoughts, because in reality, those are the person's thoughts (or mine, yours, theirs, ours).

That is why it is said in the Igbo language: A person is his or her thought; a person is with his or her thought; a person walks with his or her thought. We can also argue that it is through types of knowledge and knowledge from other places that this or that person's thought becomes what is called "intellectual property." Even when this kind of language had not come to Igboland, the Igbo had an important tradition of identifying who possesses knowledge. In Igboland, at present and in the past, the artists, native doctors, scholars, teachers, etc. were those accorded respect in many different ways.

Ndi mmadu si n'ofu ezi-na-ulo maobu ofu obodo nwere ike inwe otutu uche na otutu mmuo: dika uche na asusu, "obodo" bu ife njiko. Asusu na odinala nke ndi obodo bu ihe na-ejiko obodo ahu, bukwara ihe obodo ji ejiko onwe oge nke oga-n'iru. "Uche" na "mmuo"; "mba" na "obodo"; "mmadu" na "uwa": ihe ndia niile bu oruputa nke uzo njiko na njido. Na ngosi: oge m kwu na onye obula nwere otutu uche maobu mmuo, ihe m bu na uche bu na onye obula nwere ike imuta uzo di iche iche onye a nwere ike ibi ndu ya. Onye uche di n'ala nwere ike imuta asusu mba ozoo; mba nkea nwere ike imuta etu ndi mba ozoo ji ebi ndu, weg. Obu ezie na odinala na omenala obula nwere uzo usoro nke ha, dika etu asusu obula nwere usoro okwu ["gramma"] nke ya, usoro obula bu ihe onye nke a nwere ike ikuzi onye nke ozoo. Ya mere ndi okauche dika Hountondji ji na-ekwu na uche di ndu, dika omenala di ndu, bu nke anya yere oye. Amamihe bu ihe mmepe. Ya bugodu na uzo esi enweta ya tasiri ike, maobu na oge ufodu nsogbu na-esoro ya bata, amaihe nke obula na-eweta mmpepe uche na ewemanya, nwere ike iwetara ndi obodo na ndi uwa ezigbo oganihu.

Ya mere ojiri di mkpa ka onye obula gbaa mbo ituputa amamihe banyere mmepe nke odinala na omenala.[15] A na eji asusu Igbo kwu na odinala di "nso." Ihe eji ekwuru nke a abughi sooso maka maka na odinala a na-ekwu maka ya bu nke ndi Igbo! Ihe eji ekwu bu maka na odinala nke ndi obodo obula bu isi na njikota (a) amamihe izi adi, nke amagoro amago, site n'omenala; na (b) usoro uzo nke di nwe omenala ahu ji ajuju ajuju na na-eme nchomcho gbasara ihe ha na-amabeghi site n'omenala. Ihe anyi kwuru gbasara amamihe di n'obodo tunyekwera n'ikowa uru o naba na ndi mmandu na-enwe "ihunanya obodo" nke ha. Onye obula nwere ike isi na ya nwere omenala maobu obodo sooso oge onye a nwere amamihe gbasara uru omenala maobu obodo aha. Oge obula onye mutara etu obodo si ebi ndu, site n'ime ya ghota omenala, anyi nwe ike ikwu na onye aghota obi nke obodo a. Obu enwemnwe mmuo nke obodo ka anyi na-akpo ihumanya ndi ibe.

Mana onweghi ihe kwuru na nsopuru omenala maobu ihunnaya obodo ga akwusiriri sooso n'obodo nke m. Onye obula nwere ike imezi onweghi ka o buru na onye a bu ezigbo onye Igbo ghotakwara omenala na obodo ndi Yoruba, ndi Hausa, maobu ndi Irish. Odighi ofu uzo onye obula nwere nke iji buru onye ezioma: enwere otutu uzo iji buru ezigbo nwa, ezigbo nee maobu nna; ezigbo onye uka, onye Igbo, maobu onye Naigiria; ezigbo onye Afrika, onye Amerika, maobu onye Japan, weg.; maobu onye nwere ihunaya gbasara uwa dum, na mba obula. Ya mere na ofu onye nwere ike inweta amamihe, we nwekwa ihunanya, gbasara omenala ndi di n'obodo di iche iche. N'otu okwu ahu, enwere otutu uzo onye ji *abu* onye Igbo, nwekwa otutu uzo eji *ama* ndi Igbo.

V. OKWU NA UWA

Anyi nwere ike iji asusu ndi oyibo *one-and-many* kowa ihe omenala Igbo ghotara gbasara amahihe na ihunanya nke ezi na obodo. Onwe ihe omenala

People from one family or nation can have different thoughts and different spirits, just as the thought and language of a "nation" can unify. The language and traditions of a people are what unifies them, and what helps the community to make progress. "Mind" and "spirit," "country" and "nation," "person" and "world": all of these derive from the work of unity and understanding. To illustrate: when I said that each person has many minds or spirits, what I had in mind is that each person can learn many ways of conducting his or her life. The grounded person can learn another language; a country can learn how other countries live life, etc. It is true that each tradition and culture has its own logic, just as each language has its own grammar: these are things that people can teach each other. That is why thinkers such as Hountondji posit that thoughts that are alive and traditions that are alive are like eyes that are open. Knowledge is something to be opened. Even if the way of getting it is hard, or sometimes trouble comes with it, knowledge brings opening of thought and insight and can help bring about the progress of the nation and the whole world.

That is why it is necessary that each person should try to discover how tradition and culture could open up.[15] We say in Igbo that tradition is "sacred." They do not say this simply because the tradition being talked about is Igbo! The reason to say this is that the traditions of all nations are what unify (1) knowledge already possessed through culture, and (2) the logic that owners of a culture use to ask certain questions and do research about things they are not familiar with in a culture. What we have said about the knowledge that resides in a nation is also related to the importance of people having love for their nation. One can say that one has a culture or a nation only when one has knowledge concerning the importance of one's culture or nation. Whenever a person understands how a community lives its life, by understanding its culture, we can say the person has understood the soul of that nation. Having the spirit of the nation is what we call loving our neighbors.

But there is nothing that says that respect for culture or love of nation stops at my nation. One could position oneself to be a good Igbo who also understands the traditions and nations of the Yoruba, the Hausa, or the Irish. There is not only one way for everyone to be a good person: there are many ways of being a good child, a good mother or father; a good churchgoer, Igbo person, or Nigerian; a good African, American, or Japanese, etc., or a person who has love for every country in the world. Therefore, a person could possess knowledge and also love for the traditions of people of different nations. In the same way, there are many ways of *being* an Igbo person and also many ways of *knowing* the Igbo.

V. WORD AND WORLD

We could use the English phrase *one-and-many* to explain how the Igbo culture understands foreign and domestic knowledge and love of nation. If there is

Igbo ga-akuziri ndi omenala obodo ndi ozoo, oga aburiri eziokwu na mmadu niile di iche iche n'uwa bukwa ofu ndi ibe. Ihe tasiri ike bu ime ka mmadu niile ebe obula ghota amamighe nke omimi di n'ime eziokwu a.

Ma ka anyi nwee ndidi kowa eziokwu a site n'ikowa umu nkpuru okwu nke a: uche, mmuo, na amamihe. Nkpuru okwu obula n'ime ndi a na-egosikwa anyi ihe otosiri ighota banyere oru ndi okaechiche n'asusu Igbo. Na ngosi, n'asusu na n'omenala ndi obodo ozoo, otutu ndi okauche n'eche na mmadu obula nwere ofu "nkpuru" obi, ofu mmuo, na ofu uzo eji akowa ihe bu amamihe. Ma n'asusu Igbo, anyi ahugo na enwere ike ikwu na onye nke a maobu onye nke ozoo di otutu uche gbasara ihe nke a maobu ihe nke ozoo di ya mkpa. Anyi na-ekwu na otu ndi mmadu, na injiko, ji otutu uche. (N'otu aka ahu, a na-asi na mmadu nwere ezi uche, uche ojo, uche nzuzu, uche oma, weg.) Ebe obu na ihe anyi na-akpo "uche," "obi," na "mmuo" di sooso na nke onye mmadu nwere echiche, anyi nweziri ike ikwu, n'asusu Igbo, na mmuo onye obula di *otu* na *otutu*. N'enweghi nsogbu obula, anyi nwekwera ike ikwu na omume onye a maobu omume nke onye ozoo n'egosi uche (obi, mmuo, isi, weg.) oma, ojo, nzuzu, iberibe, weg.

Dika etu anyi nwere ike ikwu na enwere m otu ahu di n'oke n'oke, anyi nwekwa ike ikwu na uche (obi, mmuo, isi, weg.) nke ndi mmadu di n'udi di iche iche. Ofu eziokwu a bukwa ihe omimi gbasara ihe anyi na-akpo "amamihe," maka na amamihe di n'iche n'iche na n'udi n'udi. N'ezie, obu gini ka anyi na-akpo amamihe karia inwe ike iji echiche jikota, n'uzo were anya na n'uzo bara uru, nghota si n'iche n'iche bata onye na mmuo? Iwu ikpa nkata n'asusu Igbo—etu anyi si hu n'akuku ndemde anyi a nke gafere agafe—na-egosi na amamihe bu oru njikota okwu n'uche n'uzo n'enye ewe-manya gbasara ihe uwa. Obukwa ngbakoba amamihe di otu a, site na oge gboo na ugbua, ka ndi Igbo na akpo "omenala" nke amamihe. N'asusu Igbo, "filosofi" bu sooso ofu n'ime otutu omenala amamihe di iche iche, nke obula anyi nwere ike ikuzi n'ulo akwukwo maobu site n'ezi n'ulo.

Ajuju ikpazu o kwesili iza bu nkea: kedu ihe bu isi ijiko nke uche (obi, mmuo, omenala, weg.)? Kedu etu anyi ga-esi kowaa, n'uzo zuru ezu, isi okwu njiko nke obula gbasara atumatu: *one-and-many* n'asusu Igbo? Acho m izaa na obu sooso nime asusu ka anyi ga achowa mkpuru [konsept] njiko nke udi okwu ndi a. N'akuku nke ndemde anyi a nke gafere agafe, anyi akpogo konsept njiko a "mmekorita": imeekorita okwu na okwu; uche na uche; mmadu na ibe ya; maobu omenala nke a na omenala nke ozoo. N'elu nkowa nke a, anyi nwekwa ike igosi udi mmekorita di n'etiti uwa na necho. O bu site n'oru uche na oru aka ka onye obula, maobu ndi otu mmadu ndi obula, ji emeputara onwe ha amamihe, omenala, na agam-n'ihu. Dika etu anyi si kwuo: omenala bu uzo ndi mmnadu si ejikota amamihe ike ha, n'uzo amamihe ga abara ha uru, ma kita mana oganihu.

VI. MMECHI

O bu site na njiko okwu na uche ka m nwe ike ikwu na uwa a bu uwa *m*. Okwu-na-uche sokwa n'ihe mere ka m nwe ike ikwu na obodo nke a maobu

anything the Igbo culture could teach other cultures, it is the truth that all people are different but also one. What is required is that all people everywhere understand this profound reality.

But let us be patient enough to explain this truth by discussing these words: mind, spirit, and knowledge. All these words in themselves show us what we should understand concerning the work of Igbo-language philosophers. For example, in the language and culture of people from other nations, many of their philosophers think that each person has one soul, one spirit, and one way of explaining knowledge. But in the Igbo language, we have seen that one person or another could have many minds concerning a certain issue or topic. We say that many people in coming together have many minds. (In the same way, it is said that someone has a right mind, a bad mind, a foolish mind, a good mind, etc). Since what we call "mind," "soul," and "spirit" is only found in a person who has ideas, we could then say, in Igbo language, that the spirit of everyone is one and many. Without difficulty, we could state that the behavior of one person or another demonstrates mind (soul, spirit, brain, etc.), whether good, bad, foolish, stupid, etc.

Just as we can say that I have one body with different parts, we can also say that the mind (soul, spirit, head, etc.) of people is diverse. This truth is the mystery that we call "knowledge" because knowledge comes in different kinds and varieties. Indeed, what do we call knowledge if not the ability to clearly and usefully unite all the different thoughts that come to someone? The law of dialogue in Igbo—as we have seen above—shows that knowledge is the art of bringing together word and thought in a way that clarifies the world. It is the collection of such knowledge both past and present that the Igbo call "cultural" knowledge. In the Igbo language, "philosophy" is only one of many different cultural knowledges, which we can teach either at school or at home.

The last question requiring answer is this: What is at the center of the unity of mind (soul, spirit, culture, etc.)? How can we fully explain the central uniting idea of *one-and-many* in the Igbo language? I want to answer that it is only within language that we can find the concept with which to unite these words. Earlier in this writing, we identified this concept of unity as "interaction": interactions between word and word, thought and thought, person and neighbor, or between this or that culture. On top of this, we could also elucidate the interaction between the world and nature. It is through the thoughts and skills of a person or group that they create for themselves knowledge, culture, and progress. As we have said: culture is the way that people bring together the strength of their knowledge, the knowledge that will be useful to them both now and in the future.

VI. CONCLUSION

It is through the combination of word and thoughts that I can say that this world is *mine*. Word and thought also enable me to say that this nation or

obodo nke ozoo bu obodo nke *m*; maobu na omenala nke a maobu omenala nke ozoo bu omenala *m*. Na mkpemkpe, aga m akpo iwu usoro njiko okwu na uche n'uwa *gramma*. O bu oru diri ndi okaechiche ituputa etu iwu di etua si diri iche n'asusu Igbo, wee yikwara iwu ndi di ka ya n'asusu obodo ndi mba ozoo.

N'ebe a, ka m tuputa na oge onye na-ekwu maka iwu jikoro echiche nke a na echiche nke ozo, anyi ga-akpo ya "uche." Oge anyi na-ekwu banyere iwu njiko uche-na-uwa, anyi ga-akpo ya "okwu." N'ozokwa, okwu-na-uche bu nani ihe mere na asusu mmadu na-asu bu ihe n'enye amamihe na ewemanya. Ya mere onye obula ga-ekweta na obu asusu bu ihe na-ejiko imemmuo na ihe-uwa. Na ngosi, ewepu iwu na-ejiko uche na okwu, kedu etu onye nwere ike ighota ihe ndia: ihu na azu, elu na ala, maobu aka-nri na aka-ekpe; ebe nke a na ebe ozoo; oge nka a na oge ozoo; weg.? O bu iwu okwu-na-uche na usoro asusu di etu a mere amamihe di n'odinala nke ndi Igbo ji akowa na *njikoka*. "Njiko-ka" naani maka na onye na-ekwu nke a aghotago na uche di n'iche n'iche!

Filosofi nwere ike inyere anyi aka ituputa amamihe ndi ozoo si n'omenala na n'asusu ndi Igbo bia. Mana, n'uche nkem, odighi mkpa na onye okauche obula ga-aburiri onye nkuzi. Dika etu ndi Igbo nwere ndi omenka, ndi okamdemde, ndi ukochukwu, ndi okikpe, weg., o tosiri inwe ndi okaechiche nwere ike iru oru ha n'asusu Igbo. Filosofi n'asusu Igbo bu ofu uzo enwe ike iji kowara ndi Igbo ihe gbasara asusu na omenala ndi Igbo, maobu ikowara ndi Igbo ihe banyere asusu na omenala ndi obodo na ndi mba ozoo. Filosofi n'asusu Igbo nwekwa ike ikowara ndi na-aghotaghi asusu a ihe o di ha mkpa imata gbasara asusu na omenala Igbo.

NOTES

1. "Oge Ndi Igbo," Owerri Girls High School Forum, http://www.owerrigirls.net/html/modules.php?file=viewtopic&name=Forums&start=15&t=124. Accessed 2 July 2007.

2. Kwasi Wiredu, *Philosophy and an African Culture*, New York: Cambridge University Press, 1980.

3. Kwasi Wiredu, *Conceptual Decolonization in African Philosophy: Four essays*, Ibadan: Hope Publications, 1995.

4. Paulin J. Hountondji, "Langues africaines et philosophie: l'hypothèse relativiste," na *Les études philosophiques* (1982) n.4, 393-406; "Les langues, la science, le développement," na *Langues africaines et échange des connaissances*, UNESCO: Conseil Interafricain de philosophie, 1983; "Reason and tradition," na Odera Oruka na D.A. Masolo (ed.), *Philosophy and cultures: Proceedings of the 2nd Afro-Asian Philosophy Conference, Nairobi, Oct.-Nov., 1981*, Nairobi, Bookwise Limited, 1983, 137-145; "Recherche théorique africaine et contrat de solidarité," Série de recherchee, 40, Genève: Institut international d'études sociales, 1978; "La culture scientifique dans les pays de la périphérie," na *Culture pour tous et pour tous les temps*, Paris, Presses de l'Unesco, 1984, 65-78; "The Particular and the Universal," na *Bull Soc Fr*

another is *mine,* or that this culture or the other is *mine.* In summary, I will call this law governing the logic of the combination of word and thought in the world *grammar*. It is the task of philosophers to figure out how this law is different in Igbo and how it relates to similar laws in the languages of other nations and countries.

Here, let me point out that when someone is talking about the law that holds together this and that idea, we call it "thought." When we are talking about the law joining thought and the world, we call it "word." Again, word and thought are the only reason that the language spoken by someone is what provides that person with knowledge and awareness. This is why all should agree that it is language that holds together the inner spirit and the things of the world. To illustrate: If we remove the law holding thought and word, how can anyone understand the following: back and front, up and down, or right and left hand, this place or that place, this time or that time, etc.? It is the law of word and thought and the logic of language such as this that made the knowledge within the tradition of the Igbo state that *unity is strength.* "Uniting is better" only because the person who says this understands that there are different thoughts!

Philosophy can help us point out the knowledge that other people can find in Igbo culture and language. However, in my mind, it is not essential that every thinker should be a teacher. Just as the Igbos have artists, writers, priests, judges, etc., they should also have philosophers who can do their work in the Igbo language. Philosophy in the Igbo language is one way through which we could explain and elucidate to the Igbo their language and culture or explain things about the language and culture of other nations and countries to the Igbo. Philosophy in Igbo can also explain to those who do not understand this language what it is that is necessary to understand about the Igbo language and culture.

NOTES

1. "Oge Ndi Igbo," Owerri Girls High School Forum, http://www.owerrigirls.net/html/modules.php?file=viewtopic&name=Forums&start=15&t=124. Accessed July 2, 2007.

2. Kwasi Wiredu, *Philosophy and an African Culture* (New York: Cambridge University Press, 1980).

3. Kwasi Wiredu, *Conceptual Decolonization in African Philosophy: Four Essays* (Ibadan: Hope Publications, 1995).

4. Paulin J. Hountondji, "Langues africaines et philosophie: l'hypothèse relativiste," in *Les études philosophiques* (1982) n.4, 393–406; "Les langues, la science, le développement," in *Langues africaines et échange des connaissances* (UNESCO: Conseil Interafricain de philosophie, 1983); "Reason and Tradition," in *Philosophy and Cultures: Proceedings of the 2nd Afro-Asian Philosophy Conference, Nairobi, Oct.-Nov., 1981,* ed. Odera Oruka and D. A. Masolo (Nairobi: Bookwise Limited,

Phil 81 (1987), 145-189; "L'appropriation collective du savoir: tâches nouvelles pour une politique scientifique," na *Genève-Afrique* 26 (1988): 49-66; "African Cultures and Globalisation: A Call to Resistance," na *Developpement and Cooperation* 6 (1997), 24-26.

5. Paulin J. Hountondji, "Présentation," na *Rationalité: une ou plurielle*, ed. P. J. Hountondji, Dakar: Codesria, 2006, p. 2.

6. Chinua Achebe, *Hopes and Impediments*, New York: Anchor Books, 1990; *Home and Exile*, London: Canongate, 2003; na *Morning Yet on Creation Day*, New York: Anchor Press, 1976.

7. Chinua Achebe, "Echi di ime, taa bu gboo," Odenigbo Lecture, Owerri: Odenigbo House, 4 September, 1999. A version of the lecture is available at http://www.kwenu.com/lectures/achebe_odenigbo99.htm. Accessed 2 July 2007.

8. Achebe, "Echi di ime," pp. 37, 38, na 39.

9. Na ngosi, nenee Achebe, "Echi di ime," p. 40.

10. Ibid.

11. Ibid.

12. Frances Pritchett, "Translator's Introduction" to Chinua Achebe, "Echi di ime, taa bu gboo," http://www.columbia.edu/itc/mealac/pritchett/00fwp/igbo/achebe/transintro.html

13. Nee, na ngosi, Ernest N. Emenyonu, "Achebe and the Problematics of Writing in Indigenous Languages," na *Guardian* (Nigeria), Saturday, December 15, 2001.

14. Achebe, "Echi di ime, Taa bu gboo," p. 40.

15. Nee, na ngosi: Kwame Gyekye, *Tradition and Modernity: Philosophical Reflections on the African Experience*, New York: Oxford University Press, 1997; Gyekye, *An Essay on African Philosophical Thought: The Akan Conceptual Scheme*, Philadelphia: Temple University Press, 1995; Kwasi Wiredu, *Cultural Universals and Particulars: An African Perspective*, Indiana University Press, 1996; Richard H. Bell, *Understanding African Philosophy: A Cross-cultural Approach to Classical and Contemporary Issues*, New York: Routledge, 2002; Paulin J. Hountondji, *Endogenous Knowledge: Research Trails*, Dakar: Codesria Book, 1999; Hountondji, "Tradition: Hindrance or Inspiration?," http://www.quest-journal.net/Q14a.txt, accessed 20 July 2007; weg.

1983), 137–45; "Recherche théorique africaine et contrat de solidarité," Série de recherches, 40 (Genève: Institut international d'études sociales, 1978); "La culture scientifique dans les pays de la périphérie," in *Culture pour tous et pour tous les temps* (Paris, Presses de l'Unesco, 1984), 65–78; "The Particular and the Universal," in *Bull Soc Fr Phil* 81 (1987): 145–89; "L'appropriation collective du savoir: tâches nouvelles pour une politique scientifique," *Genève-Afrique* 26 (1988): 49–66; "African Cultures and Globalisation: A Call to Resistance," *Developpement and Cooperation* 6 (1997), 24–26.

5. Paulin J. Hountondji, "Présentation," in *Rationalité: une ou plurielle*, ed. P. J. Hountondji (Dakar: Codesria, 2006), 2.

6. Chinua Achebe, *Hopes and Impediments* (New York: Anchor Books, 1990); *Home and Exile* (London: Canongate, 2003); *Morning Yet on Creation Day* (New York: Anchor Press, 1976).

7. Chinua Achebe, "Echi di ime, taa bu gboo," Odenigbo Lecture, Owerri: Odenigbo House, 4 September, 1999. A version of the lecture is available at http://www.kwenu.com/lectures/achebe_odenigbo99.htm. Accessed July 2, 2007.

8. Ibid., 37, 38, 39. [I have used the English translation by Frances Pritchett, cited in note 12 below —Ed.]

9. See, for example, Achebe, "Echi di ime," 40.

10. Ibid.

11. Ibid.

12. Frances Pritchett, "Translator's Introduction" to Chinua Achebe, "Echi di ime, taa bu gboo," http://www.columbia.edu/itc/mealac/pritchett/00fwp/igbo/achebe/transintro.html.

13. See, for example, Ernest N. Emenyonu, "Achebe and the Problematics of Writing in Indigenous Languages," in *Guardian* (Nigeria), December 15, 2001.

14. Achebe, "Echi di ime, Taa bu gboo," 40.

15. See, for example: Kwame Gyekye, *Tradition and Modernity: Philosophical Reflections on the African Experience* (New York: Oxford University Press, 1997); Gyekye, *An Essay on African Philosophical Thought: The Akan Conceptual Scheme* (Philadelphia: Temple University Press, 1995;) Kwasi Wiredu, *Cultural Universals and Particulars: An African Perspective* (Bloomington: Indiana University Press, 1996); Richard H. Bell, *Understanding African Philosophy: A Cross-cultural Approach to Classical and Contemporary Issues* (New York: Routledge, 2002); Paulin J. Hountondji, *Endogenous Knowledge: Research Trails* (Dakar: Codesria Book, 1999); Hountondji, "Tradition: Hindrance or Inspiration?," http://www.quest-journal.net/Q14a.txt. Accessed July 20, 2007; etc.

APPENDIX 1

The late Dr. Eze thought it would be useful to include along with his essay the following provisional glossary:

Isi Nkpuru Okwu [Key Words]

Amamihe: knowledge, skill, savvy

Anya: sight, knowledge, "eye"

Anya-odinala: common sense, good sense

Anya-oma: wisdom, (good) judgment

Asusu: language

Echiche: idea, (a piece of) thought

Edemede: writing

Ekwumekwu: discourse

Ewemanya: consciousness, awareness

Ezi: external, foreign

Ezi na obodo: foreign and domestic

Ibiputa: to publish

Idee: to write

Ijiri: to hold (a thought, an idea, or a belief)

Iko ikpe: to plead a case

Ikpebi: to judge; to conclude

Ile-anya: to expect

Imechi (okwu, ndoro-ndoro, nkowa, weg.): to conclude

Isi: mind, brain, "head"

Isi-oma: intelligence; analytical or discerning (mind)

Kpakapii: absolutely

Kpatakpata: with certainty; no exception

Mba: country

Mmuo: spirit

Mmuta: scholarship

Nchekwube: faith

Nchomcho: research

Ndemde: writing profession

Ndiobodo: a people, nation

Ndoro-ndoro: argument

Necho: nature

Nka: art

Nkowa: explanation

Nkpakori (okwu, uka, uche): conversation

Ntumanya: hope

Obi: soul

Obodo: nation, state

Odinala: tradition, custom

Ofu: one

Oka: expertise, profession

Okaechiche: philosopher

Okammuta: scholar

Okandemde: writer

Okwu: speech, word

Okwukwe: belief

Olu: voice, tongue

Omenala: culture

Omenaka: artist

(Onye) Okauche; thinker

Onyeoka: expert, professional

Onyeoru: worker

Oru: work

Ọ́tu: single; singular

Ōtū: united

Uche: thought, mind

Uchiche (iche uche): thinking

Ebumkpemkpe Okwu [Abbreviations]

weg. = wegabazia (*etc.)*

n.g. = na ngosi (*e.g.; for example*)

y.b. = ya bu (*i.e.*)

APPENDIX 2

The late Dr. Eze thought it might interest readers—especially Igbo readers—to hear some of his thoughts on why he wrote in the way he did. I reproduce some of those thoughts, originally expressed in a cover letter accompanying his original essay and in a subsequent e-mail exchange, below:

From Eze's cover letter:

Dear Chike,

I have written without—as some prefer to do—the many pronunciation marks usually placed over Igbo vowels. I am assuming that a translator who can read Igbo half as well as s/he reads English will have no problem with this. For example, in English, "i" can be pronounced as in light, little, Creighton, leisure, etc. in the same way as "o" can be pronounced as in do, dough, tough, round, etc. Igbo vowels have similar variations, all of which should be familiar to a translator with functional knowledge of the language.

Yet, I recognize that philosophy in any language could be quite a technical matter. Where I used non-everyday Igbo words, in addition to making them clear by context, I have also provided their most obvious translations in a glossary.

Currently, I put the glossary under the subtitle "Key Words" . . . But, of course, I do not consider the words "key" in the sense that they cannot be substituted. I have no desire to hinder either the independence or the creativity of any translator.

Speaking about your own point of view as Editor, however, I would like to request that my glossary of terms be published along with the rest of the text. Because of their technical nature, these terms could become, I hope, part of the necessary building blocks in the future work of generating a new shared philosophical vocabulary in the language.

From an e-mail dated August 2, 2007:

I believe that anyone with functional literacy in Igbo does not need the help of accents on written Igbo. Moreover, for those whose mastery of the language is above average, I truly believe that the accents constitute a distraction. (For example, accents help only when a word is written utterly alone, with zero context. However, in a context (of even as little as two other words), the meaning of any Igbo word is almost always completely obvious.)

[Any exceptions to the above observation might be cases where, for the heck of it, a linguist goes out of his or her way just to prove a point. But such artificial and excessive demonstrative effort usually produces sentences that are either meaningless or a hundred percent comical.]

So, for practical reasons, my preference would be to publish my essay without accents. This doesn't rule out compromises about putting accents on some individual words, where necessary. As I see it, writing in this way should be part of the conversations about how to move the language forward.

Papa ne Bɔne

Kwasi Wiredu

Sɛnea yɛn mpanyingfoɔ kaayɛ no, ahotɔ na onipabiara pɛ. Ɛnti, ereyɛ ayɛ sɛɛ yɛbetumi aka sɛ papa ne adeɛ a ɛde ahotɔ brɛ onipa, na bɔne ne adeɛ a ɛde ɔhaw anasɛ yaw brɛ onipa. Nanso ɛto da bi a, adeɛ a ɛde ahotɔ brɛ obi no de ɔhaw na ɛbrɛ ne yɔnko. Afei nso nnyɛ adeɛ a ɛde yaw brɛ nnipa nyinaa na ɛyɛ adeɛ bɔne. Yɛfa nea ɛdi kan no, a yɛbetumi akyerɛmu sei: Obi bɛtumi akowia aban sika kɛse bi de atoto adan ɛne neama pii ma watɛnase ama ne ho atɔ no fɔmm. Nanso ahotɔ a ɛtesaa yɛ adeɛ a yɛbɛfrɛ no ahotɔ bɔne. Ɛna yɛfa asɛm baako no nso a, yɛbetumi ahu se sɛ onipa yare sei a, ebɛtumi aba sɛ yɛbebɔ no paneɛ. Woi yɛ adeɛ a ɛtumi yɛ ya papaapa. Nso yɛtumi hu sɛ, enyɛ ade bɔne.

Saa nsɛm yi ma yɛhu sɛ papa ne bɔne nyɛ onipa baako ho asɛm. Eyɛ amansan asɛm. Sɛ yɛ ka sɛ adeɛ bi a obi ayɛ, anasɛ suban bi a wayi adi akyerɛ yɛn nyɛ a, yɛkyɛrɛ sɛ anka oyɛ onipa a odwen ne yɔnko nipa ho a, anka orenyɛ saa adeɛ no. Sɛ saa na ɛte dea, ɛnde yɛbetumi aka sɛ papa ne adeɛ a ɛtumi de ahotɔ bre nipa okwan bi so a ɛmfa ɔhaw ana yiaw ana abufuo mma nipa foforo biara so.

Ɛmmom obi bɛtumi abisa sɛ, ɛbɛyɛden na bere biara yɛbetumi ahu sɛ adeɛ bi a yɛpɛsɛ yɛ yɛ no yɛ adeɛ a ebɛtumi de ɔhaw anasɛ neama basaa saa aba nkrɔfuɔ so. Eha no adeɛ bi wo ho a ɛsesɛ yɛ de yɛn adwɛne ba so paa. Ɛne sɛ emrɛ pii no, enyɛ ɛneɛma a adeɛ a yayɛ no de ba nkoaa na ekyerɛ sɛ yayɛ adeɛpa anasɛ yayɛ bɔne ana sɛ yɛyɛ nipa bɔne. Bere biara no ɛsesɛ yɛ de nea onipa no *dwen* sɛ ɔpesɛ oyɛ no kɔ adwendwen mu papaapa. Yɛnfa no sɛ opanyiun bi ahu sɛ akwadaa kɛtewa bi reko to amɛna mu. Odimirika reko pagya akwadaa no afi nea ɔwɔ ho, nso oduru ho no a osɔɔ akwadaa no mu pe wapatri de akwadaa no ahwe fom ma neti akɔbɔ ɔboɔ bi so ama wawu. Yei yɛ ahomɛtesɛm kɛse. Nso yɛrenka sɛ owura no adi awu, ɛfisɛ yɛnim sɛ na papa na opɛsɛ ɔyɛ. Eha no yɛrɛnka sɛ adeɛ a oyɛe no yɛ adeɛpa anasɛ adebɔne. Nea yɛbɛka ne sɛ na opɛsɛ ɔyɛ ade pa, na asane na esanee no. Ɛnti seisei de nea yɛbɛka ne sɛ papa yɛ adeɛ a onipa ayɛ na (1) ɛde

Good and Evil

Kwasi Wiredu, *University of South Florida (emeritus)*
Translated by Joseph Osei, *Fayetteville State University*

According to our Akan elders, everyone desires her well-being. For that reason, it might appear that we can say that good is what brings well-being to people and evil what brings trouble or suffering to people. However, sometimes what brings well-being to someone brings trouble to others. Also, not everything that brings suffering to people is evil. Consider the first claim for example: someone can steal a huge amount of state money and make himself contented by buying huge mansions and acquiring luxuries. That kind of contentment will, however, be considered contemptible. If we come to the second point, we can understand why a sick person could be given an injection that might be painful and still agree that the injection or the pain is not evil.

Evidently, determining right and wrong is not a personal issue but a universal problem for all humans. When we criticize a person's behavior, we imply that if he were considerate of others s/he would not have behaved that way. In that case, we can say that good is what brings happiness to a person in a way that does not bring hurt or anger to others.

One might rightly ask how we can ever determine that any action we take will not bring harm or inconvenience to others. This question points to a critical issue in this discourse. Very often it is not only the consequences of our actions that determine whether the action is right or wrong. It is important to consider carefully, in addition, the *intention* of the person who did the action. Take for example the case of an adult who finds a child who has slipped and is about to fall into a pit. This adult rushes to rescue the child but unfortunately the child slips from his grip and crashes his head on a rock and dies instantly. "A great misfortune," we would all say. However, none of us would consider this person a murderer because we know that what he wanted to do was good. Here we would not even debate whether what he did was good or bad. What we would say is that the good he wanted to do was thwarted by an accident. So now, for the time being, what we may say about the good is that it is something done by a human being that (1)

ahotɔ aba na (2) amfa ɔhaw amma obiara so na (3) ɔreyɛno na ɔwɔ anidaso sɛ saa na ɛbɛba.

Sɛ yɛ bisa sɛ ɛdɛn ne bɔne a, yɛbetumi adi kan aka se biribiara a ɛde ɔhaw anasɛ yiaw ana amane ba no yɛ bɔne, gyesɛ ɛyɛ adeɛ a yɛ hyia. Nanso ɛsesɛ yɛ de ka ho sɛ enyɛ bɔne nyinaa na efi onipa nkyɛn. Yɛnfa no sɛ mframa kɛse bi abɔ mpofirim mu abubu adan akum nipa. Saa adeɛ no yɛ asɛm bɔne kɛse. Nso ɛnfiri onipa. Afei nso, sɛ yɛre ka bɔne a efiri nipa nkyɛn ho asɛm a, ɛsesɛ yɛ hunu sɛ eto da bi a adeɛ a ɛyɛ bɔne wo baabi, nnyɛ bɔne wo baabi foforo bi, ɛfisɛ ɛtumi ba sɛ adeɛ a ɛyɛ bɔne wo amaane bi mu nu nyɛ bɔne wo amaane foforo bi mu. Fa no sɛ wo yɛ [O]kanii ba a wote Akan man mu. Enneɛ wunim sɛ te te no na yɛ di ennɔbɔa. Ɛnti sɛ obi wɔhɔ na sɛ nafuo ben wo na obesrɛ wo sɛ bɛboa no mbo ne kookoo a wabɔa ano de akogu faako no a, ense sɛ wo ka kyerɛ no sɛ wunni adaagye ɛnti ɔnkɔ na ɔnkɔ hae nkrofo na wombɛyɛ saa adwuma no. Wo ka saa a, wayɛ no bɔne.

Ɛnso sɛ ɛyɛ aburokyiri tesɛ ebia London sei na Londonni baako, a nadwuma ne sɛ oton loory, koka kyerɛ Londonni foforo bi sɛ omra me boa no ɛfisɛ saa da no adwuma abɔbo no so a, obɛtumi aka akyerɛ no sɛ ɔnkɔpe nkrofoɔ mɛyɛ adwuma no ma no na ontua won ka. Londonfo biara rɛntumi nkakyerɛ no sɛ waka asɛm bɔne anasɛ wayɛ neyɔnko bɔne. Ne nkyerɛmu ne sɛɛ Londonfo amaanneɛ mu no biribi tesɛ enɔbɔa nni mu pii.

Sɛ yɛdwen saa asɛm yi ho a, adeɛ baako a ebɛtumi aba yɛntrimu nesɛ yɛ be bisa sɛ biribi wo wiase yi mu a yɛbetumi aka sɛ ɛyɛ anaasɛ enyɛ wo baabiara ma nipa nyinaa anaa? Saa asɛm yi yɛ asɛm hia pa paa pa ɛnti yɛbe fa mrɛ kakra de ahwehwɛ mu. Nea edi kan no yɛbefa neema a enyɛ. Yɛnfa no see obi wo ho a akunkum akunkum yɛ no de paa. Ɔka asɛm na wokoka bi a, ofa etuo paa na wato abɔ wo aku wo. Oyɔnkoɔ nso de adeɛ a oyɛ a nesɛ, onya abaayaa, akwadaa kɛtewaa a wadi bɛyɛ mfie miensa pe a, na ɔno obarima panyim mu no ate asi ne so pesɛ one no da ama ɛnti wapirapira akwadaa no. Obi nso de, adeɛa oyɛ a ne sɛ owia adeɛ. Sɛ wanhwe yie na wogya wofie pɔno to ho ko baabi na sɛ ohu pe a, ɔbɛkɔ wodan mu ako sesa wo neɛma de adwane. Saa neɛma miensa a mabɔbo so yi nyinaa yɛ neema bɔne wo baabiara.

Onipa biara nni asaase yi so a ope sɛ obi bekum no sɛ waka asɛm na ɔnonso akokabi nti. Ɛna obiara mpɛ sɛ obi be pira nɛba, anasɛ obi bewia ne neama. Enyɛ sɛ yɛmpɛsaa keke. Wodwen ho kakra bi a, wuhu sɛ, sɛ ɛyɛ adeɛ a okwan wo ho sɛ nea wompɛsɛ obi de yɛ wo no, wo bɛtumi de ayɛ obi a, ɛneɛ ɛntumi mma sɛ kuro biara wɔ wiase yi mu a onipa bi ne neyɔnko onipa bɛtumi atna hɔ. Yei titiriw nti na yɛ nananom ka too ho sɛ adeɛ a wompesɛ obi de yɛ wo no ɛmfa nyɛ no.

brings well-being (2) does not bring any trouble to anyone, and (3) was the intended outcome.

If we ask what evil is we can say, to start with, that anything that brings trouble or pain or suffering is an evil, unless it is something needed. To this we should add that not every evil is human-made. For example, when strong winds, such as hurricanes or cyclones, blow, destroying many buildings and killing many people, that is a great evil, but it is not due to humans. We should also notice in discussing evil that what is wrong in some place may not necessarily be wrong in another place because it can happen that what is evil according to certain customs is not evil according to other customs since what makes an action wrong in one place might not necessarily make the same action wrong in a different place. Suppose, for example, that you are an Akan living in Akanland. You would know that mutual aid in farming is an old Akan cultural practice. So if a neighboring farmer should appeal to you to come and help him in, for example, scooping out the beans from the cocoa pods he has heaped up in his farm, you ought not to tell him that you can't spare the time, and that he should go and hire laborers for the service. This would be considered wrong in Akanland.

However, if a car salesman in Europe, say, in London made a similar request for a neighbor's assistance on an overwhelmingly busy day, the person could refuse and ask the dealer to find someone to hire to assist him. No one in London could tell him that he has said or done something wrong to his fellow human being. The reason is that there is not in London culture anything much like the kind of communal mutual aid practiced in Akanland.

Upon further reflection on this matter, it might occur to us to inquire whether there is anything in the world that can be said to be good for everybody everywhere. This is a very critical question and so we will take quite a bit of time to investigate it. Let us begin our inquiry with things that are bad. Imagine a person who enjoys killing people. If he says something and you say the contrary, he takes a gun and shoots you to death. As for another fellow, all he does is that if he gets a little girl, say three years of age, he, a grownup, would descend upon her, raping and injuring her. As for yet another fellow, what he does is go about stealing things. If you are not careful and you leave your door open when going out, he would enter your room and take your belongings and escape with them. All these three things we have mentioned are evils everywhere.

No one on earth would like somebody to kill him just because the latter said something and he dissented. Similarly, no one would like her child to be raped or her property stolen. We don't just say we dislike such actions. Rather, we want to indicate that they are evils. If you think just a little about the foregoing, you will see that if it were permissible to do to others what you don't want them to do to you, then there could not possibly be any place in the world where a human being could live together with another fellow human being. It is principally for this reason that our Akan elders laid it down that you should not do to another person what you would not have him do to you.

Saa adeɛ a yɛreka ho asɛm yi yɛ ewiase yi mu abrabɔ ho mra a ɛdi kan. Mmom, ɛsesɛ me kyerɛkyerɛ mu se, sɛ mefrɛ no mra a menkyerɛ sɛ ɛyɛ mra a yahyɛ ato hɔ. Nea ɛte ne sɛ ɛyɛ mra a onipa biara a otumi dwen kakra biara tumi hu se ɛsesɛ obiara gye tu mu. Saa mra yi sɛ obi bu so a, yɛka sɛ *bɔne* aba nafa mu, wayɛ bɔne. Sɛ onipa bu mra yi so a, enkyerɛ sɛ onnim sɛ ɛsesɛ odi so. Mmrɛ pii no, onipa nim sɛ adeɛ bi yɛ adebɔne, nso obɛyɛ. Ɛfisɛ etodabi a mra no so di yɛden. Yɛmfa no sɛ obi akopie sika kɛse bi a newura were afi ama akoka baabi a sɛ obi fa a obiara renhu. Fa no sɛ sika no yɛ mpem mpem. Nea wakopie so no nso oyɛ adwuma deɛ, nso eto dabi a nɛho timi kyerɛ no kakra. Anokwa sɛm, nipa pii wɔhɔ a sɛ sei na won asetna mu te a, ɛnde wobefa sika no akodi. Ebinom koraa de, sɛ wɔwɔ sika koraa a, wobɛfa akoka nea wo wo no ho. Enyɛ sɛ wonnim sɛ ɛyɛ bɔne sɛ wo befa sika no. Wonim sɛ adeɛ a wompɛsɛ obi de yɛ wo no, ɛnsɛ sɛ wode yɛ obiara. Onipa a oyɛ saa no yɛfre no onipabɔne. Oyɛ onipa a ne suban nyɛ fe. Yɛbe kasa atia ne suban ɛfisɛ, onipa a obɛyɛ saa bɔne yi yɛ onipa a mmrɛ pii no obɛyɛ neema basaa a ɛnfata.

Onipa pa ɛne onipa a sɛ okoto bribi tesɛ sika a yɛre ka ho asɛm yi a, obefa na wabɔ moden ahwehwe ne wura na ode ama no. Wanyɛ bi koraa no, ode asɛm no beto dwa. Oyɛ saa a, wa yɛ ade pa, na sika no wura beda nase papaapa. Afei nso nipa pii be yi no ayɛ aka sɛ oyɛ onipa pa. Yɛ beka sɛ oyɛ onipa pa ɛfisee adeɛ a oyɛe no kyerɛ sɛ odwen ne yɔnko nipa ho. Oka kyerɛ ne ho sɛ, sɛ ɛyɛ ɔno na newerɛ firii ne sika ma ekaa baabi saa a, anka obepe sɛ nea obɛkopie so no de bɛ brɛ no. Yei kyerɛ sɛ mra a yɛkaa ho asɛm no ayɛ adwuma wo onipa no adwen so.

Sɛ nipa nyinaa te saa a, anka ɛyɛ papaapa. Nanso, sɛnea yaka no, nipa pii wo ho a worenyɛ saa. Ebinom koraa de sɛ wofa saa sika no a, won tiboa mpo renhaw won. Wotumi kakyerɛ won ho sɛ "Obi de yɛ me a, mempɛ. Ɛnti den?" Sɛ onipa adwen te sei a, yɛnka sɛ oyɛ onipa bɔne; nea yɛka ne sɛ nadwen nyɛ, edam bi na erebo no. Yɛ ti yɛ sɛ nnipa a wɔte saa nnɔɔso pii wɔ wiase yi mu. Ɛfisɛ sɛ wɔ dɔɔso a anka ewiase ha asetra bɛyɛ den papaapa; ɛnokware, anka ebɛyɛ den abroso. Ebi koraa anka erenyɛyie mpo. Whae na ne ho bɛtumi ato no, sɛ nnipa a one won te kuro baako mu no emu pii nyano a wobefa ne neɛma anasɛ wo beku no koraa mopo? Yɛ nfa no sɛ mpanyin fo a wɔwɔ ho no asɛm a wobeka ara ne se nea onipa pe na oyɛ.

What we are talking about here is the First Law of human conduct. I ought to explain, though, that by calling it a law, I do not mean that it is something that has been legislated. But the point is that it is a kind of law that anybody who can reflect a little can recognize to be valid for everybody. If anyone violates this law, we say evil has entered his behavior; he has done wrong. If someone violates the law, it does not mean that he does not know that he ought to obey it. Very often a person knows something to be bad, and yet he will do it. The reason is that sometimes it is difficult to obey the law. Imagine that someone has come upon a large sum of money, which the owner has forgetfully left in a place where anybody can take it without being noticed. Let's say that the money amounts to a million dollars and that, although the discoverer is not unemployed, his finances are sometimes quite tight. In truth, there are lots of people, who, if their finances are like this, will take the money for their own use. Indeed, as for some people, even though they are wealthy, they will still take the money to maximize their wealth. It is not that they do not know that it is wrong for them to take the money. They know that you ought not to do to anyone what you would not want him to do to you. One who does the contrary is called a bad person. He would be said to be a person who has no beauty of character. We would deplore his character because usually anyone who breaks the First Law has the habit of doing things that are not befitting of a virtuous person.

A good person is one who, coming upon something like the money we are talking about, will try his best to find the owner and return it to him. At the very least, he would make the matter public. If he does so, he has done something good, and the owner of the money will thank him very much. Also, many people will praise him, calling him a good person. We would say he is good because what he did showed that he had concerns for the interests of his fellow human beings. He told himself that if it was he himself that had left his money in a place like that in forgetfulness, he would have liked the one who came across it to return it to him.

It would be good, indeed, if everybody was like that. But, as we have noted, there are many people who won't do that. There, in fact, are some who would take the money without any problem of conscience. They are able to say to themselves, "If somebody does the same to me, I won't like it. So what?" If someone thinks like this, we don't say he is a bad person. What we say is that there is something wrong with his mind; it is caught up in some kind of insanity. We are lucky that there are not too many people like that in the world. This is because, if there were a great lot of them, life in this world would be difficult; indeed, it would be too difficult. It probably would not be feasible. Who could possibly have any sense of well-being, if many of the people with whom he lives in the same community would make off with his belongings or even kill him, if they had the opportunity? Let us suppose that all that the elders of the community would say is that people can do what they want.

Nea edi kan no, ɛyɛ madwen sɛ nea ɛnti a bribi a ɛte saa nni ho ne see onipa biara wo ahumɔbrɔ kakra wɔ ne koma mu. Ɛyɛ adeɛ a yɛde woo yɛn. Enyɛ adeɛ a edɔɔso pii wo yɛn nyinaa mu, ɛnso ɛyɛ adeɛ a ɛtumi ma nipa pii hu sɛ adeɛ a wompesɛ obi de yɛ wo no ensɛsɛ wode yɛ obi. Ɛto da bi a neɛma neɛma bi tumi ka saa ahumɔbrɔ no hyɛ ma onipa tumi yɛ bɔne. Nanso esane sɛ saa adeɛ no wɔhɔ kakra no nti mrɛ pii no onipa a wayɛ bɔne no tumi hu sɛ wayɛ bɔne. Ɛna nea onyɛɛ bɔne nso tumi hu sɛ papa yɛ. Enyɛ saa nkoaa; otumi yɛ papa nso.

Nea eto so mienu ne sɛɛ: mrɛ pii no sɛ onipa benya ahotɔ gyina sɛ ahotɔ bɛba oman mu. Sɛ asumdwee nni oman mu a, asumdwee nni ho mma onipa baako biara. Ɛyɛ nokware sɛ wofa nipa maako maako a, mrɛ pii no esɔno nea obiara pɛ, anasɛ ohia. Nso wodwen ho kakra a wuhu sɛ yɛ nyinaa hia se asomdwee ne ahotɔ bɛba oman mu. Ɛnti sɛ yɛredwen papa ne bɔne ho a, ɛsesɛ ye hwehwɛ mu ma yɛhu sɛnea saa neama mienu yi tumi hyia. Eduru ɛha a na yɛ hu asɛm a yɛfrɛɛ no ɔbra mu mra a edi kan no ho mfaso. Saa mra no na ema yɛtumi whewhɛ mu hu sɛ adeɛ a obi pɛsɛ ɔyɛ, anaasɛ wayɛ dada no, odii kan susu whɛɛyɛ se nahotɔ ne amansan ahotɔ hyia anaa.

Saa neama mienu a yɛreka ho asɛm yi yɛ neɛma a yɛn nananom huu no pefee. Na okwan baako a wofaa so de kaa asɛm no too ho nesɛ, anyansafo, a wotumi de neama tesɛ dua anasɛ dote di adwini, de wonsa yɛɛ adɛnkyɛm mienu a won yafunu yɛ baako na won ti yɛ mienu, na worekọ aduan ho. Esane sɛ wɔwɔ eti mienu no nti won ano ne won tekrema nso yɛ mienu mienu. Wo dwen ho saa a, wo be te aseɛ sɛ won mienu no obiara bɛ pɛ sɛ obenya aduane a ɛwo ho no bi awesa wo nanum ansa na ako ne yafunu mu. Emfa ho sɛ won yafunu yɛ baako; ɛsɛsɛ won mienu nyinaa nya aduane no bi di fa won tekrema so. Eyi yɛ adeɛ a sɛ ɛwɔ won adwen mu sɛ aduane no beko yafunu baako mu a ebema won atumi de ntoboaseɛ ahyɛhyɛ sɛnea wobekyɛ aduane no. Wo yɛ saa a, ntokwa biara remma. Eha no yɛtumi hu sɛ etiri mienu no gyina ho ma nipa baako baako, ɛna yafunu baako no nso gyina ho ma amanfo nyinaa.

Ɛnso eto dabi a saa asɛm yi a ekyerɛ sɛ yɛnyinaa yafunu yɛ baako no timi fi yɛn adwen mu. Nea emano ba saa nesɛ, ɛneema a ehia yɛn wo yɛn whenano no tumi so yɛn adwene mu dendeedɛn wo okwan bi so a emma yɛn ndwen dwen neɛma ho nkɔ akyiri nhu sɛ yɛne amanfoo nyinaa wo yafunu baako. Ɛba saa a na akoyɛse nea onipa no were afiri Ɛmmra Kɛse no, anasɛ yɛnka no sɛ emra no ntimi nyɛ adwumah papa wo onipa no adwen so. Onipa adwen yɛ saa a, opɛsɛ ofa neema a edɔɔso kyɛn nea nteaseɛ wo mu sɛ obɛtumi afa. Asɛm a ɛte sei tumi de akasakasa anasɛ ntokwa ba, ɛfisɛ nipa pii wo ho a worempeneso mma obi mfa nea edooso kyɛn nea okwan wɔhɔ sɛ ɔmfa.

First, it seems to me that the reason why we don't have such a situation is that human beings have some measure of compassion in their hearts. We are born with it. It is not abundant in all of us, but it is enough to enable many people to recognize that we ought not to do to others what we would not like them to do to us. Sometimes certain circumstances can extinguish the compassion and facilitate wrongdoing. Yet, because there is a certain measure of it in us, a person who has done wrong is frequently able to understand that he has done wrong, and he who has not done wrong is able to appreciate that goodness is good.* That is not all; he may actually do the good.

Second, the well-being of an individual generally depends on the well-being of the community. If the community has no peace, the individual has no peace. It is true that if you take people one by one, you will often find that what any individual wants is different from what others want or need. Yet, if you reflect a little on the matter, you will find that we all need peace and well-being in the community. Therefore, when thinking about good and evil, we ought to investigate how these two things (individual and community interests) can be harmonized. It is here that we find the importance of what we have called the First Law of conduct. It is this law that enables us to check regarding something that somebody is planning to do or has already done whether he first considered whether his interests were consistent with the interests of the community.

Our ancestors saw clearly the two things we have just spoken about. And one way in which they expressed their thinking on the matter was this. Some among the wise who had the talent for symbolizing ideas in such media as wood or clay constructed an art motif showing two crocodiles with one stomach and two heads fighting over food. Because they had two heads, they had two mouths and two tongues. If you bear this in mind, you would understand why each of them would like to have some of the available food to chew in his mouth before it goes down into the stomach. It does not matter that they have one stomach; each of them ought to have some of the food to eat on his own tongue. Still, if they take cognizance of the fact that the food will go into one common stomach, it would encourage them to be patient and come to an agreement as to how the food is to be shared. If they do so, there will be no fighting. Here, then, we can see that the two heads stand for individuals considered one by one, and the stomach for the community taken as a whole.

However, sometimes the thought that we all have the same stomach can disappear from the mind. What brings this about is that sometimes our immediate desires can seize our minds so forcefully that we are unable to think deeply enough to recognize that we all have one stomach. When that happens it is as if the person has forgotten the First Law of human conduct. Or let us put it in this way: that law is no longer able to work effectively on his mind. In that state of mind a person will try to take more than his fair share. This kind of thing is apt to cause quarrels or even fighting, since there are a lot of people who cannot accept that anybody can take more than his fair share (of common assets).

Sɛ yɛre dwen ɔbra papa ne ɔbra bɔne anaasɛ suban papa ne suban bɔne ho a, Ɛmmra Kɛse no tumi boa yɛn papaapa. Ɛfisɛ, ɛno ka ho bi na yɛtumi bu atɛn sɛ ɔbra bi anaasɛ suban bi yɛ anaasɛ enyɛ. Nanso enyɛ saa mmra no nkoaa na yɛhia. Ɛyɛ nokware sɛ adeɛ biara a etia Ɛmmra Kɛse no yɛ bɔne, nanso sɛ biribi ntia no a enkyerɛ sɛ ɛyɛ adeɛ papa.

Mɛde asɛm bi bekyerɛkyerɛ nea mere ka yi mu. Ewiase yi mu no mmeae, mmeae bi wɔ ho a ɔbaa tumi ware mmarima mienu anaaso nea ekyɛn saa. Yɛmfa no sɛ wako baabi a ɛtesaa ne nipa a wɔwɔ ho no bi redi nkomɔ. Nnipa no baako yɛ obarima a one ɔbaa a one obarima baako wo aware mu dada rebeware. Wo bisaa no sɛ "Ɛnti sɛ ɛyɛ wo na wone ɔbaa wo aware mu na obarima bi nso ne no rebeware aka wo ho a anka ebɛyɛ wo de ana?" Na mmuae a ode maa wo ne sɛ "Aane." Saa na ɛte dea, ommuu Ɛmmra Kɛse no so; ɛnso ɛnkyerɛ sɛ awaree a ɛtesaa yɛ ade papa. Ɛbɛtumi aba sɛ enyɛ wo baabi, nso ɛyɛ wo baa bi. Ebia baabi wɔhɔ a kyee, kyee wo saa aware no mu dodo, ɛnti enyɛ. Na ebia baabi nso de ɛyɛ papaapa, ɛfisɛ ɛho no onipa asetra mu hia sɛ ɔbaa baako benya mmarima dodow kakra wo ne ho. Akwantufo a wɔnom ako baabi a saa aware suo yi kɔɔso tete mmrɛ mu anaaso edaso koso ennemrɛ mu ka saa nsɛm yi. Na yɛ dwen ho a yɛbetumi ahu sɛ ebɛtumi aba saa.

Nea ɛnti a mɛde biribi te sɛ aware suo a yɛreka ho asɛm yi baa ɛneama a yɛredwen ho no mu nesɛ, ema yɛ hu sɛ neama a nipa yɛ no, ebi wɔhɔ a sɛ ɛyɛ papa anasɛ ɛyɛ bɔne gyina sɛ edi anasɛ enni Ɛmmra Kɛse no so; ɛna neama bi nso wɔhɔ a ɛnte saa. Nea ente saa no ne papa anaa ne bɔne gyina sɛ ɛbɛtumi ana so ɛntumi nfa ahotɔ ɛmma. Sɛ bribi bɛtumi de ahotɔ aba a ɛnso eremmu Ɛmmra Kɛse no so a, enne ekyerɛ sɛ ɛyɛ adeɛpa. Saa asɛm yi erɛyɛ ayɛsɛ asɛm bi a Enyiresi ni bi a na wofrɛ no John Stuart Mill (1806-1873) kaayɛ. Nanso Mill no na sɛ oreka nasɛm no ntia ntia mu a na onnfa Ɛmmra Kɛse no mma mu. Eye a oka bribi te sɛ: Adeɛ a ɛyɛ adeɛ pa ne adeɛ a ɛde ahotɔ ba. Ahomɛtesɛm no nesɛ, sɛ wamfa Ɛmmra Kɛse no amma mu a, asɛm no nsi pi. Migyidi sɛ na Mill nim se ɛsesɛ Ɛmmra Kɛse no ba mu, nanso enyɛ me sɛ ohuu pefee baabi a ɛsesɛ ode hyɛ.

Madwen ne sɛ saa nsɛm a mereka ɛdefa papa ne bɔne ho yi ɛne yɛn nana nom adwen nam okwan baako so. Ɛnso sɛ obi nim sɛ w[o]akan Mill nhoma a okyerɛw de faa papa ne bɔne ho na ohu sɛ woreka sɛ ahotɔ ho asɛm hia papaapa ansa na onipa ate papa ne bɔne nkyerɛkyiremu ase a, na ɛyɛno sɛ saa adeɛ yi wonya fii Mill ho. Ɛnte saa. Afei nso adeɛ a yɛfre no ahotɔ no sɛ me ka sɛ merekyerɛ kyerɛ mu sɛnea medwen sɛɛ te wo ha a, masɛm be ware. Nea mɛka ara ne sɛ madwen ne Mill adwen nnhyia wo neama no nyinaa ho.

When thinking about good and bad conduct or about good and bad character the First Law helps a lot, because it does play a role in our ability to determine whether an act or show of character is or is not good. Nevertheless, that law is not the only instrument we need. It is true that anything that goes contrary to it is wrong, but if something does not go contrary to it, it does not mean that it is good.

I will illustrate what I am saying with an example. There are some places in this world where a woman can marry two men or more. Let us take it that you are visiting a place like that and are having conversations with some indigenes. One of them is a man who is going to marry a woman already married to another man. You ask him, "So if you were married to a woman and another man is also going to marry her in addition to you, would you think it is all right?" And his reply is "Yes." In that case he has not violated the First Law. But that does not show that a marriage of this kind is a good thing. It may be that is good in some places but not in others. It may be that there are places where a marriage of this sort creates too much friction. But there also may be places where it is quite a good arrangement because local living conditions make it necessary for a woman to have more than one man around her. Travelers who have been to where this kind of marriage went on in olden days and still goes on today testify to this.

The reason why I brought a reference to something such as the marriage system just mentioned into the discussion is that it enables us to see that of the things that human beings do there are some whose goodness or badness depends on whether or not they conform to the First Law and others that are not like that. Goodness or badness in the latter case depends on whether or not the action in question will maximize human well-being. If something can bring well-being without breaking the First Law, then it is a good thing. This formulation sounds somewhat like a view that was put forward by an Englishman called John Stuart Mill (1806–1873). However, whenever Mill was engaged in providing brief statements of his position, he tended not to include the First Law. He habitually said something to the effect that an action is good if it maximizes human well-being. The lamentable thing is that if you don't bring in the First Law, then your theory cannot stand. I do believe that Mill understood that the First Law was needed, but he does not seem to have found where best to invoke it.

I think that what I have been saying about good and evil conforms to the thought of our ancestors. Yet, if somebody knows that you have read what Mill said about good and evil, then when you say something such as that understanding the importance of the idea of human well-being is necessary for understanding good and evil, he thinks that you it got it from Mill. That is not the case. If I were to try to explain my conception of human well-being here, I might become prolix, but I should mention that I do not agree with Mill on all the issues involved.

Seisei de mepɛsɛ yɛ hu nkyɛkyɛ mu bi. (1) Ɛnesɛ, neama a Ɛmmra Kɛse no nkoaa tumi kyerɛ sɛ ɛyɛ anasɛ enyɛ no yɛ neama a ɛte saa wo wiase nyinaa. Neama tesɛ nokwaredi, ne ahumɔbɔro yɛ neama a Ɛmmra Kɛse no kyerɛ yɛn wo ewiase yi mu baabiara sɛ ɛyɛ. Ɛkyɛrɛ yɛn soso sɛ neama te sɛ nkontompo, adwamanmo, kɔnkɔnsa, anibre, ahooyaw, pɛsɛmankomenya, atrimuɔden beberebe, krɔnobɔ, ensisie, ɛne neama a ekeka ho yɛ neama a enyɛ. Na yɛtumi hu sɛ ɛnyɛ wo baabiara.

(2) Sɛnea yahu dedaw no, neama pii wo ho a nnipa yɛ a yɛrentumi ngyina Ɛmmra Kɛse no nkoara so nka sɛ ɛyɛ anaa enyɛ. Yɛ betumi akyerɛkyerɛ mu sei: Yɛnfa nnɔboa. Tete no na nnɔbɔa yɛ asɛmhia papaapa wo Akan mae mu. Nanso, sɛnea yahu dadaw no, sɛ woko baabi tesɛ London na wo ko ka kyerɛ obi a ote ben wo sɛ omɛyɛ nnɔbɔa adwuma ma wo na sɛ oka sɛ daabi a, yɛrentumi nka sɛ wabu Ɛmmra Kɛse no so. Sɛ yɛbisa no sɛ, sɛ obisa obi saa mmoa yi bi na ɔno nso ka daabi a obe ka sɛ ɛyɛ ana a, obɛtumi Aka sɛ aane.

Nea yɛ hu wo ha ne sɛ, Mmra Kɛse no nkoara ntumi nkyerɛ yɛn sɛ nnɔbɔa yɛ anaasɛ enyɛ adeɛpa. Ɛgyina ho ma baabi ne bere a yɛre whehwe asɛm no mu no. Sɛ wo fa Akanfo man mu a wuhu pefee sɛ nnɔbɔa yɛ adeɛpa, ɛfisɛ na ɛboa akuafo ma wotumi yɛ won adwuma kama, ma wonya ahotɔ fi adwumah no mu. Wo ko baabi te sɛ London a wu hu sɛ biribi tesɛ nnɔbɔa nyɛ adeɛ a sɛ wɔɔnom anyɛ a ɛbɛha won pii biara. Sɛ wofa mmrɛ nso a, wu hu see ɛtumi sesa sɛnea yɛhu nneama tesɛ nnɔbɔa. Seisei sɛ woko Akan man mu a wobehu sɛ nnoboa nni ho tesɛ kanee tete no. Edaso wo ho, nanso ento sɛnea na ɛte tete bere no.

(3) "Ɛmmra" ne nsusue a yɛgyina so de hwe sɛ onipa suban anaa nabrabɔ yɛ anasɛ enyɛ no nea efa neama tesɛ nnɔbɔa ho no yɛfre no *amanne*. Nea yahu nesɛ sɛ ɛyɛ anaa enyɛ no tumi sesa. Ntease womu sɛ ebɛyɛ saa, ɛfisɛ adeɛ a ɛtumi de ahotɔ ba ɛnnɛ no bɛtumi de ɔhaw aba ɔkyɛna; ɛna adeɛ a *ɛyɛ* ma yɛn wo yɛn kurom bɛtumi de yiaw abre obi wo nekro mu. (Emmom saa nsɛm yi sɛ yɛreka a, ɛsesɛ yɛkae sɛ neama a Ɛmmra Kɛse no nkoara tumi ma yɛhu sɛ ɛyɛ anasɛ enyɛ no nka ho). Amanne yɛ adeɛ a ɛno na ema yɛhu nsonee a ewo sɛnea nnipa a wofiri mmeae mmeae wo wiase ha no yɛ won neama.

(4) Adeɛ bi wɔhɔ a ɛsɛsɛ yɛdeka neama a yaka ho asɛm wɔ saa nkɔmɔ a yɛredi yi mu. Ɛne adeɛ a yɛ nananom frɛ no *musuo*. Akanfo ka se musuo yɛ ade bɔne bi a nananom asamanfo tia papaapa. Ɛyɛ adeɛ a sɛ obi yɛ a won bo fu ma wode asotwe to saa onipa no ne nabusuafo so. Saa adeɛ no ebi ne awudi, anasɛ sɛ obi bewia adeɛ a ɛyɛ asamanfo dea anasɛ sɛ obi didi ohehe atem (wo petee mu), ana sɛ, sɛbe, one ohɛne yɛre be da. Sɛ obi yɛ adeɛ a ɛte sei bi a, gyese se otwa dwan na ode nsa ko ma mpanyinfo de gu fom ansa na nananom nsamanfo bo adwo.

For now I want to emphasize or reemphasize the following points, which are in part elucidatory restatements of earlier findings: First, the things that are determinable as good or as bad on the basis of the First Law alone are of that character everywhere in the world. Things such as truthfulness and compassion are things that the First Law teaches us to be good everywhere. It teaches us also that things such as lies, debauchery, false witness, resentfulness, envy, selfishness, wickedness, cheating, and stealing are intrinsically bad. And we can see that they are bad everywhere.

Second, as already noted, there are many human actions that cannot be said to be good on grounds of the First Law alone. We can explain this in this way. Let us take mutual aid in farming. In the past, this was very important in Akan life. But, as we saw early on, if in a place like London you ask a neighbor to render you some mutual aid service, and he declines, you cannot say he broke the First Law. If we ask him whether he would think it all right if he himself made a request for this same kind of help and was rebuffed, he could say yes.

What we see illustrated again here is that the First Law alone cannot tell us whether mutual aid in farming is good or not. It depends on where and when the investigation is made. If we take the question in the context of Akan life, mutual aid was a good system because it helped the Akan farmers to do their work well and to get a sense of well-being from it. If you go to a place like London, you see that it does not bother them too much not to have something like the Akan practice. If you take the time dimension, you realize that it can change the way we view things such as the practice of mutual aid. Right now, if you go to Akanland, you will see that the practice is not as animated as it was in the distant past.

Third, of the "laws" and principles on the basis of which we evaluate character or conduct, those that involve cultural practices, such as mutual aid practices, are called *customs*. What we have just seen is that whether they are good or bad can change with time. This is understandable, because what can bring well-being today can bring suffering tomorrow, and what is good for us in our community can bring trouble for somebody in his community. (We should remember, though, that those things that the First Law is alone able to determine to be good or bad are not included.) Custom is what enables us to see the diversity of the ways in which people from various parts of the world conduct their lives.

Fourth, there is something that we need to add to the topics we have touched upon in this conversation. It is what our ancestors called *musuo*. The Akan say that *musuo* is an evil much detested by the ancestors. It is something that, if done, upsets them very seriously and causes them to punish the culprit and his relatives. Some instances of it are murder, stealing things that belong to the ancestors, insulting the ruler in public or, worse, seducing his wife. If somebody does something of this sort, he will have to sacrifice a sheep and offer drinks to the elders for libation before the ancestors can be pacified.

Ɛsane sɛ nananom nsamanfo ho ba asɛm no mu no nti, nipa bi ka sɛ saa neama a yabobɔ so yi yɛbetumi afrɛ won *taboo* wo abrofo kasa mu. Ɛnso yɛ ka no saa a, enyɛ yie, ɛfisɛ *taboo* yɛ adeɛ a sɛ wo bisa sɛ edɛnti na onipa yɛ a enyɛ a, mmuae a ebɛtumi aba ara ne sɛ asaman fo no mpɛ saa adeɛ no. Yei kyerɛ se sɛ yɛ bisa sɛ ɛdɛnti na asamanfo no mpe saa adeɛ no a, asɛm *foforo* biara nni ho a obi bɛtumi aka akyerɛ yɛn. Nea obɛtumi aka ara ne sɛ pɛ ara na asmanfo no mpɛ adeɛ no. Saa na ɛte dea, ende neama a yɛbobɔɔ so te sɛ awudi anasɛ obi rekowia asamanfo adeɛ no rɛntumi nyɛ tabɔo. Sɛ wobisa Okaniiba sɛ ɛdɛn nti na ensɛsɛ onipa biara sore na oko te si obi so di na wuo a, obekyerɛ wo sɛ obiara nni ho a obɛpɛ sɛ obi bekum no saa. Ɛnti no sɛ wompe sɛ obi de saa yɛ wo dea wo nso okwan nni hɔ sɛ wode saa bɛyɛ obi. Ekyerɛ sɛ Ɛmmra Kɛse no na ɔde bebua wo. Wofa neama a yɛ boo din sɛ nkrɔfoɔ bi ka sɛ ɛyɛ *taboo* no na wodwen ho sɛnea yahu yia, wo be hu sɛɛ, emubiara nyɛ *taboo.* Enyɛ nea obi pe na ekyerɛ adepa; ɛyɛ nea ɛsɛsɛ obiare pe. Saa asɛm yi gyina ho pintiin ma obiara.

Afai yɛnsan nko musuo so. Yɛtumi hu sɛ ansa na yɛ bɛtumi afrɛ bribi musuo no ɛsesɛ adeɛ no yɛ adeɛ bɔne. Na sɛ yɛpɛsɛ yɛhu sɛ ɛyɛ adeɛ bɔne a, yɛ be hwe sɛ Ɛmmra Kɛse no nkoara tumi kyerɛ yɛn saa anaasɛ ɛsesɛ yɛde amanne ba mu. Yɛyɛ woi ho adwuma wie a, na afei yɛ be hwehwe mu sɛ yɛnananom asamanfo wɔ adeɛkese bi tia adeɛ no. Sɛ yɛhu sɛ ɛtesa a na yɛbetumi aka sɛ adeɛ no yɛ musuo. Woi kyerɛ pefee sɛ musuo a yaka ho asɛm yi de enyɛ *taboo.*

Ɛneɛ obi bɛtumi abisa yɛn sɛ *taboo* wɔ Akanfo abrabɔ mu anaasɛ ɛbi nni mu koraa. Sɛ wo hwɛ neɛma bi a ema no yɛsɛ yɛ wo *taboos*. Musuo baako ne sɛ obarima de ne ho be ka ɔbaa wo wira mu. Sɛ wo bisa sɛ adɛnti na saa adeɛ no yɛ bɔne a, nea yɛbɛka akyerɛ wo ne see ɛyɛ adeɛ a Asaase Yaa mpɛ. Saa nti sɛ obi yɛ saa a, Asaase Yaa, a oyɛ asaase hemaa, be ma aduane kom aba wɔ onipa a oyɛɛ saa no ne nabusuafo afuo mu. Wo hwe a na ereyɛ ayɛ sɛ nea ɛnti a adeɛ no yɛ bɔne ara ne sɛɛ Asaase Yaa mpe saa. Yei kyerɛ sɛ nkyɛrase biara nni ho. Saa de a, na erɛyɛ ayɛsɛ ɛsɛsɛ yɛ gye tumu sɛ nea yɛre ka ho asɛm yi yɛ *taboo* wo Akanfo abrabɔ mu.

Ɛyɛ madwen sɛ ente saa. Migyedi sɛɛ yɛn mpanyinfo no hyɛɛ ɛmmra no too ho sɛnea ebɛyɛ a mmarima a won adwɛne mu nnɔ mfa won ahoɔden enkɔ haw mmaa a ebia biribi nti aka wɔnkoaa wo ewira mu. Mmarima a wote saa no sɛ woka sɛ wore kyerɛkyerɛ won nea ɛnti a ensɛsɛ wɔkɔ e te si mmaa so saa a worɛnte ase; ɛnso se wo huna huna won sɛɛ, sɛ woyɛ saa a Asaase Yaa bɛma ekɔm aba a, ɛbema wɔn asuro sɛ wɔbɛyɛ saa. Mmarima a won adwen mu dɔ de, wonim sɛ ɛmmra no yaanyɛ ama wɔn, ɛfisɛ wonhia.

Because the departed spirits of our ancestors are taken to be involved in the idea of *musuo,* some have suggested that we can call it "taboo" in English. But that usage won't do at all, because a taboo in this context is something such that if you ask why it is bad the only kind of reason you can be given is that the ancestors don't like it. This means that if we ask why the ancestors don't like it there is no reason that anybody can give us other than that they just don't like it. But if this is so, then the things we mentioned, such as murder and the stealing of things that belong to the ancestors, cannot be taboos. If you ask any cultured Akan why one ought not to just descend on somebody and kill him, she will tell you that there is nobody in the world who would like to be killed like that. If then you would not like that to be done to you, then there is no way you can be within your rights to do that to somebody. This means that she will answer you with an appeal to the First Law. If you take all the things we mentioned as being taken by some people as taboos, you will see in the same way that none of them can be a taboo. It is not what somebody wants that determines what is good; it is what everybody ought to want. This proposition stands unshakable before everybody.

Now let us return to *musuo*. It is obvious that before we can call something *musuo,* it has to be something bad. If it is bad, we need to find out whether this is so on the sole basis of the First Law or on the basis of custom. With this done, we may then investigate whether our ancestors had any major objections against it. If they did, then we can now say that we are dealing with is a *musuo*. All this shows clearly that *musuo* is not taboo.

Suppose all that is granted; still, someone can ask whether or not there are any taboos in Akan life. If you look at certain things, it might appear that there are. For example, one *musuo* is for a man to have sex with a woman in the bush. If you ask why such an act is bad, you are told that Asaase Yaa, the Earth goddess, disapproves of it, and that if anybody does that Asaase Yaa will bring food infertility upon the farms of the culprit and his close relatives. When you think of it, this sounds pretty much like saying that the reason why the thing is bad is that the Earth goddess very much dislikes it. And it seems that there is no other reason. If that is so, then it is beginning to look as if we must acknowledge that here is at least one taboo in Akan life.

It seems to me that this is not the case. I believe that our elders made this prohibition to discourage men incapable of deep thought from using their physical strength to molest women who may happen for some reason to be alone in the bush. If you try to explain to men of that kind the reason why they should not invade lone women, they will not understand. But if you terrify them with the story that if they do that the Earth goddess will punish him and his relations with famine, they might fear to do that. As for sound thinking men, they knew that the prohibition was not made for them, because they don't need it.

Adeɛ baako a ɛma me dwen sɛ yɛn mpanyingfo no ndwen sɛ, paani paani, obi bu ɛmmra no so a Asaase Yaa bɛ ma ekom aba nesɛɛ, na wongyendi sɛ obi wohɔ a oyɛ Asaase Yaa. Na ɛyɛ asɛm ka kɛkɛ wo won tirimu. Asɛm baako a na yɛnpanyinfo ka ne sɛ Asaase Yaa yɛ Onyankopon yere. Yei yɛ adeɛ a ɛsɛsɛ yɛ tumi hu sɛ ɛyɛ asɛm ka keke.

Adeɛ bi a ɛnonso ɛsɛsɛ ema yehu sɛ saa emmra a ebinom dwen sɛ ema *taboo* tumi ba Akanfo abrabɔ mu no yɛ asɛm kae kɛkɛ ne sɛ yɛnim sɛɛ Akanfo wo emmra a ɛsɛ saa ma mofra. Yɛ ka kyerɛ mofra see, sɛ wɔredware a ensesɛ wɔ to nyom, ɛfisɛ wɔyɛ saa a wɔn maame be wu. Afei nso yɛ ka kyerɛ won sɛɛ ensɛsɛ wɔbɔ hwerema anadwo kɔnkɔn.

Enhia sɛ onipa bedwen pii ansa na wahu sɛ saa nsɛm yi yɛ adeɛ a yɛde hunahuna mofra sɛnea ɛbeyɛ a worenyɛ neama bi. Nea ɛnti a yɛmpɛ sɛ woto nyom bere a woredware ne sɛ, ensu fi bɛtumi ako won anum ama yare abɔ won. Sɛ wo fa wherema deɛ no nso a, wutumi hu sɛ, nkwadaa bɛtumi—sɛ wo dooso a—abobɔ hwerɛma pii ahaw mpanyinfo asomu ama ayɛ den sɛ wobɛ da. Saa nkyerɛkyerɛmu yi nti na ensesɛ nkwadaa yɛ neama a yɛbɔbɔo so no; na enyɛ sɛ mofra no maame bewu nti. Nso mpanyingfo nim sɛ woka woi nyinaa kyerɛ nkwadaa nkɛtenkɛte a wɔrente ase; na wɔ be kɔ so ayɛ neama a yɛmpe sɛ woyɛ no. Ɛnti asɛm a wɔkae sɛ abɔfra yɛ saa a, ne maame be wu no yɛbetumi aka sɛ ɛyɛ asɛmka kɛkɛ. Yɛ betumi ahu sɛɛ nea mpanyingfo kae de fa Asaase Yaa ho sɛ, sɛ nnipa yɛ neama bi a, ɔbema ekom aba no nyinaa yɛ asɛmka kɛkɛ.

Adeɛ a yɛtumi hu wo ha ne sɛ Akanfo abrabɔ paa de biribiara a yɛbetumi afrɛ no *taboo* nni mu. Ɛte saa dea a, ende ɛyɛ asɛm bi a eso papaapa. Ɛfisɛ ende yɛbetumi aka sɛ onipa abrabɔ mu emmra biara nfi esoro ana efom ne ɛba. Nenyinaa firi onipa adwem mu na ɛba. Nea mekyerɛ ne sɛ, sɛ bribi wo ho na obi ka sɛ ɛyɛ anasɛ enyɛ a, enyɛ Onyame ana asamanfo anaa abosom biara ɛnti na ɛtesaa. Nkyerɛase wohɔ a ebɛtumi ama ya hu papa anasɛ bɔne a ewo adeɛ no mu. Sɛ wo hwɛ mu a, wu hu sɛ saa nyansa yi yɛ adɛ a na yen nana nom wɔ.

Yei nkyerɛse Onyankopɔn ho adwen mma nipa pii abrabɔ mu. Nokware ni, sɛ enni nnipa tirim sɛ Onyame mpe bɔne, na woyɛ bɔne a ɔbetwe waso a, anka nkrɔfuɔ be yɛ bɔne pii paa. Nso nea yahu ne sɛ, sɛ opanyin yɛ saa a, na wayɛ sɛ akwadaa. Ɛyɛ nkwadaa na wɔka sɛ, "Merenyɛ saa ɛfisɛ, sɛ me yɛ saa a, me maame (anasɛ me papa) be bo me" Ɛnti sɛ onipa a wanyin ka bribi a ɛte sɛ yei a, ɛyɛ ahɔmɛte kɛseɛ. Sɛ opanying mu ka bribi te sɛ "Merenwia adeɛ no ɛfisɛ, sɛ miwia a, Onyame be twe maso" a, ende na nadwen ayɛ sɛ abɔfra adwen! Berebiara a obi bɛka asɛm a ɛtesɛ "Merenyɛ y ɛfisɛ, sɛ mɛyɛ a **A** be twe maso" no ore kasa te sɛ abɔfra.

One reason why I do not think that our elders well and truly believed that if someone broke the prohibition, Asaase Yaa would punish him with famine, is that they did not believe that there was anybody who actually was Asaase Yaa. The reference to Asaase Yaa was, in their own minds, merely a manner of speaking. Another thing that our elders used to say is that Asaase Yaa is the wife of God. We should be able to see that this is only a manner of speaking.

Another thing that should make us see that what some people take as evidence of taboo in Akan life is just a manner of speaking is that we know that the Akan have somewhat similar prohibitions for children. We tell little children that they should not sing while having a bath, because if they do, their mother will die. We also tell them that they should not whistle in the dead of night for the same reason.

It does not take a lot of reflection to see that these are merely ways of frightening children into abstention from certain activities. The reason why we don't want them to sing while taking their bath is that they might swallow dirty water and get sick. Concerning the matter of whistling at night, you will see that children, especially if they are many, could whistle so much as to impede sleep for adults. These are the explanations of why children should not do the various things mentioned and not the ones given them, such as that their mother will die if they do certain things. But the adults know that if they told the little children all this, they would not understand, and they would continue doing what we don't want them to do. So now we can say that the warning, for example, that if they did certain things their mother would die, was merely a manner of speaking. We can see now that what our elders said about Asaase Yaa to the effect that if you did certain things, she would bring about famine, was, just like these, a manner of speaking.

What we see here is that in Akan moral life there is nothing that can be called a taboo. If that is right, then this is matter of great significance. Because, for example, we can say that no rule of behavior comes from the heavens above or the earth below. They all come from the human mind. What I mean is that if someone says of something that it is good or that it is bad, it is not because of God or the departed spirits or the fetishes that it is or is not so. In all probability, our ancestors had this insight.

This does not show that thinking about God does not play a part in the moral life of many people. In truth, if it were not in a lot of heads that God hates evil and will punish it, there would be much more evildoing than now. However, what has emerged is that if an adult does so, he is acting like a child. It is children who say, "I won't do that, because if I do that mama (or papa) will spank me." And so it is a great pity if an adult says something such as, "I will not steal because if I do so God will punish me." Generally, anyone who says a thing such as, "I will not do A, because if I do it, B will punish me" is talking like a child.

Ɛsesɛ yɛ te aseɛ sɛ nsɛm a yɛreka yi nnkyerɛ sɛ onipa a wanyin rɛntumi misa afotuo mfi obi ho. Obɛtumi abisa afotuo afi obiara a odwen sɛ onim nyansa ho. Saa nipa koro no bɛtumi ayɛ ne tipen anaasɛ ne panyin. Ɛbɛtumi koraa aba sɛ nea oreko srɛ afotu no anyin kyɛn nea ore be ma afotuo no. Anyɛ bribi koraa no, afotuo bɛtumi ayɛ neama miensa: Ebɛtumi ama obisa fo no ahu adeɛ bi a ɛwo ho anasɛ asɛm bi a asi dadaw a ɛbɛma adeɛ a ɛrehaw nadwen no agyae. Ebɛtumi nso akyerɛkyerɛ neama mu ama ntease aba nnipa ntɛm. Afei nso afotu bɛtumi akyerɛ nea ɛnti a bribi a obisafo no pɛsɛ oyɛ yɛ papa ana bɔne. Nea ɛto so miensa no hia kyɛn nea aka no nyinaa.

Ansa na yɛbewie nkomɔ yi, me pe sɛ ye hu sɛ papa ne bɔne nyɛ neama a ɛno ankasa wo ho. Ɛyɛ neama a yehu no wo onipa abrabɔ mu. Sɛ onipa bo bra pa a, ekyerɛ ne suban; yɛ ka sɛ ɔwɔ suban pa. Na sɛ ɔbɔ bra bɔne a, yɛka sɛ ɔwɔ suban bɔne. Ɛnti suban yɛ adeɛ a, sɛ yɛredwen onipa abrabɔ ho a, ɛsesɛ yɛhu sɛ ɛho hia papaapa. Ɛmmom, sɛ eduru se yɛ pɛsɛ yɛkyerɛkyerɛ suban papa anaa suban bɔne mu a, endeɛ yɛhia sɛ yɛ bekyerɛkyerɛ papa ne bɔne mu. Ɛnti papa ne bɔne ho nsɛm na edikan, nanso ɔbra ne suban pa ho nsɛm nti na papa ne bɔne ho nsɛm hia.

Afei nso bere a yɛ fii ase rekyerɛ papa ne bɔne mu no yɛ yɛɛ nkyɛkyɛ mu bi. Yɛ kaa sɛ neama bi wo ho a Ɛmmra Kɛse no nkoara tumi ma yɛhu sɛ ɛyɛ papa anasɛ ɛyɛ bɔne. Nanso sɛ edu baabi a Ɛmmra Kɛse no nkoara ntumi nkyerɛ nea ɛyɛ papa anasɛ bɔne. Yɛkyerɛɛ mu sɛɛ, sɛ ɛba saa a, amanne so na yɛgyina de hu nea ɛyɛ ne nea enyɛ. Esane sɛ amanne tumi sesa firi oman de kɔ oman anasɛ bere de kɔ bere nti ɛsesɛ yɛfri papa ne bɔne nkyerɛkyerɛ mu a yɛko amanne nkyerɛkyerɛ mu. Yei yɛ adeɛ a nebere bɛba. Eha de nea yɛbɛka ara nesɛ, sɛ yɛ hwehwe mu a, yɛ behu sɛ Akanfo adwen de fa suban pa ne ɔbra pa ho no gyina sɛnea won abusua nhyehyɛe te. Ebɛboa yɛn nso ama yanya enteasɛ ɛdefa tete amanmue ho. Na ɛba saa a, ebia yɛbetumi anya nyansa bi a ɛbɛboa yɛn wo ɛnemmrɛ yi mu asetra ne ammanbu mu. Migyidi sɛ yei yɛ nokware ɛdefa Abibirim fa kɛse.

It should be understood that we are not saying that an adult cannot ask for moral advice from another person. He can ask for advice from anyone she considers wise. That person may be his age-mate or senior or even junior. At the minimum, advice can do three things for him. The consultant may be able to call his attention to some aspect of the problem that could stop her worries. She might also be able to analyze away misunderstandings among the people concerned so that there is harmony. Also, she may be able to show him reasons why something he wants to do is good or bad. The third possibility is the most important.

Before we finish this conversation, I would like us to understand that good and evil do not have existence of their own. They are only an aspect of human life and conduct. If a person is upright in his conduct, it shows his character; we say he has good character. And if he is not upright in his conduct we say he has bad character. Therefore, in our thinking about human conduct we should note that character is of incalculable importance. However, when it comes to clarifying the notions of good or bad character, we do have first to elucidate the notions of good and evil. So the theory of good and evil comes first, but it is because of conduct and character that we need it.

At the outset of our discourse on good and evil we made the following analysis. We noted that there are things that could be identified as good or evil on the basis of what we called the First Law of conduct alone. We noted also cases in which that law could not alone show us what is good and what is bad. We explained that in such cases we depended on custom to determine what was good and what was evil. Because customs can change from culture to culture or from time to time, we need, after dealing with the general theory of good and bad, to explain the idea of custom in detail. This is something whose time will come. For now, all we can say is that if you study Akan conceptions of good character and conduct, you find that these depend on their system of kinship relationships. Such a study will also help us to have an insight into traditional politics. From this perhaps we might gain some wisdom about present-day life and politics. I think that this is mostly true in Africa.

NOTE

*This is an Akan adage, which may be interpreted to be saying that doing good to others is morally good.

Contributors

EDITOR

Chike Jeffers was born in Toronto, Canada, to parents hailing from Dominica and Guyana. He received his PhD in philosophy from Northwestern University in 2010. He is now an assistant professor in the Department of Philosophy at Dalhousie University (Halifax, Nova Scotia). He specializes in Africana philosophy and philosophy of race, with general interests in social and political philosophy and ethics. Some of his recent and forthcoming work includes: "Do We Need African Canadian Philosophy?," *Dialogue: Canadian Philosophical Review/Revue canadienne de philosophie* 51 (December 2012): 643-666; "The Cultural Theory of Race: Yet Another Look at Du Bois's "The Conservation of Races," *Ethics* 123 (April 2013): 403–426; "Embodying Justice in Ancient Egypt: *The Tale of the Eloquent Peasant* as a Classic of Political Philosophy," *British Journal for the History of Philosophy* 21 (May 2013): 421–442; and "Appiah's Cosmopolitanism," forthcoming in *The Southern Journal of Philosophy*.

AUTHORS

Souleymane Bachir Diagne was born in Saint-Louis, Senegal. He is a professor in the Department of French & Romance Philology and the Department of Philosophy at Columbia University. He previously taught for twenty years at Cheikh Anta Diop University in Dakar, Senegal, before spending six years at Northwestern University. His areas of research include history of philosophy, history of logic and mathematics, Islamic philosophy, African philosophy, and Francophone literature. His books include *Boole: l'oiseau de nuit en plein jour* (Paris: Belin, 1989); *Islam et société ouverte: la fidélité et le mouvement dans la pensée de Muhammad Iqbal* (Paris: Maisonneuve et Larose, 2001); *Léopold Sédar Senghor: L'art africain comme philosophie* (Paris: Riveneuve, 2007), which has been translated as *African Art as Philosophy: Senghor, Bergson, and the Idea of Negritude* (London: Seagull Books, 2011); *Comment philosopher en*

Islam? (Paris: Panama, 2008); and *Bergson postcolonial: L'élan vital dans la pensée de Léopold Sédar Senghor et de Mohamed Iqbal* (Paris: CNRS, 2011).

Messay Kebede was born in Addis Ababa, Ethiopia. He is a professor of philosophy at the University of Dayton in Ohio. He previously taught philosophy for many years at Addis Ababa University in Ethiopia. His research interests include African philosophy, culture and modernity, political and social philosophy. He is the author of five books: *Meaning and Development* (1994), *Survival and Modernization* (1999), *Africa's Quest for a Philosophy of Decolonization* (2004), *Radicalism and Cultural Dislocation in Ethiopia* (2008), and *Ideology and Elite Conflicts: Autopsy of the Ethiopian Revolution* (2011). He has also published numerous articles.

D. A. Masolo was born at Mahero in Siaya County, Nyanza Province, Kenya. He teaches philosophy at the University of Louisville in Louisville, Kentucky. He taught philosophy at the University of Nairobi and other universities in Kenya until 1991 when, as one of the victims of the anti-academic dictatorship of then-president Daniel arap Moi, he relocated to the United States. The focus of his training was the history of modern and contemporary European philosophy, a background that, in conjunction with interests and studies in the social sciences, later influenced his research interests toward comparative modes of thought, and African philosophy in particular. His publications in this area include *African Philosophy in Search of Identity* (1994), *African Philosophy as Cultural Inquiry* (co-edited with Ivan Karp, 2000) and, more recently, *Self and Community in a Changing World* (2010), all published by Indiana University Press.

Frederick Ochieng'-Odhiambo comes from Ugenya constituency in Siaya County, Nyanza Province, Kenya. He is professor of African Philosophic Sagacity and head of the Department of History and Philosophy, University of the West Indies, Cave Hill Campus, Barbados. He previously taught philosophy at the University of Nairobi and the National University of Lesotho in southern Africa. His areas of research include African philosophy, moral and social philosophy, and logic; areas in which he has written several journal articles and book chapters. His books include *Logic and Induction* (Nairobi: Stantex Publishers, 1996); *Introductory Symbolic Logic* (Nairobi: Consolata Institute of Philosophy Press, 2003); *Conversations in Philosophy: Crossing the Boundaries* (Newcastle: Cambridge Scholars Publishing, 2008); *Foundations of Ethics: A Critical Reader in Moral and Social Philosophy* (Nairobi: University of Nairobi Press, 2009); *A Companion to Philosophy* (Nairobi: Consolata Institute of Philosophy Press, 2010); and *Trends and Issues in African Philosophy* (New York: Peter Lang, 2010).

Betty Wambui was born in Nairobi, Kenya. She is an assistant professor with a dual appointment in Africana and Latino Studies and Women's and Gender Studies. She received her PhD in philosophy from Binghamton University and her MA from the University of Nairobi. Her areas of specialization include African philosophies and social, political, and legal philosophy. She is particularly interested in the questions raised by feminist philosophies, critical race theories, critical legal studies, social contract theory, discrimination, and morality. Her most recent publication is "The Challenge of Provenance: Myth, Histories and the Negotiation of Socio-Political Space" (*Phoebe* 19, no. 2, Fall 2007).

Emmanuel Chukwudi Eze (1963–2007) was born in Enugu State in Nigeria. A specialist in postcolonial philosophy, Eze wrote as well as edited influential postcolonial histories of philosophy in Africa, Europe, and the Americas. Educated in Nigeria, the Democratic Republic of Congo, and the United States, Eze received his PhD in philosophy from Fordham University in 1993. Eze taught at Bucknell University and at Mount Holyoke College; in addition, he was a postdoctoral visiting scholar at Cambridge University (1996–1997), a visiting professor at the New School for Social Research (1997) and at the University of Cape Town (2003). Eze was most recently associate professor of Philosophy at DePaul University, where he also edited the journal, *Philosophia Africana*. He died December 30, 2007, after a short illness. His most recent work included the posthumously published *On Reason: Rationality in a World of Cultural Conflict and Racism* (Durham: Duke University Press, 2008). One of his lifelong projects was to bring together the study of philosophy with Igbo language and culture, thus demonstrating the importance of the essay included in this volume.

Kwasi Wiredu is an Akan Ghanaian, born and bred in Kumasi, Ashanti. He did his undergraduate studies at the University of Ghana, and his graduate studies at Oxford. He returned to Ghana in 1961 and taught philosophy at the University of Ghana till 1983. From January 1987 he taught philosophy at the Department of Philosophy, University of South Florida, retiring in 2007 as a Distinguished University Professor Emeritus. Consistently with these dates, he has held visiting professorships at the University of California, 1979–1980; University of Ibadan, Nigeria, 1984; University of Richmond, Virginia (N.E.H. Distinguished Professor), 1985; Carleton College, Minnesota (Donald J. Cowling Visiting Professor), 1986; and Duke University, North Carolina (Visiting Professor), Aug. 1994–95 and 1999–2001. Three fellowships complete the list: Birbeck College, University of London Honorary Visiting Fellow 1966–67; Woodrow Wilson International Center for Scholars, Washington, D.C., May-Dec.1985; and National Humanities Center, North Carolina, May-Dec.1985. Some of his publications are *Philosophy and an African Culture* (Cambridge University Press, 1980) and *Cultural Universals and Particulars: An African Perspective* (Bloomington: Indiana University Press, 1996). He edited *A Companion to African Philosophy* (Malden, MA: Blackwell, 2004).

TRANSLATORS

Omar Ka was born in Dakar, Senegal. He is presently teaching linguistics, Wolof, and French in the Department of Modern Languages, Linguistics and Intercultural Communication at the University of Maryland, Baltimore County. His areas of specialization include sociolinguistics, specifically language planning and language policy, phonology and morphology, and second language teaching. He has authored or co-authored books and articles on language planning in Senegal, Wolof phonological structure, as well as textbooks for learners of Wolof. His most recent book is titled *Nanu Dégg Wolof: A Multidimensional Approach to the Teaching and Learning of Wolof as a Foreign Language* (Madison, WI: NALRC Press, 2009).

Bethlehem Hailu Dejene was born in Addis Ababa, Ethiopia. She is a PhD candidate in the Department of Anthropology at Northwestern University. Her research interests include religious change in post-Socialist Ethiopia, competitive sources of healing (i.e., spirit possession and exorcism), and anthropology of Orthodox and Pentecostal/charismatic Christianity. She is currently writing her dissertation on the Ethiopian Orthodox Tewahdo Church's reform movement since 1991.

Stephen Omondi Owino is a native of Siaya, Kenya. He is currently a doctoral candidate in philosophy at the University of Nairobi and a tutorial fellow in the Department of Philosophy and Religious Studies at Kenyatta University. His areas of interest and research are: logic, philosophy of language, exact philosophy, postcolonial philosophy, history of philosophy, and subaltern philosophy. Some of his recent publications include: "Ethnicity and Globalisation" (co-authored with Francis Wokabi), in *The Dialogue of Cultural Traditions: A Global Perspective* (Washington, DC: CRVP, 2008), and "Beyond Quantity: Higher Education in Kenya" (co-authored with Susan Waiyego) in *Universités et Universitaires en Afrique de l'Est* (Paris/Nairobi: Karthala-IFRA, 2012).

Oriare Nyarwath was born in Kisumu County, Kenya. He is a senior lecturer of philosophy in the Department of Philosophy and Religious Studies, University of Nairobi, Kenya. His areas of research interest include African philosophy, social philosophy, and logic. His recent works include "The Luo Care for Widows (*Lako*) and Contemporary Challenges" (*Thought and Practice* 4, no. 1, June 2012), "Ethnicity and Ethnicism: What is Wrong?" (*Horizons: A Journal of Philosophy* 1, 2010), and *Traditional Logic: An Introduction* (Nairobi: Consolata Institute of Philosophy Press, 2010).

Evan Maina Mwangi is from Mũrarandia in Mũranga County, Central Kenya. He studied for his PhD at the University of Nairobi. A Gikuyu speaker and writer, he teaches English (twentieth-century Anglophone African literature) at Northwestern University. He is the co-author of *The Columbia Guide to East African Literature Since 1945* (with Simon Gikandi). His latest book is *Africa Writes Back to Self: Metafiction, Gender, Sexuality* (Albany: State University of New York Press, 2009). He is currently finishing work on a book about the centrality of gender in the translation of postcolonial literatures.

Mary Gloria C. Njoku was born in Mbano in the southeast of Nigeria. She holds a PhD in psychology from DePaul University, Chicago, and is currently the director of academic planning and senior lecturer in psychology at Godfrey Okoye University in Enugu, Nigeria. Mary Gloria's areas of interest include research ethics, psychology of Nigerians, sense of community, understanding of the mind, personality and peace, and quality of life. Her most recent contributions are in the *Annals of Research, Stories of Peace,* and *Psychological Health.*

Joachim Oforchukwu is born in Isu-Njaba in Isu Local Government Area, Imo State, Nigeria. He is a priest of the Holy Ghost Congregation. He works at Ancora, the New Jersey State Psychiatric Hospital, as chaplain, advisor, and counselor. He serves on the State of New Jersey Psychiatric Advisoral Committee, Ancora. He is also teaching pastoral theology at St. Charles Borromeo Seminary in Wynnewood, Pennsylvania. Dr. Oforchukwu is the author of many books including *Towards a Just Nigerian Society* (1996), *Improving the Christian Marriage-Relationship in Our Society* (2000), *Education Among Nigerian Youths: Can Our Educational System be Redeemed?* (2002), *Perspectives on Leadership: A Synthesis of Types and Theories* (2011), and *A Theological and Biblical Appraisal of Ozo Title Taking and its Implications for Current Leadership Issues in Igbo Catholic Church (Nigeria)* (2011).

Uchechi Ukaegbu was born in Evanston, Illinois, and is of Igbo descent. She completed her PhD in the field of biological sciences from Northwestern University where she studied the regulation of bacterial enzymes with renewable energy potential. She is currently a postdoctoral fellow at Weill Medical College of Cornell University where her research interests are focused on understanding epigenetic memory in malaria virulence genes.

Chikwendu Christian Ukaegbu was born in Aba in Southeast Nigeria. He is a distinguished senior lecturer of sociology at Northwestern University. He had previously held the positions of senior lecturer at the University of Nigeria and professor and head of the Department of Sociology at the University of Wyoming. His areas of interest include development and change, political economy, organizations, and African studies. Some of his recent publications include, "War and the Making of a Scientific and Technological Intelligentsia" (in A. Nwauwa and C. Korieh, *Against All Odds: Igbos in Postcolonial Nigeria*, 2011), "Leadership Fatalism and Underdevelopment in Nigeria: Imaginative Policymaking for Human Development" (*Philosophia Africana,* 2007), "Business Environment and Entrepreneurial Activity in Nigeria: Implications for Industrial Development" (with Mary Agboli) (*Journal of Modern African Studies*, 2006), and "Lessons from Biafra: The Structuration of Socially Relevant Science in the Research and Production Directorate" (*Social Forces*, 2005).

Joseph Osei was born at Kokofu in the Ashanti Region of Ghana. He is a full professor of philosophy in the Philosophy/Government & History Department at Fayetteville State University (University of North Carolina). His research interests include social and political philosophy, theoretical and applied ethics, Africana philosophy, philosophy of religion, and philosophy of education. His most recent publications include: *Ethical Issues in Third World Development: A Philosophy of Social Change* (Lewis, NY: Edwin Mellen Press, 2011); *The Challenge of Sustaining Emergent Democracies: Insights for Religious Intellectuals and Leaders of Civil Society* (Bloomington, Xlibris: Academic Publishers, 2009); "Toward a New Philosophy of Education for Sustaining Democracy and Development in Africa: Seven Foundational Principles," *Journal of International Studies and Development* 2 (Spring 2012); "Democracy and the Challenge of Religious Extremism in Ghana," in *Christianity, Missions and Ecumenism in Ghana* (Accra: Asempa Publishers, 2009); and "On the War Against Terrorism and Poverty: What Would King Do?" *Quest: An African Journal of Philosophy* (2008).

Index